CLASSICS OF NAVAL LITERATURE
JACK SWEETMAN, SERIES EDITOR

This series makes available new editions of classic works of naval history, biography, and fiction. Each volume is complete and unabridged and includes an authoritative introduction written specifically for Classics of Naval Literature. A list of titles published or currently in preparation appears at the end of this volume.

Sea Devils

Italian Navy Commandos
in World War II

J. Valerio Borghese

Translated by James Cleugh and adapted
by the author
With an Introduction by Paolo E. Coletta

NAVAL INSTITUTE PRESS
Annapolis, Maryland

Naval Institute Press
291 Wood Road
Annapolis, MD 21402

This book was originally published in Italian as *Decima Flottiglia Mas* in 1950.
This translation was first published in 1952 by Andrew Melrose Ltd., London.

ISBN-13 978-1-59114-047-4

Library of Congress Cataloging-in-Publication Data
Borghese, Iunio Valerio, 1907–1974.
  {Decima Flottiglia Mas. English}
  Sea Devils : Italian navy commandos in World War II / J. Valerio Borghese ; translated by James Cleugh and adapted by the author ; with an introduction by Paolo E. Coletta.
       p.   cm. — (Classics of naval literature)
Originally published: London : A. Melrose, 1952.
Includes bibliographical references.
ISBN 1-55750-072-X
1. World War, 1939–1945—Commando operations—Italy. 2. World War, 1939–1945—Naval operations, Italian. I. Title. II. Series.
D794.5.B67   1995
940.54'5945—dc20

                                                                      95-32082

Printed in the United States of America on acid-free paper

15 14 13 12 11 10 09   9 8 7 6 5 4 3 2
First printing

Introduction

The stereotype of the Italian navy in World War II is that it was commanded by admirals dominated by fear of losing ships and manned by "incompetent and cowardly 'greasy Eyeties.'" Adm. Sir Andrew B. Cunningham, commander in chief of the British Mediterranean Fleet, 1939–43, declared that his sailors "had nothing but a healthy contempt" for what Rear Adm. Samuel E. Morison, author of the almost-official *History of United States Naval Operations in World War II*, referred to (in quotation marks) as the "'Dago Navy.'"[1] To Anglo-Saxon eyes, Italy's naval doctrine called for action only when its forces were superior to the enemy's. However, studies by Glen John St. Barclay and Italian-speaking James Sadkovich and the testimony of Marc'Antonio Bragadin, Vice Adm. Giuseppe Fioravanzo, and J. Valerio Borghese all note that despite its handicaps the Italian navy was able to sustain the struggle with the Royal Navy in the Mediterranean for thirty-nine long months.[2]

The fleet against which the Regia Marina Italiana had measured its strength after World War I was the French. Such a measure was clearly insufficient for the situation that arose on

10 June 1940, when Italy's entry into World War II pitted it against the navies of both France and Britain. France's surrender later that month eliminated its lesser antagonist but left it confronting the Royal Navy, at that date arguably the world's most powerful navy. Allied planning had called for the French fleet to control the Mediterranean to the west of Malta and the British Mediterranean Fleet to secure the east. To replace the French, the British quickly constituted Force H, a powerful squadron based at Gibraltar. Still, its global commitments dictated that the Royal Navy could not bring its full strength to bear in the Mediterranean. The assets available to Force H and the Mediterranean Fleet usually made the two of them slightly superior to the Italian fleet; but the latter, which enjoyed the advantage of interior position, was often superior to either one in every category of combatant except aircraft carriers—and the importance of that exception was not immediately apparent.

If the numerical odds it faced were not entirely unfavorable, the Regia Marina operated under numerous other disadvantages. Some were apparent when Italy entered the war, others became evident in its course, and still others were not discovered until afterward. Perhaps the most serious (and the most obvious) of its problems were logistical. Although Italy ranked as a great power, it did not possess a great-power economy. Its industrial capacity was only about one-fifth that of Germany, and it lacked essential natural resources, especially iron and oil. It would be impossible for the Regia Marina to replace significant losses among its major units promptly.[3]

This consideration alone sufficed to cause the naval high command to forswear any idea of promoting a decisive battle in pursuit of a Mahanian "command of the sea," and instead to concentrate on the navy's fundamental strategic missions: maintaining the seaborne flow of men and supplies to the Axis forces in North Africa and interdicting enemy convoys in the central Mediterranean. Veterans and historians of the

Royal Navy have made these priorities the subject of many caustic witticisms. For example, in his memoirs Admiral Cunningham recalled that on a peacetime ship visit Adm. Arturo Riccardi (later Italy's naval chief of staff) pointed out that he kept a copy of *The Life of Nelson* on his bed table; however, his "subsequent actions . . . showed that he had not greatly profited by his nightly reading."[4] Such quips to the contrary, its limited resources gave the Regia Marina good reason to conclude that it could not afford to accept battle on British terms.[5]

The first nine months of the Mediterranean war revealed that the Italian naval effort was also handicapped by operational deficiencies unsuspected at the onset of hostilities. Chief among these were inadequate air support and the lack of radar. The Regia Marina was the only major navy that had not built at least one aircraft carrier between the world wars. The decision to refrain from doing so was based on two assumptions, both of which proved false: first, that planes of the independent Regia Aeronautica Italiana flying from bases in Italy and Libya would provide all the air support the navy needed, and second, predominant even in navies that built carriers, that such vessels would be at best auxiliaries to the battle line. To the Italian navy's leaders, therefore, it seemed preferable to spend construction funds on the battle line itself. Even after a strike from a single British carrier on the fleet base at Taranto on 11 November 1940 disabled three Italian battleships—one for the duration of the war—the high command remained skeptical, persuading Mussolini to withdraw the order he immediately issued to convert the liner *Roma* into a carrier. A little more than three months later, at the Battle of Cape Matapan, a British carrier strike on an Italian fleet devoid of air cover set the stage for the major surface engagement of the Mediterranean conflict, a night action in which three Italian heavy cruisers and two destroyers were sunk at no cost to their opponents. As a result of this reverse, the conversion of the *Roma* (subsequently renamed the *Aquila*) and, later, a still larger liner was actually set in motion, but work had not been completed on either vessel by the time of the Italian armistice in September 1943.[6]

It was also at Matapan that the nighttime performance of enemy formations made the Regia Marina realize that the Royal Navy had radar, a technology in which Italian electronic firms had vainly tried to interest the armed forces before the war. The significance of this discovery was all the greater because unlike their British counterparts, Italian heavy surface units were not trained in night fighting. Efforts to overcome the radar gap could not make up for lost time. Although an experimental set was installed in the battleship *Littorio* in September 1941, satisfactory units did not become available until October 1942, and only twelve had been mounted by the time of the armistice.[7]

Not until long after the war did it become known that, in addition to the other difficulties under which the Regia Marina labored, the Ultra-secret codebreakers at Bletchley Park outside London were eavesdropping on the Italian armed forces' radio communications (and those of their German allies as well). Ultra's importance can be exaggerated. Changes in ciphers caused it to "lose" codes for varying periods; signals in codes that had been cracked could not always be read and evaluated in time to be of use; and even when they were, friendly forces might lack the resources to react. Still, there can be no doubt that Bletchley Park did the Regia Marina great harm. It was, for example, an Ultra intercept that alerted the British to the Italian sortie that climaxed in the Battle of Cape Matapan. By far the most influential of Ultra's achievements in terms of its impact on the Mediterranean sea war, however, was the penetration of the machine cipher used to notify North African port authorities of the departure, route, and composition of convoys, which could then be tracked and ambushed. The British sought to disguise the source of their information by such means as sending aircraft to "discover" convoys they knew all about. These measures notwithstanding, the frequency with which their convoys were attacked led the Italians to suspect that their security was being breached. But they assumed that the explanation must lie in treason or conventional espionage. Like the Germans, they remained confident in their codes.[8]

Italian naval operations were further complicated by a pair of faulty strategic decisions: the failure to seize Malta, the British air and naval base athwart the sea lanes to Libya; and the German rejection of Italy's request to compel Vichy France to open Tunisian ports to Axis shipping early in the war. For the former, the Italian high command was in part to blame, having no plan prepared to invade Malta at the time Italy entered the conflict and the island's defenses were weak. The subsequent depredations by forces based there revealed the extent of that oversight. In 1942 the Italians urged the Germans to join them in a combined assault on the island, but the latter eventually backed out of a reluctant commitment to do so. When the Luftwaffe Fliegerkorps seconded the Regia Aeronautica's air siege of the island—from January through June 1941 and again from January through April 1942—Malta was effectively neutralized; but between those periods and increasingly after June 1942 its striking forces wreaked havoc on traffic to Africa. The Tunisian ports finally became available to Axis convoys in November 1942 after Germany responded to the Allied invasion of French North Africa by pouring troops into that country—but by then it was too late. Malta was on the rebound, and the majority of the Italian fast merchantmen that would have benefited most from the shorter voyage was at the bottom of the sea.[9]

The result of these circumstances was an inevitable attrition of the operational capability of the Italian navy and merchant marine. Despite German promises of aid, fuel stocks plummeted to a fraction of their prewar level. Fleet operations came to a close in August 1942; the fifty thousand tons of fuel per month reserved for running convoys left virtually nothing for the big ships. The strength of the combat and merchant fleets underwent a similar shrinkage in consequence of Italy's anemic industrial base. The commissioning of the battleship *Roma* in 1942 offset the effective loss of the *Cavour* at Taranto in 1940, bringing the number of Italian capital ships back to the original six; but only three of the eleven cruisers lost between June 1940 and September 1943 could be replaced (all from prewar construction), and no more than five of the forty-five destroyers. The only combatants that increased in number were the relatively small, quickly produced corvettes, subchasers, and motor torpedo-boats upon which the burden of convoy escort increasingly fell. The tempo of operations also took a toll on the ships that survived them: as of January 1943, two-thirds of the Regia Marina's existing escorts were unserviceable. Losses to merchant shipping proved even more devastating. Excluding those caught overseas in June 1940, Italy lost 1,278 merchantmen during the war. Of the 597 displacing more than 500 GRT (gross registered tons), a mere sixty were replaced.[10]

The Axis capitulation in Tunisia in May 1943 brought Italian surface operations to an end. There was no chance that the remnants of the Regia Marina could raise meaningful opposition to the invasion of Sicily in July, and the armistice had been secretly negotiated before the invasion of mainland Italy in September. Yet for all its tribulations, for most of the war the Regia Marina had succeeded in its all-important task of assuring the flow of supplies to North Africa. In terms of tonnage dispatched, 98 percent reached port in 1940; in 1941 the annual average was 83.9 percent, despite heavy losses suffered late in the year as a result of the temporary revitalization of Malta; and in 1942 it was 84.2 percent, although the monthly average for the last quarter was a calamitous 59.1 percent. The use of Libyan ports was abandoned in December of that year, and thereafter the convoy effort faltered. Only 68.3 percent of the supplies sent to Tunisia on what soon became known as the *rotta della morte*—the road to death—arrived safely.[11] Until then, however, the logistical problems about which Rommel complained arose from the quantity of supplies dispatched and the difficulty of getting them to the front after they entered North African waters.

But if mission, logistics, and other factors confined Italy's surface fleet to the central Mediterranean, its navy included a formation that carried the war across the Mediterranean from Alexandria to Gibraltar and beyond: the Tenth Light Flotilla, to whose exploits its last wartime commander, J. Valerio Borghese, devoted this book.

The Italian navy was the first to practice special operations, two pioneer frogmen having ridden a slow-speed torpedo with a detachable warhead into the Austrian naval base at Pola (now Pula) on the Adriatic to sink the twenty-thousand-ton dreadnought *Viribus Unitis* in the closing days of World War I. But interest in such undertakings evaporated upon the return of peace. It was not until the Italian invasion of Ethiopia in 1935 briefly raised the specter of war with Britain that two young submariners took the initiative to begin work on an improved version of the device that had sunk the *Viribus Unitis;* not until 1938 that the development of this and other special weapons was given an institutional foundation by being made a branch of the First Light Flotilla; not until August 1940—two months after Italy's entry into the war— that the unit attempted its first operation; and not until early 1941 that it attained organizational independence as the Tenth Light Flotilla (*Decima Flottiglia MAS,* often abbreviated X MAS, the initials standing for *Motoscafo Armato Silurante,* or motor torpedo-boat), a cover name intended to disguise its true character.

The Tenth's special weapons department had two divisions, surface and underwater. The former's craft consisted of high-speed explosive- and torpedo-carrying motorboats. The latter's arsenal included the famous *maiale* ("pig"), two-man "human torpedoes" carried to the vicinity of their targets by transport submarines that embarked a trio of them in canisters on deck; a variety of small but potent explosive charges for combat swimmers to attach to ships' hulls; and the two-man midget submarine CA. With the exception of the CA, which was never operationally employed, all of these weapons achieved success.

As Borghese makes clear, these successes were neither easy nor cheap. Unforeseen circumstances caused some missions to be aborted; others ended in failure, sometimes disastrous. Radar transformed the flotilla's attack on La Valletta, one of its most ambitious undertakings, into a bloody shambles; three of its transport submarines were lost, one with all hands; and unit members killed in action included one of its commanding officers and two division heads. But the Tenth learned from its mistakes, and it persevered.

The most spectacular of its successes occurred in the harbor of Alexandria, Egypt, on the night of 19 December 1941, when two pigs released from a submarine under the author's command disabled the British battleships *Valiant* and *Queen Elizabeth*. (A third pig badly damaged a tanker and a destroyer lying alongside.) The battleships were the last two in the Mediterranean Fleet, the *U-331* having sunk the *Barham* off Cyrenaica on 25 November; and their incapacitation, coupled with Fliegerkorps II's assignment to Sicily and the withdrawal of Malta's surface striking force, gave the Axis almost untrammeled use of the central Mediterranean for five months. The *Valiant* was back in service by the summer of 1942, but the *Queen Elizabeth*, Cunningham's flagship, did not become operational again until June 1943. As the admiral—who recalled being "tossed about five feet into the air" by the explosion—rather ruefully observed, "One cannot but admire the cold-blooded bravery and enterprise of these Italians. Everything had been carefully thought out and planned."[12]

But for the armistice, the Tenth Light Flotilla might have

scored an even more spectacular success: an attack on shipping on the Hudson River in downtown New York. The operation, scheduled for December 1943, was to be carried out by its midget submarine, which would be piggybacked across the Atlantic by one of the oceangoing Italian submarines based at Bordeaux. Borghese proudly notes that this represented "the only practicable plan, so far as I am aware, ever made to carry the war into the United States" (261). Like the Halsey-Doolittle raid on Japan not quite two years earlier, the action could not have done much material damage; but Borghese expected it to have an immense psychological effect.

In an appendix recording the vessels that the Tenth damaged or sank, Borghese lists four warships totaling 75,690 tons and twenty-seven merchantmen totaling 189,662 tons, for an aggregate of 265,352 tons. More recent research by the Italian Naval History Office has revised these figures to five warships of 72,190 tons and twenty-three merchantmen of 130,572 tons, for a total of 202,762 tons. Deleted were two of the three merchant vessels supposedly hit at Suda in March 1941 (nos. 5–7 on Borghese's list) because only one, the 8,234-ton tanker *Pericles,* was actually damaged; the Soviet motorship believed to have been torpedoed in the Black Sea (no. 12); and the U.S. motorship reputedly disabled at Algiers (no.22). Added was HMS *Jervis,* the destroyer damaged at Alexandria in December 1941. The tanker that fell victim to the same attack (no. 8) was identified as the 7,544-ton *Sagona,* and the unknown "destroyer of the *Jervis* class" sunk off El Daba in August 1942 (no. 4) as the Type 2 *Hunt*-class destroyer escort *Eridge.*[13]

That all of these successes took place after March 1941— by which time the British had had nine months to get their guard up—makes them all the more impressive. Indeed, after the war Adm. Angelo Iachino, who commanded the Italian fleet from November 1940 to April 1943, concluded that the Regia Marina would have been well advised to emphasize the *"mezzi insidiosi"* of light forces, submarines, and naval assault teams instead of big ships from the beginning. James J. Sadkovich, the author of the most recent scholarly study of the Italian naval effort, suggests that Iachino may have been right: "Rather than building big surface ships, the Italian navy might have better spent its budget constructing more 'insidious' craft, especially given the performance of the X MAS. . . . [I]t seems obvious that had this unit been fully trained and equipped in June 1940, it would have had a crucial impact on the war. Yet 'insidious' units depended upon surprise, and they were much less effective once British port defenses were improved." [14]

Junio Valerio Borghese was uniquely qualified to tell the story of the Tenth Light Flotilla. Born a prince with four hundred years of Tuscan antecedents, he graduated from the naval academy at Livorno and was a lieutenant with two submarine commands to his credit when Italy entered the war. After three patrols in command of the *Vittor Pisani* in the summer of 1940, he was selected to attend a German submarine school course on Atlantic convoy warfare. Returning home in the expectation of receiving one of the big submarines at Bordeaux, he was instead offered command of the *Scirè,* a 620-ton Mediterranean boat then being modified to carry pigs. "I accepted this offer with enthusiasm," he writes (40). He participated in five operations between September 1940 and December 1941 and then relinquished command of the *Scirè,* having been ordered to devote himself full time to his previously additional duty as head of the Underwater Division. In May 1943 he assumed command of the flotilla, a position he retained until the armistice.

Borghese writes well and offers clear descriptions of the Tenth's matériel and vivid characterizations of its personnel. Much of the story he could relate from personal experience. In his accounts of operations in which he was not involved, he makes extensive use of quotations from the reports, letters, and diaries of the men who carried them out. The result is a history that possesses the immediacy and excitement of a first-person narrative. It is also a striking testimonial to the ability of determined, well-trained men to overcome apparently insurmountable obstacles in the service of a cause for which they are ready to risk all. "What was it," Borghese asks, "that made these men so different from the majority of their fellows, so indifferent to personal and material interests, so superior in their mentality to the common run of mankind?" It was not, he answers, ambition, the hope of wealth or professional advancement, or the attraction of being identified as a hero. "It was one faith alone that inspired them; their strength came from but a single source; it was one quite innocent of hidden or transcendental motives. As Italian seamen, they felt it to be their duty to devote themselves entirely to the service of their country . . . ; their offering was comprehensive and absolute, arising solely from an instinctive sentiment, part of their very essence: the sentiment of patriotism" (53).

Borghese's occasional comments on political and international affairs indicate that he retained a degree of identification with the government for which he had fought so well. The conquest of Ethiopia, an act of unameliorated aggression that destroyed the credibility of the League of Nations, is characterized as "a victory . . . achieved by a people fighting in unison for its right to live" (18); the invasion of Greece, equally unprovoked, is glossed over by the declaration that "Greece became involved in the war" (74); and the secret negotiations that led to the overthrow of Mussolini and the Italian armistice are "the insidious intrigues of those who plotted against their own country from within" (241). But these and a handful of other such remarks are throwaway lines in what is essentially a story of high adventure and heroic achievement.

The history of the Tenth Light Flotilla is sketched in such works as Richard O'Neill, *Suicide Squads: Axis and Allied Spe-*

cial Attack Weapons of World War II (London, 1981), and
Aldo Cocchia, *Submarines Attacking: Adventures of Italian Naval Forces* (London, 1956), as well as studies by Bragadin and
Sadkovich. The Tenth's exploits are the subject of William
G. Schofield and P. J. Carisella, *Frogmen: First Battles* (Boston, 1987). Lazzero Ricciotti, in *La Decima Mas* (Turin,
1984), devotes more than half of his book to Borghese's activities following the Italian surrender. The only known article is that by Paul Kemp, "Decima MAS," *MHQ* 7 (Autumn
1994): 74–81. The assault craft used by the Tenth and Borghese's operations with the *Scirè* are amply covered by publi-
cations issued by the Italian Naval History Office. But *Sea
Devils* remains the classic account.

The Imperial Japanese Navy, which committed five midget
submarines to an unsuccessful attack on Pearl Harbor at the
time of the air raid, was the only other navy that entered the
war with the ability to carry out the type of operations at
which the Tenth excelled. But the latter's exploits soon inspired imitation. The British used a pig lost at Gibraltar as
a model for human torpedoes called chariots and developed
midget submarines known as X-craft. An attempted attack
on the German battleship *Tirpitz* in October 1942 by two
chariots towed across the North Sea by an innocent-seeming
fishing trawler failed when the tow lines parted ten miles
from the target's Norwegian base, but three months later a
chariot sank the unfinished Italian light cruiser *Ulpio Traiano*
at Palermo. X-craft towed to Norway by a full-sized submarine put the *Tirpitz* out of action for six months in September
1943, and others severely damaged the Japanese heavy cruiser
Takao at Singapore in July 1945. The Germans produced
midget submarines, radar-controlled explosive motorboats,
and a new type of weapon consisting of two torpedoes, one
of which served as a vehicle for a single operator, his head
above water in a plastic dome, who fired the other projectile.
These weapons achieved modest success off the Normandy

beaches in July and August 1944, permanently disabling the old British cruiser *Dragon* and sinking a destroyer escort and seven other small vessels.

Late in the war the Japanese produced *kaiten* ("turn toward heaven") piloted torpedoes, initially deployed in November 1944, and *shinyo* ("ocean shaking") explosive motorboats, a few of which made fruitless sorties off Okinawa in March 1945. *Kaiten*s definitely sank the fleet oiler *Mississinewa* and may have been responsible for the sinking of the destroyer escort *Underhill* and the cruiser *Indianapolis,* although the submarine commander involved in the loss of the latter insisted that he had used conventional torpedoes. For its part, the U.S. Navy organized underwater demolition teams (UDTs) to reconnoiter invasion sites and blast paths through natural and man-made underwater obstructions. First employed in the assault on the Marshall Islands in February 1944, UDTs were used on an increasingly large scale in both the European and Pacific theaters during the remainder of the war.

Italian assault units did not cease operations in 1943. Their subsequent targets were Italian warships seized by the Germans at the time of the armistice. A mixed force of Italian and British frogmen sank the heavy cruisers *Bolzano* and *Gorizia* at La Spezia in June 1944, and in April 1945 an Italian team immobilized the unfinished aircraft carrier *Aquila* to prevent it from being used as a blockship at Genoa.

These operations were not conducted under Borghese's command, however. Following the armistice, the Tenth was the only Italian force in the La Spezia area not attacked by the German troops that entered the city the next day. Soon thereafter Borghese rallied to the Salò Republic, a shadow state Mussolini established behind German lines. Until the end of the war Borghese used the Tenth, a land army of six thousand men scattered throughout northern Italy, against the forces of the Italian Republic, communists (especially Tito's Yugoslavs, who tried to annex northeastern Italy), and

partisans of all stripes. His extremely rough handling of partisans earned him the sobriquet "The Black Prince." Late in
April 1945 the German front—and with it, the Salò Republic—collapsed. In Milan when Mussolini was executed on the
twenty-eighth, Borghese put on a lieutenant's uniform furnished by a U.S. liaison officer and was driven to Rome,
where he appeared in civilian clothes. No one could offer a
postwar Italian court evidence to sustain the allegations about
his mistreatment of partisans—and he remained a free man.
He died in Cadiz, Spain, on 28 August 1974.

An Italian colleague told this writer that "Borghese was
one of the 'damned souls' of Italian history. For this reason
in Italy it's not 'politically correct' to write books about him
(just for historians) or better yet don't buy these books (just
for libraries)." Borghese is therefore best remembered as the
bright, stealthy, and audacious commander of the *Scirè* and
of the Tenth Light Flotilla until September 1943. His organization set the pattern for similar elite groups maintained
by all major naval powers since World War II.

Capt. Paolo E. Coletta,
USNR (Ret.)

Notes

1. Viscount Cunningham of Hyndhope, *A Sailor's Odyssey* (New York, 1951), 240; Samuel Eliot Morison, *History of United States Naval Operations in World War II*, vol. 2, *Operations in North African Waters, October 1942–June 1943* (Boston, 1947), 189.
2. Glen John St. Barclay, *The Rise and Fall of the New Roman Empire: Italy's Bid for World Power, 1890–1943* (New York, 1973); James J. Sadkovich, *The Italian Navy in World War II* (Westport, Conn., 1994); Marc'Antonio Bragadin with Giuseppe Fioravanzo, *The Italian Navy in World War II* (Annapolis, Md., 1957); Giuseppe Fioravanzo, "Italian Strategy in the Mediterranean, 1940–1943," U.S. Naval Institute *Proceedings* 84 (September 1959): 65–72.
3. Sadkovich, *Italian Navy in World War II*, 34–39.
4. Cunningham, *Sailor's Odyssey*, 190.
5. Sadkovich, *Italian Navy in World War II*, 54, 345.
6. Alberto Santoni, "The Italian Navy at the Outbreak of World War

II and the Influence of British ULTRA Intelligence on Mediterranean Operations," in Jack Sweetman et al., eds., *New Interpretations in Naval History: Selected Papers from the Tenth Naval History Symposium* (Annapolis, Md., 1993), 295–96.

7. Sadkovich, *Italian Navy in World War II*, 41–42, 132.
8. Santoni, "Outbreak of World War II," 298–301.
9. Sadkovich, *Italian Navy in World War II*, 79–80, 239, 249, 272–74, 314–18, 346.
10. Ibid., 32, 37, 39, 103, 286, 317, 337, 338.
11. Ibid., 301, 318, 321, 343, 344.
12. Cunningham, *Sailor's Odyssey*, 433, 435.
13. Sadkovich, *Italian Navy in World War II*, 217, 335.
14. Ibid., 1–2, 5, 336.

Sea Devils

H.M.S. *Valiant.*

CONTENTS

CONTENTS

7

CONTENTS

LIST OF ILLUSTRATIONS

LIST OF ILLUSTRATIONS

LINE DRAWINGS IN TEXT

CHAPTER I

HOW A NEW ARM WAS BORN

Origins: The Sanctions and British hostility during the Abyssinian war—Precedents: Pellegrini's Grillo *('Cricket') and the* Mignatta *('Leech') of Paolucci and Rossetti—Toschi and Tesei—The human torpedo is born—First experiments—The training centre on the Serchio—The first pilots—Origin of the explosive boat—The Duke of Aosta—Two years lost—Fresh start in 1938—Aloisi in command—Finishing touches in 1940—The first full practice with the submarine* Ametista *(Amethyst)—What might have been done and was not.*

'*2nd October, 1935*

ITALY is on the march to East Africa. The Navy is standing by; things may begin to happen any moment now. We may not be ready for them and the prospect of a clash with the British Fleet, the most powerful in the world, may give us plenty to think about, but that doesn't worry us; every officer and every seaman is at his post, ready to accept responsibility and do his duty.'

The story of the origin of the Italian assault craft and of the reasons for their adoption must begin with the date quoted above rather than with the events of the First World War: for it was really the menacing situation in those days that obliged us to create the new arm.

How could Italy have resisted an attempt to overwhelm her with the crushing power and weight of the British Fleet? In a war, such as that to be expected, Italy's chances would be discounted in advance: the disproportion of strength would be immense, both by sea and by air; so, too, would be the inequality of industrial capacity and ability to maintain supplies. We should have been hemmed in within our small and cramped peninsula and bound to be soon starved out by the British blockade. How could we break out?

And then an idea began to form in our minds: to create a destructive weapon and employ it unexpectedly and at the right moment, thus causing the enemy's fleet a substantial initial weakening by attacks launched during the first days of war and based upon the novelty of their means and the impetus of the assailants.[1]

Some kind of new, unforeseen weapon, rapidly produced and instantly employed, to carry destruction into the enemy's camp from the very start of hostilities, would put us in a position to face the conflict on terms of equal strength or, at any rate, of less disadvantage. The effectiveness of this weapon would be its surprise value—that is to say, its being kept secret; yet its employment would have to be on a massive scale and against a number of different objectives at the same time, for, once the secret weapon became known, its opportunities would be vastly reduced and its employment very much more difficult and risky.

Teseo Tesei and Elios Toschi were two Sub-Lieutenants serving as engineers on submarines belonging to the La Spezia flotilla. They had been occupied for years with long mutual discussions on such topics; they had studied in particular the enterprises of those who had preceded them during the First World War in the invention and employment of new weapons: there was Commander Pellegrini, who had entered Pola harbour with his *Grillo*, a motorboat equipped with caterpillars enabling it to climb over the defences (he had been surprised at a critical moment of his negotiation of these obstacles and captured before he could reach his final objective); there was also Sub-Lieutenant Raffaele Paolucci, a young surgeon who afterwards achieved great distinction in his profession—he was the man who, together with Naval Engineer Major Raffaele Rossetti, began the series of individual forcings of enemy harbours in the distant days of 1918. Paolucci gives the following account of the origin of his idea:

"In February 1918 I had formed a project to take a motorboat to the entrance of Pola harbour, as near as about a kilometre outside a gap in the breakwater, and swim from there, with a special mine of my invention, to one of the nearer of the *Radetzky* type battleships which were anchored directly behind the defences. The mine was to be 160 cm. long, about 60 mm. in diameter, and shaped to a point, with two air tanks, one astern and one forward. The charge, consisting of a quintal (220.46 lb.) of compressed T.N.T., would occupy a central position, and between it and the forward point a time-fuse with external control would be placed

[1] Elios Toschi: *Escape Over the Himalayas*. Ed. Eur., Milan.

for the ignition of the detonator and, consequently, the explosion of the charge. On arrival under the enemy vessel I would open the air tank astern and the position of the mine would then change from horizontal to vertical. A rope something over four metres in length, which I would bring with me wound round my waist, and with one end already made fast to the mine, would then be attached to a scupper terminal or any other structural protuberance or, if the worst came to the worst, to the bottom step of a davit. I should then set the time-fuse for explosion in an hour, open the forward air tank, and the mine would then sink about four metres, the length of the rope suspending it. The hour of grace before the explosion would permit me to retrace my route, this time relieved from the weight of the mine, again negotiate the defence nets and, just outside, await the effect of the explosion. After it had taken place I should swim further out to sea and, with my back to the enemy, flash a small, waterproofed electric torch in order to show the waiting Italian motorboat where I was."[1]

This first project was abandoned, after months of dogged and solitary training by night, during which Paolucci swam distances up to 10 kilometres, towing a barrel to represent his mine. He was ordered eventually by Captain Costanzo Ciano of the Navy to join up with Naval Engineer Major Rossetti, who had been working since the beginning of the war at the construction of a device which would enable him to enter the base at Pola in order to sink enemy vessels. This apparatus consisted of a compressed-air special torpedo, controlled by an external lever.

"Two charges, each containing 170 kg. of T.N.T., are fitted to the head of the casing. Ignition takes place automatically at any moment desired by means of a time-fuse. There was also a special magnetic device (a 'leech') for automatically attaching the charge to the enemy's hull. These magnetic contrivances, about 20 cm. long and not more than 6–7 cm. thick, are lodged in a kind of recess inside each charge: as soon as they are brought beneath the enemy vessel, they adhere to the hull. They have attached to them a strong, thin rope about four metres long, so that the charge does not sink below that depth. The charge is detached from the special

[1] Raffaele Paolucci: *My Little Lost World*. Privately printed.

torpedo with the greatest of ease. Propulsion strength amounts to 40 h.p.: a speed of from three to four miles an hour can be attained with an air-load sufficient for a maximum range of eight or 10 miles."[1]

It is well known, and an exploit which belongs to the honoured records of naval enterprise at all times and in all countries, how, on the 31st of October, 1918, Paolucci and Rossetti, after months of training with and perfecting of the new weapon, set out from Venice on the torpedo-boat 65 PN, Costanzo Ciano being in command of the operation. They took to the sea at the mouth of Pola harbour that evening. After enormous difficulties caused by the very strong current and having overcome several lines of defences, they succeeded in mining the *Viribus Unitis*, which blew up and sank at dawn on the 1st November.

Such was the example which was to inspire the research of our two young engineers, Tesei and Toschi. Their careers, their persons and their ideals were united in a common love of their profession, for which they had a missionary zeal; both were imbued with the simple and healthy conviction that patriotism is the primary duty of man and the highest honour open to his achievement.

Toschi was a tall, strong, well-proportioned man with a frank, honest countenance and shrewd bright eyes; Tesei was shorter, equally robust but of a more nervous type; the sharpness of his features was mellowed by his deep, dark eyes, indicative of the maturity of his intelligence and the resolution of his character.

These men saw the problem in its technical aspect. Their object was, starting from the *Mignatta* of Rossetti, to work up to a weapon which should improve upon its predecessor by enabling two men, a pilot and an assistant, to live, navigate, approach and attack an objective *without ever emerging to the surface of the water*.

They spent entire nights, closeted in their little room at the submarine shore quarters in La Spezia, discussing and planning the technical and nautical details involved. At last the project took shape.

"The new weapon is in size and shape very similar to a torpedo but is in reality a miniature submarine with entirely novel features, electrical propulsion and a steering wheel similar to that of an aeroplane. The innovation of greatest interest is the point that the

[1] R. Paolucci, *op. cit.*

14

crew, instead of remaining enclosed and more or less helpless in the interior, keep outside the structure. The two men, true flyers of the sea-depths, bestride their little underwater 'airplane', barely protected from the frontal onrush of the waters by a curved screen of plastic glass . . . at night, under cover of the most complete darkness and steering by luminous control instruments, they will be able to aim at and attack their objective while remaining quite invisible to the enemy. The operators, unhampered by the steel structure, are free to move and act at will, to reach the bottom of the sea and travel along it in any way and direction, and are able to cut nets and remove obstacles with special compressed-air tools and, therefore, reach any target. Equipped with a long-range underwater breathing-gear, the operators will be able, without any connection whatsoever with the surface, to breathe and navigate under water at any depths up to thirty metres and carry a powerful explosive charge into an enemy harbour. Being utterly invisible and beyond the reach of the most delicately sensitive acoustic detector, they will be able to operate in the interior of the harbour till they find the keel of a large unit, fasten the charge to it and thus ensure an explosion which will sink the vessel."[1]

As soon as the finishing touches had been put to the blue-prints, they were submitted to the Naval Ministry for approval and the authorization to build one or two prototypes for practical testing.

The reply of Admiral Cavagnari, Chief of the Naval Staff, was prompt and favourable: two specimens were immediately to be constructed. Thirty mechanics of the San Bartolomeo (La Spezia) Submarine Weapons Works were ordered to do the job. The two inventors were not released from their duties as submarine engineer officers and were therefore only free to devote themselves to the carrying out of their project when not performing their service on board. Nevertheless, in a few months, after considerable difficulties had been overcome and improvised expedients used—the first motor-engine came from a lift which was being demolished!—the two prototypes were ready.

"The first tests were satisfactory," Toschi wrote. "They were carried out in the chilly waters of the bay in January and gave us

[1] Toschi, *op. cit.*

15

unexpected results and extremely novel sensations when our submerged bodies stiffened convulsively as we were carried along by the machine we had ourselves created. We felt a thrill of delight in the dark depths of the sea our tiny human torpedo was penetrating so obediently."

After the demonstration tests an official one was held in the presence of Admiral Falangola, who was sent down from the Ministry, in one of the repair docks of La Spezia arsenal, which was cleared for the occasion and surrounded, for reasons of secrecy, by police. In spite of the low temperature and a number of constructive short-comings, and the restricted extent of the waters of the dock, the tests of manœuvrability and of submersion survived the rigorous nature of the experiment and overcame the incredulity of those present. These two determined and courageous men had in fact created a new weapon; there could be no doubt about it when their heads were seen to show on the surface of the muddy water and then to disappear entirely beneath it without leaving a trace, only to reappear farther on, in accordance with the manipulation of an invisible device which was obviously under perfect control by the pilots.

Admiral Falangola saw the advantages of the new weapon and gave permission for the construction of a certain number of units; they were duly ordered. At the same time, during the early months of 1936, several officers, who volunteered and had the necessary out-standing physical and moral qualifications, were appointed for training in the difficult task of operating the piloted torpedo. Their names should not be forgotten: besides the Naval Engineer Sub-Lieutenants Toschi and Tesei, they were Lieutenant Franzini, Gunner Sub-Lieutenant Stefanini and Midshipman Centurione.

Such was the nucleus of what was to be the Tenth Light Flotilla; that is to say, the division of the Italian Navy destined for the research, construction, training and employment in war of assault craft.

But this did not develop along conventional lines; a new invention inevitably provokes reaction, distrust and scepticism. There were fanatics, progressive spirits, who now supposed that fleets were a thing of the past; how could they ever survive the employment of the new weapon? On the other hand, there were the conservatives; guns alone, in the future as in the past, could decide the question of naval superiority; what could only two men, immersed in chilly water and

16

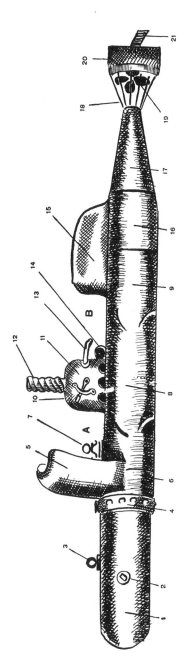

SLOW-SPEED TORPEDO—CALLED THE 'PIG'.

(a) Pilot's seat. (b) Diver's or second man's seat.

(1) Warhead (300 kg. of explosive). (2) Time-fuse. (3) Suspension-ring. (4) Clutch for warhead. (5) Wind-screen. (6) Fore trimming-tank. (7) Trimming-tank control pump. (8) Battery compartment. (9) Electric motor. (10) Crash submersion control lever. (11) Crash submersion tank. (12) Crash tank exhaust valve. (13) Security grip for second man. (14) 20 *atm* air container for tank crash exhaust. (15) Can containing reserve breathing set and working tools (net-lifters, net-cutters, rope, clamps, etc.). (16) Stern trimming tank. (17) Propeller shaft compartment. (18) Protective grid for propeller. (19) Propeller. (20) Vertical rudder (direction). (21) Horizontal rudder (for depth).

The midget submarine "C.A."

the darkness of night, do against the insuperable defensive measures taken by a fleet at anchor at a naval base? Was it permissible to waste time and money and sidetrack officers, so urgently needed on account of the great development of the Italian Navy, for training in an employment which stood so little chance of a successful issue and was in any case unprecedented? And what was to be thought of the claim of these two young engineer officers in desiring themselves to be the first pilots to take machines of their own construction into action in the event of war? The regulations were definitely against it: the piloted torpedo was a unit of the Navy; the command of naval units is the prerogative of deck officers; engineers may plan, but not operate, units at sea.

Thus, while a first tiny nucleus of pilots was being formed under the orders of Commander Catalano Gonzaga of the submarine flotilla at La Spezia, Toschi and Tesei, the inventors, remained aboard their submarines, often away from their base on cruises, so that they could only turn to the perfecting of their new machine and to training in its use in the few odd hours of leisure their normal duties left them.

At the mouth of the River Serchio, on the estate of the Dukes of Salviati, far from any road and from any prying eye, in the thick of the magnificent pine-woods, centuries old, which run down almost to the seashore, stood, right from the start, first in a tent, then in a farmhouse, the training centre of the human torpedoes; the grandeur and beauty of nature were a worthy setting and a safe refuge for the silent, secret, fervent and assiduous work of the handful of seamen who were one day to endanger the British Fleet and arouse the unreserved admiration of the whole world for their audacity.

Meanwhile, under the stimulus of the same reflections as had inspired Tesei and Toschi while the sanctions were in force, the General of Aviation Duke Amedeo of Aosta, was planning to achieve the same results by wholly different methods. Small and very fast motorboats, containing explosives and carried between the two floats of the S.55 hydroplanes (the glorious old *Santa Maria* type), were to be released in great numbers in front of enemy naval bases immediately after the beginning of hostilities. After penetrating the harbour they were to be launched against the ships at the same time as an air attack took place to distract the attention of the defence. The Duke of Aosta confided this idea to his brother Aimone, Duke of Spoleto, admiral and devotee of motorboat sport. The Duke Aimone took the matter up personally and, in association with Commander Giorgis, who attended to the naval construction required, and with the engineer Guido Cattaneo, who took care of the mechanical side, two specimens were soon constructed of a craft which corresponded in size and weight with the desired purposes. The extremely light hull was composed of a wooden frame covered with waterproof canvas; the engine, to save space, was placed horizontally; the bows contained a charge which would explode on impact against the objective, causing it to sink. The pilot would have to throw himself into the sea a few moments before impact, after making sure that his little vessel was dead on the target.

Such was the origin of the first rudimentary assault craft, which, after a number of alterations and improvements, was to become the perfect weapon enabling us to attain the glorious victory of Suda Bay.

The work carried out with such enthusiasm was soon brought to an abrupt end.

The swiftness with which the war in Africa terminated in a victory actually achieved by a people fighting in unison for its right to live, caused the responsible military commanders to believe, now that Ethiopia had been outfought and the Empire proclaimed, that the situation had improved and the threat of a European conflict was less imminent. Accordingly, the small special weapons department had no sooner been set up than it was casually dissolved. This was a grave error, the consequences of which were severely felt at the outbreak of hostilities with Britain; it was an error which should never have been committed, in view of the fact that the consolidation of our position in East Africa not only failed to mitigate British enmity but actually rendered it more positive, uncompromising and relentless.

From the end of 1936, therefore, until 1938, the few new weapons in existence, which had been made ready with so much patient industry, were stored away in depots carefully shielded from prying eyes; the few volunteers already trained for the risky employment which had seemed soon to be required, were diverted to other tasks; technical research and planning for the employment of the new arms were interrupted.

In 1938 Commander Paolo Aloisi, an officer with an enthusiastic interest in and talent for engineering, was appointed, at La Spezia, to the command of the First Light Flotilla, consisting of very fast vessels; he was also directed by the Ministry to take over the special weapons.

The old materials were retrieved and Aloisi devoted his inventive gifts to their improvement; the original piloted torpedo devised by Toschi and Tesei underwent considerable alterations for the better, and the canvas-covered motorboats were replaced by others with wooden hulls. Cattaneo and the dockyard staff of Baglietto at Varazze took an active share in this work.

It was only in July 1939, in view of the rapid approach of an international crisis and the now obvious imminence of war in Europe, that the Naval Staff issued the following order:

"The Command of the First Light Flotilla is entrusted with the duties of training a nucleus of personnel for employment with given special weapons, and of carrying out, under the general supervision of Admiral Goiran, experiments and tests concerned with the perfecting of the said weapons."

Accordingly, at the beginning of 1940, the old pilots returned at intervals to the Serchio, retaining, however, the appointments to their vessels; Toschi, Tesei, Stefanini, Catalano and Centurione were joined by other officers to begin training: the latter were De Giacomo, Di Domenico, Vesco, Birindelli, Bertozzi, de la Penne and Aloisi himself.

Admiral Cavagnari, Chief of the Naval Staff, to whom a documentary film had meanwhile been shown on the subject of the new explosive craft, at once perceived the possibilities they afforded and ordered a series of 12 to be constructed. He also commissioned Captain De Pace to form and direct, within the planning department of the Naval Staff, a division for the study of special weapons. An initial organization thus came gradually into practical being.

Aloisi had resurrected the new weapons, had contributed much to their technical improvement, to the formation of a first nucleus of personnel in training and, above all, to overcoming the distrust and opposition of the many who saw in the Secret Department merely a useless waste of energy, not to say a convenient method adopted by some men to evade professional discipline by taking a brilliant line of their own. Highly placed quarters were beginning to be impressed by the idea of a bold move on the first night of war as a decisive factor in the outcome of the conflict. But owing to the two years which had been lost, neither the material nor the personnel were yet ready, while events marched rapidly and fatefully on and the time of testing came swiftly nearer.

It was at the beginning of 1940 that I had the opportunity to make personal acquaintance with the group of pilots of the new weapon. I was at that time in command of the submarine *Ametista*, which had been selected for the first full practice with human torpedoes. The idea of using air transport for these craft had now been given up; the absence of a naval air force and the lack of close collaboration between the Navy and the Air Force had made it impracticable (this was only one of the minor detriments which the failure to co-ordinate caused during the war, to the prejudice of our armed forces' chances of success). The submarine, therefore, replaced the aeroplane.

In the presence of Admiral Goiran, commanding the North Tyrrhenian Sector, Captain De Pace and Commander Aloisi and all the pilots of the group, three of the craft were lashed on the deck of the *Ametista* and, with their operators aboard, the submarine put to sea. The Gulf of La Spezia, at a point south of the island of Tino, with the submarine surfaced, was the scene of the manœuvre of releasing personnel. After the craft had got clear, with the operators astride of them, two for each torpedo, in single file, we saw the three little vessels disappear rapidly into the windy darkness of the night; six diminutive black points indicated their presence, where the operators' heads just showed above water; in an instant more even these had vanished. The plan was to approach the harbour, enter it by the eastern gate and attack the *Quarto*, which was anchored in the roadstead. The practice lasted all night. At daybreak one of the three operators reached the objective (the other two craft had got into trouble) and a powerful (dummy) charge was fixed to the keel of the target; in real warfare the target could not have escaped certain destruction. On that occasion a system was tried out, based upon the transmission of very short waves from the submarine, to guide the torpedoes, which were equipped with receivers, back to the parent ship on the conclusion of their mission. Results being unsatisfactory, the system was abandoned, but mainly because it was considered, by the pilots in particular, that no plans should be made for return to the submarine, the pilots preferring to feel that from the moment of their release communication was cut off; no energy was to be held in reserve for eventual escape but all of it was to be used up, to the point of utter exhaustion, in inflicting the greatest possible damage on the enemy. Tesei especially,

20

who was one of the pilots that night, maintained this principle, carrying it to the heights of the most sublime and impersonal mysticism. "The success of the mission is not very important," he used to say, "nor even the outcome of the war. What really counts is that there are men ready to die in the attempt and really dying in it: for our sacrifice will inspire and fortify future generations to conquer." In these words he was consciously foretelling his own death; this innermost conviction gave him great prestige among his colleagues, who considered him their guide and conscience as well as their technical adviser.

This practice and others, in which I took part, made a deep impression upon me. I had specialized in underwater weapons and had experience in that sphere, having, in fact, many years' experience as a diver, and was thus able to realize how effective in war the new weapon might be. Despite the undoubted difficulties of employment of the torpedo, men of exceptional physical and moral endowments, working to the limit of the resources of human energy, endurance and will power, would be capable of performing actions hard to match for surprise value. In the piloted torpedo and in the explosive motorboat the Italian Navy and it alone possessed resources which would positively have enabled it to carry out a sudden unexpected mass attack. Delivered in a number of harbours simultaneously, so as to take full advantage of the element of surprise, the attack could have led to a resounding and substantial victory at the beginning of hostilities which might have equalized the potentials of the opposed fleets.

The explosive motorboat was a true 'assault weapon', while the piloted torpedo would be better designated an 'insidious weapon'; this terminological difference well expresses the contrast between the traits of character required in volunteers for either arm.

Impetuosity is as necessary to the one as a cool head to the other; the former concentrates his whole store of energy in an action of a few seconds, while the latter must economize it for hours and hours; the former is all nerves and the other must not have any; the former defies, in a single supreme instant, an enemy who faces him and whom he can see; the latter, submerged in the utter darkness of the nocturnal depths of the sea, is guided on his blind course by the luminous dials of his instruments and becomes aware of his target only when his bare hands touch the mighty keel of the enemy vessel; the former, finally, is the infantryman who, exposed to a hostile barrage, leaps from a trench to the attack with grenade or bayonet; the latter is the pioneer making his way through enemy lines, overcoming all obstacles, surrounded by snares and perils, entrusted to an extremely vulnerable apparatus, and protected from the paralysing chill of the waters only by a thin rubber diving-suit.

Different characters, different men and, therefore, different methods and different bases for training them.

Motorboats at La Spezia with classes in engine practice, pilotage, navigation, negotiation of obstacles and methods of attack; human torpedoes on the Serchio with training in diving with the breathing gear, torpedo pilotage, navigation, underwater negotiation of defences by cutting or lifting nets, and, finally, attack on keels.

Identical moral and ethical qualities required in all; firmness of character, quick decision, tenacity, contempt for danger, unswerving resolution, unrestricted devotion of one's own life to the Fatherland.

With this mentality and in this atmosphere the preparations went forward, at the beginning of 1940, among this small group of officers and seamen; but this high level of personal responsibility was contrasted with scanty resources, the distrust for the new weapons and the vague conception of their real possibilities, doubt as to their success and, finally, the lack of any organized and far-seeing plan for their use. Thus the way was barred to a great Italian victory which might have changed, perhaps even reversed, the course of the war.

And that a well-timed attack in mass at the beginning of hostilities would have been wholly successful is confirmed by the results achieved with our still imperfect weapons against the British Fleet, victoriously attacked in its most heavily fortified bases at an advanced stage of the war, when highly effective precautionary and defensive measures had already been taken. And even after the British had become acquainted with and obtained actual possession of the new weapons, through the attacks they had undergone, and their existence was no longer a secret, Alexandria and Gibraltar were several times forced with positive results.

It is not for polemical reasons that the errors committed and the opportunites lost are here recalled; it is because I consider that History ought to be impartially written for future generations: from the knowledge of their predecessors' mistakes, they should learn not to commit them again.

CHAPTER II

TYPES OF ASSAULT CRAFT

Description of special types—The midget submarine CA—The human torpedo SLC and its employment—A typical operation —The San Bartolomeo SSB torpedo—The explosive assault boat MTM—Its submarine-borne sister craft MTR—The torpedo assault boat MTS and its subsequent forms MTSM and SMA—The 'leeches' or 'bugs' carried by 'frogmen' or assault swimmers—Explosive limpets.

THE types of assault craft of the Italian Navy underwent, as war proceeded, modifications and transformations suggested by experience and by the need to counter the defensive measures taken by the enemy as he became acquainted with the methods of attack.

The principal types of assault craft were:

The midget submarine CA. A small submarine of about 12 tons, built by the Caproni works and based on an original model dating back to the First World War. Its armament consisted of two torpedoes of 450 mm. and its crew of only two men. It was the idea of Lieutenant-Commander Angelo Belloni to employ this type of submarine for entering an enemy harbour in submersion and for launching underwater saboteurs there to mine ships.

Scientific progress in the field of underwater detectors, the great distance of enemy harbours from the Italian starting bases (as opposed to the situation in the previous war), in relation to the limited range of the CA, and the existence of the human torpedo, a new, handier weapon, with greater power of penetration and lower costs, spoke against the employment of the CA in the originally planned manner. It was, however, about to be employed for an attack on New York harbour when the armistice was proclaimed.

A certain number of a more seaworthy type, the CB, having a displacement of 30 tons, a crew of four and a considerably greater range, were also built; these were used with remarkable success in the Black Sea, where they were employed as submarines, not as assault craft.

The SLC human torpedo, called the 'pig'. (An improved model by Tesei and Toschi of Rossetti's *Mignatta*.) A kind of torpedo 6.7 metres long, with a diameter of 53 cm., ridden astride by two men: the pilot (always an officer) was in front and his assistant behind him. Their legs were held in place by stirrups; a windscreen was used as a break-water. The maximum speed was 2.5 m.p.h. (hence the official designation SLC, the initials, in Italian, of 'slow speed torpedo'), action range was about 10 miles, the limit of submersion depth 30 metres (often exceeded in war-time emergencies). Submersion and surfacing were carried out by flooding or emptying tanks with electric pumps. Propulsion was electrical, energy being provided by an accumulator battery of 30 elements with tension capacity of 60 volts; speed could be regulated in four stages by a flywheel connected to a rheostat. The rudders were controlled on the same principle as that of the *cloche* in aviation and for similar purposes. In front of the pilot stood the panel of control instruments consisting of a depth gauge, a magnetic compass, a voltmeter, an ampère meter, a manometer for registering pressure in the trimming tanks and a spirit-level. The control instruments were all luminous so as to allow them to be read at night under water.

Let us now examine the 'pig' from stem to stern. The head (1.8 metres long), which contains 300 kg. of explosive, can be detached from the rest by means of an easily manipulated clutch. Next comes, within the body of the torpedo, the fore trimming tank and above it the seat of the first pilot, with windscreen and panel of guide and control instruments. In the centre are the accumulator batteries and the motor compartment with the crash submersion tank above, worked by a lever for the exhaust valve. Exhaustion of the crash submersion tank is obtained by high-pressure air from containers placed at the rear of the tank. Then comes the seat of the second man, who leans his back against a chest containing the working tools: compressed air net-lifters and net-cutters, scissors, the kind of clamps called 'sergeants', used in attacking the keels of enemy ships, plenty of rope, also required for this operation, and coiled round a billet of wood: it is called in our jargon a 'lift'. In the body of the torpedo there is next placed the stern trimming tank, the compartment containing the propeller shaft, the propeller itself surrounded by a protective grid, the horizontal rudder for depth and the vertical rudder for direction, both controlled by the *cloche*.

The pilots wear a special rubber diving-suit which covers every part of them except head and hands: a Belloni overall (named after its inventor) consisting of a hermetic garment into which one gets through a central opening provided with an ingenious zip-fastener. The pilot uses an underwater breathing apparatus fed by bottles containing high-pressure oxygen good for about six hours. The rubber breathing bag of the apparatus is connected with a corrugated flexible tube which carries the oxygen (at greatly reduced pressure) to the mouthpiece. Exhalation takes place through the same tube and the air is expelled into a canister of soda lime crystals for detaining and absorbing the carbon-dioxide produced by respiration.

And now let us see how all this works.

We may imagine ourselves inside the submarine approaching the enemy harbour; our two-man torpedoes are contained in watertight steel cases clamped on to the deck. After a few days we get near the base to be forced. We shall be released at the shortest distance from the enemy's harbour permitted by the natural obstacles and those created by the defence.

Immediately after passing out of the escape hatch, both members of the crew pull their apparatus out of the cylinder and apply various tests to ensure that it has not been damaged during the approach. If all is well, the pilot, guided by the luminous compass, goes full speed ahead, by the courses previously laid out, to the entrance of the harbour; during this phase our heads will be kept above water enabling us to see our way and to breathe without the mask, so as to avoid undue fatigue.

Speed will be gradually reduced as we approach the zone of enemy observation; if we are threatened with discovery by a patrolboat, or the beam of a searchlight hovers over us, we submerge rapidly, continuing along our approach course. Now our 'pig' bumps against the nets guarding the harbour entrance. We shall pass beneath them if there is a gap or else we shall make one with the net-cutter or net-lifter. We are now inside the harbour; at slow speed, with only the tops of our heads above water ('observation level'), we crawl up to our assigned target; we know exactly where it is anchored and, therefore, the course of approach to it. We are also familiar with its outline, for we have studied it a thousand times in all its possible aspects.

At last we catch sight of the ship we are after; we have identified it.

How are we going to attack it? I shall use the words of one who has carried out many such operations and lived to tell us the tale.

"You see the outline of your target against the sky. You have dreamed of this moment for months, you have been training for it for years. This is the decisive minute. Success means glory; failure, a unique opportunity lost for ever. You approach, at 'observation level', to within about 30 metres of the target. There may be some lights on deck: the gleam of a match for a cigarette; or a snatch of singing from the crews' quarters may remind you that what you are seeking to destroy is something alive. You take a compass bearing, then you flood the diving-tank and the water closes over your head.

Everything is cold, dark and silent. Now you are deep enough; you close the flooding valve, put the motor into low gear and glide onwards. It gets suddenly darker; you know that you are underneath the ship. You shut off the motor and open the valve for pushing the water out of the diving-tanks. As you rise, you lift a hand above your head. You wonder whether it will touch smooth plates or knife-edged barnacles which will play the devil with your fingers or, worse still, tear your rubber overall and let the sea seep through.

Now you have found the hull. You push the torpedo back, so that your assistant can catch hold of the bilge keel, a couple of hands' breadths wide, which runs along each side of the keel of every large ship. You feel a thump on the shoulder: your assistant has found the bilge and is fixing a clamp on it. Two thumps on the shoulder: the clamp is in position. Now you go ahead to get at the bilge keel at the other side. Your second is paying out a line from one side to the other. He fixes the second clamp. And now back again, pulling oneself along by the line stretched under the hull, as far as the centre of the ship. While you clutch the rope with your hands, holding the torpedo between your legs, your second leaves his seat and passes you till he reaches the warhead in front. In the darkness you know that he is fastening the warhead to the rope stretched under the ship between the bilge keels. Now he has detached the head; the firing clock which will cause the 300 kg. of the charge to explode in two and a half hours begins to measure off the seconds. Your assistant returns to his seat: three thumps on the shoulder: the job is done. You start the motor, glide away from under the ship and gently surface. Now you may think of escape."

Simple, isn't it?

We shall see later how things work out in practice and what serious difficulties were encountered by those who attempted and often successfully completed a real attack; but before examining it as it is, with all its dramatic and unexpected features, we wanted to take you along with us on this exceptionally favoured and easy mission. Even that simple account may give the reader an idea of the energy and endurance of those men who volunteered to be dropped off at sea, only protected by a thin diving-suit, thousands of miles away from their bases and their homes; and who, astride of a fragile apparatus moving under water with a terrible cargo of explosive, penetrate a harbour at night and challenge the enemy by placing, with their own hands, the charge under the hull of his ship.

This weapon, employed at Gibraltar, Malta and Algiers, enabled Italy to score the great victory at Alexandria.

The San Bartolomeo SSB torpedo. An improved model of the previous type, with the sea-going qualities of range, speed, navigability and submersion considerably increased. Built in the secret assault craft workshop, at the Submarine Weapons department of La Spezia dockyard, in accordance with the blue-prints of Major Mario Masciulli and Captain Travaglini, it was never used in action, because its imminent employment was prevented by the armistice.

The modified touring motorboat MTM, called the 'explosive boat (E-boat)'. A flat-bottomed motorboat, 1.9 metres wide, 5.2 metres long; driven by an Alfa-Romeo 2500 engine, giving it a speed of 32 m.p.h., five hours without refuelling at maximum speed. The combined propeller and rudder, a one-piece unit outside the hull, as in an outboard craft, can be easily lifted out of the water: hence the boat can slip over defence nets without getting stuck. The forepart of the craft contains a keg of 300 kg. of explosive, bursting upon impact or hydrostatic pressure. This craft is piloted by one man; after cautiously negotiating possible obstacles and torpedo nets, he identifies his target; he aims the bows of the E-boat at it; as soon as correct aim has been taken, he shifts to maximum speed, clamps the rudder and instantly throws himself into the sea. While the pilot, so as not to be caught in the water at the moment of explosion, rapidly climbs on to the wooden life-saver which had been serving him as a back-rest on board and which he had detached by pulling a lever an instant before plunging, the motorboat rushes on and hits the target: the afterpart is severed from the forepart (the impact leads to the bursting of a ring of small explosive charges forming a belt round the hull, so that the craft is split in two) and sinks rapidly, while the keg with the main charge, on reaching a depth fixed according to the ship's draught, explodes as the result of hydrostatic pressure, tearing an enormous leak in the hull.

This type of assault craft was used in the attacks on Suda Bay and Malta.

The light touring motorboat MTR. A motorboat derived from the preceding model, having the same characteristics and employed in the same way, but of reduced dimensions, enabling it to be placed, for approach to the enemy waters, in cylinders on the deck of a submarine.

The torpedo touring motorboat MTSM. A motorboat designed for attacking vessels not only in harbour but also in the open sea and while in motion. Seven metres long and 2.3 metres wide. Two engines (Alfa-Romeo 2500), one on each side, developing a speed of about 30 m.p.h. A small torpedo is carried in a special launching tube between the engines; it is launched from aft by a telescope ejector working on compressed air; as soon as the torpedo reaches the water it begins to run, doubling back on its tracks, and passes beneath the launching vessel. Two special depth-charges, acting under hydrostatic pressure, are the only defence measures against a pursuing vessel. The MTSM carries a crew of two, a first and a second pilot. It is a development of the MTS (carrying one engine and two torpedoes) which was employed at Santi Quaranta and Port Edda; it is a precursor of the final type, the SMA, which was only completed towards the end of the war.

The MTSM was widely used: in the Black Sea it was employed by the 'Moccagatta column', in North Africa by the 'Giobbe column', and was also employed in Tunisian, Sicilian and Sardinian waters.

The 'Leech' or 'Bug'. An explosive charge of about 2 kg., adhering to the hull by air-cushion pressure. Four or five bugs are carried round the waist of an 'assault swimmer', who is equipped with a small breathing gear, giving him a diving range of about 40 minutes (thus enabling him to place the bugs against the hull). The 'leech' has a time-fuse.

The 'assault swimmer' is a front-rank seaman who wears an

extremely close-fitting rubber overall and can swim six to seven thousand metres at a speed of about 1500 metres an hour. He is trained to approach an enemy ship, in spite of the eager and experienced eyes of the watches aboard, and without letting himself be discovered or even arousing suspicion. With invisible and silent movements, he slips down beneath the hull; he is equipped for propulsion purposes with a pair of frog-like rubber fins fitted over his feet; he wears a net over his head in which seaweed or other objects are entwined, giving them the appearance, from above, of flotsam carried along by the current.

Explosive 'limpet'. These are improvements on the 'bugs': a cylindrical case containing 4.5 kg. of very high explosive for application by the swimmer, by means of two clamps, to the bilge keels of the doomed vessel; so as to ensure that the explosion does not occur in harbour but in the open sea, the charge is provided not only with 'time' fuses but also with those of 'space'. The 'space fuse' is a small propeller set in motion at sea as a result of the movement of the vessel, but only after the latter has attained a speed over five miles. After a given distance covered by the ship, the propeller releases the lock of the firing clock and the latter is then set in motion and causes the explosion.

When the British, so as to discover these weapons, adopted the expedient of frequently running a steel cable under the hull of their ships, the limpet was given a kind of trestle, over which the cable slipped without getting stuck; and when, subsequently, the enemy undertook a regular series of explorations of the hulls by sending down divers and anti-limpeteer frogmen, a booby trap was placed which would provoke their explosion when an attempt at removing them was made.

Many other devices of various kinds were studied and occasionally constructed, for experimental purposes, by the technicians of the secret weapons workshop, but as they were never used, and for other obvious reasons as well, I can see no object in describing them. During the war a very large number of 'inventions' reached us from private sources. The great majority were fantastic and impracticable to construct or use; others were inferior to the material already being employed. There were very few of any real help in prosecuting the offensive by sea against the enemy.

On the whole, private inventions did not afford, in this field of war production, any useful assistance.

The weapons described above all had a limited range of action. Therefore, they had to be brought as close as possible to the objectives. In the absence of aircraft, which in many cases would have been the ideal means of transport, we had to modify certain naval units, usually destroyers and submarines, so as to adapt them to the special duties of 'assault craft transports'. The destroyers, with certain adaptations (deck chocks, electric cranes), proved to be useful transports for the E-boats; while a few submarines were adapted to take human torpedoes to enemy bases by carrying them on deck in watertight steel cylinders with easily working doors. The swimmers provided with 'leeches' or 'limpets' could be taken to their objectives in various ways: some were released from motorboats or torpedo-boats; others from submarines; in some cases, when the geographical circumstances were favourable, they started their operations from a neutral coast.

CHAPTER III

AT WAR—THE FIRST OPERATION:
THE SUBMARINE *IRIDE* (AUGUST 1940)

*First stage of the war—The assault craft unprepared for the
emergency—The sea-pioneer training centre and its commander
Belloni—Military secrecy—Operation of the submarine* Iride
against Alexandria—Aircraft attack on the Iride *in the Gulf
of Bomba—Rescue of the trapped men—A melancholy stock-
taking.*

10th June, 1940

ITALY declares war against Britain and France and is allied with
Germany which has concluded a non-aggression pact with Russia.
It is logically by the Italian Navy that the massive weight of British
naval supremacy will be felt, all the more since, our only war-front
being the Libyan, the Navy has to ensure the continuity of reinforcements in men and materials overseas.

What happens on our intervention? In which way do we make
use of the advantage we derive from having ourselves chosen the date
of initiating hostilities? What plan of military action, swift and sudden,
accompanies our declaration of war? Absolutely nothing happens;
from a military standpoint we enter the war from scratch, on the
pre-existent balance of forces. No plan is developed, no objective is
in view: we are marking time.

On the French front we stand on the defensive; on the Libyan front
there is only a little patrol activity (Egypt was at that time almost
completely devoid of British troops); Malta, the British naval base
situated in the heart of the Mediterranean, on the route from Italy to
Libya, the neutralization of which base should have been for years the
aim of the studies and plans of our General Staffs, and the air defence
of which consisted, on the 10th of June, 1940, of FOUR *Gladiator* aircraft, is left undisturbed; the British Mediterranean Fleet, sharing t
bases of Gibraltar and Alexandria, is inaccessible.

Such are the facts: responsibility for them will be assessed by the historian of the future.[1]

The assault craft, when the war began, suffered from the results of this general situation. They formed a small section of the Italian Navy, consisting of a few dozen men and a very few craft, which were still not ready for action; the many shortcomings in material and organization were made good, so far as it was humanly possible, by the steadiness, the conviction, the endurance, and the determination of the volunteers; they were men for whom insurmountable obstacles, insuperable difficulties and dangers impossible to overcome did not exist.

In order to deal with the need to recruit and train volunteers, there was set up, on the 1st of September, 1940, at San Leopoldo, near the Naval Academy at Leghorn, the Training Centre of Sea Pioneers, which Commanding Officer Belloni, the dean of all Italians devoted to submarine research, had been advocating for years. He was himself recalled and appointed, by a wise decision, despite his age and total deafness, to direct the training and advise the technicians of the department of insidious weapons. Officers of all arms, petty officers and seamen of all categories, who volunteered, were admitted to the Centre; they were taught the use of the underwater breathing apparatus, that is to say of the device by which it is possible to dive and remain underwater for hours, without the connection with the surface the ordinary diver needs, since he is supplied with air from a pump situated afloat.

During the training a preliminary strict weeding-out took place; all those who did not inspire confidence that they possessed, in the high degree required, the necessary physical and moral endowments, and seriousness of purpose, were returned to their units as 'certified expert breathing-gear divers'. The others were admitted to the department of secret weapons after an exhaustive inquiry into their antecedents in regard to their families and the personal motives which might have induced them to volunteer. Financial reverses, for instance, or disappointment in love, or family quarrels were valid reasons for turning down an applicant. Then came the most important test of all: a personal conversation with the commanding officer, who questioned the candidate closely with a view to gauging his spirit, ideas, stamina and

[1] In a conversation which took place in 1942 at the Palazzo Chigi (the Italian Foreign Office), Galeazzo Ciano casually told me: "When the Duce decided to declare war, he asked Badoglio: 'What plan have you got for Malta?' 'We haven't got one,' was the reply."

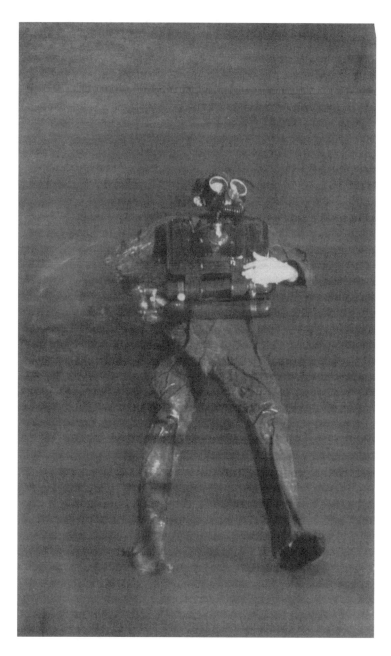

Diver with long-range breathing apparatus.

Target aimed at, rudder set, engine at full power,
whilst pilot prepares to fall into water.

Pilotless *E*-boat heads straight for target.

To avoid effects of explosion, pilot climbs quickly on
to raft he has himself launched.

mental formation. This was the decisive test. Provided the rigorous medical examinations had been passed, the commanding officer had the last word, which he based upon his personal impressions, his knowledge of men and the analytical perspicacity which came naturally to him from his professional training and career. Next came assignment to one of the special branches, suitable to the psycho-physiological characteristics of the candidate: either to surface crafts or to underwater units. Now began a long period of training (experience had taught that a good torpedo pilot needed not less than a year's coaching) so as to develop the volunteer gradually into an expert professional and, above all, to produce in him the 'ready for anything' mentality which distinguished his seniors in the use of the specialized weapon.

Secrecy, the necessity of the most absolute secrecy, not only with regard to weapons, practices, the size of the department and its location, as well as the names of mates and superiors, but even with regard to personal membership of it, was the first demand made upon the volunteers and the first test which they had to undergo. No one must know the precise type of specialization upon which a member was engaged, not even his parents or his betrothed. When one considers the extent to which most Italians feel a communicative urge, to show that they are well informed and to boast, one can realize what exceptional qualities were required in these young men; for it is sometimes easier to get an Italian to lay down his life than to make the sacrifice of holding his tongue. Yet even this miracle was achieved by way of instruction, example and character training. I do not remember that, throughout the whole duration of the war, there was a single case of any important lapse from discretion among the assault craft volunteers; neither in Italy during the long months of preparation and waiting, nor in prison-camps, when those unlucky enough to be so fated were subjected to the ordeal of ceaseless questioning.

Preparations for the first war-time operation of the Italian assault craft were in full course at the Serchio training centre; every man felt that steady, unrelenting intensity resulting from stored-up energy under continuous tension.

The British warships stationed in the harbour of Alexandria (two battleships and an aircraft-carrier) were to be attacked by human torpedoes on the night of the 25th–26th of August, 1940, at moonrise, about midnight.

The submarine *Iride* was to move from La Spezia to the Gulf of

C

Bomba, to the west of Tobruk, and there make contact with the torpedo-boat *Calipso*, carrying four SLC human torpedoes and their operators. These torpedoes were the same as had been used for training and had now been pitched up to maximum efficiency (the specimens for employment on war missions were still under construction). In the Gulf of Bomba these two-man torpedoes were to be transferred from the torpedo-boat to the submarine and there lashed to their chocks on deck. After having then carried out a submersion test off Bomba, the *Iride* was to leave for Alexandria on the evening of the 22nd of August, following a course which would bring her to a point four miles from that harbour on the night of the 25th. As the 'pigs' had a resistance to water pressure limited to 30 metres of depth, the submarine would not be able to exceed that depth of submersion during the approach; it was a dangerous limitation, for, owing to the clear water there, enemy air reconnaissance had identified submarines even at 50 metres below the surface. After receiving wireless confirmation from headquarters of the presence of units of the British Fleet in the harbour, revealed by air observation, the submarine was to release the two-man torpedoes for an attempt to force the harbour, and then to turn back. Five crews, one for each craft and one for reserve, were to embark on the *Iride*. The operators, selected among those who had volunteered, were: Lieutenant Gino Birindelli with P.O./diver Damos Paccagnini; Naval Engineer Lieutenant Teseo Tesei with P.O./diver Alcide Pedretti; Lieutenant Alberto Franzini with P.O./diver Emilio Bianchi; Naval Engineer Lieutenant Elios Toschi with Leading Diver Enrico Lazzari. The reserve crew consisted of Sub-Lieutenant Luigi Durand de la Penne with Sergeant/diver Giovanni Lazzaroni.

The submarine *Iride* was commanded by Lieutenant Francesco Brunetti; in charge of the operation was Commander Mario Giorgini, who had succeeded, shortly after the commencement of hostilities, Commander Aloisi as head of the First Light Flotilla and special weapons department.

The *Iride* (a submarine that I knew well: she had been my first command in 1937 and I had retained her for over a year and half, experiencing some lively episodes during the civil war in Spain) duly arrived in the Gulf of Bomba on the morning of the 21st of August; the torpedo-boat *Calipso* (commanded by Lieutenant Zambardi), with the human torpedoes and their operators aboard, cast anchor shortly afterwards. In the bleak and desolate bay there were also the motorship

Monte Gargano, flying the flag of Rear-Admiral Bruno Brivonesi, Commander-in-Chief of the Libyan naval forces, a small steamer unloading petrol and some light craft.

In the afternoon of the 21st, British aircraft bombed the hydroplane base of Menelao in the Gulf of Bomba; they had undoubtedly noticed the unusual presence of ships in those normally deserted waters. The next morning a British reconnaissance 'plane flew over the Gulf, a signal for intense but unsuccessful anti-aircraft fire from our units. At 11.30, transfer of the materials from the *Calipso* to the *Iride* having been completed, while the torpedo-boat went alongside the *Monte Gargano* to refuel and the submarine was leaving the bay to carry out a test submersion with the human torpedoes on deck, three British torpedo-carrying aircraft were sighted about 6000 metres away, flying at a level of 60–70 metres. The aircraft veered suddenly and headed for the submarine in an open V formation, the central 'plane being somewhat behind the other two.

In view of the shallow depth (15 metres), which precluded emergency submersion, the commanding officer, Brunetti, gave the following orders: "Full speed ahead—clear for action—stand by to open fire." He kept head on to the central aircraft, thus hoping to give it a smaller target. At a range of just over 1000 metres he opened with machine-gun fire on the lateral enemy aircraft, which had meanwhile descended to 10–15 metres. These two aircraft passed on either side of the submarine without firing their torpedoes, but machine-gunning and killing some of the gun's crew, who were at their action station. The central aircraft fired its torpedo from a distance of about 150 metres. The torpedo crashed straight into the bows of the submarine and exploded at the level of the officers' quarters. The *Iride* sank immediately. Only 14 men came to the surface: those who had been on deck and on the conning tower (among whom were Toschi and Birindelli). Two men had been killed by machine-gun fire.

The commanding officer, Brunetti, though wounded and in the water, set himself, assisted by Birindelli, to collect the survivors and succour the wounded, among whom was the navigation officer, Sub-Lieutenant Ubaldelli. Meanwhile the British aircraft continued their daring performance by attacking the *Monte Gargano*; by a lucky chance the torpedo aimed at the *Calipso* missed it.

It took just a few seconds to create such a disaster!

The *Calipso* cut the moorings connecting her with the *Monte*

Gargano, which was sinking, bore down upon the point at which the *Iride* had disappeared and began to pick up the survivors. From a trawler which hurried to the scene the operators, stripped and minus their underwater equipment (for it was all on the *Iride*), dived at once, plunging again and again, to lower and lower depths, till they reached the clearly visible hull and took down a rope to it, with a floating buoy.

The *Iride* lay on the sea-bed in 15 metres of water, almost entirely on her side and split in two at the level of the gun position. As soon as some underwater breathing sets and a diver had arrived from Tobruk on the *Calipso*, a systematic examination of the wreck began. Birindelli, Tesei, Toschi, Franzini, de la Penne and their second men took it in turns to dive, incessantly, in the hope that some member of the crew might still be found alive. At last Tesei reported that he could hear voices! Acoustic communication was at once effected; nine men, including two petty officers, the sole survivors, were imprisoned in the torpedo compartment aft.

A dramatic struggle now began; the 10 operators who had set out for the forcing of the harbour at Alexandria applied their whole energies, underwater experience and diving endurance to rescue the survivors of the sunken submarine. It was to be a struggle lasting uninterruptedly for 20 hours, with dramatic developments: men against steel! The escape hatch aft, the only possible way to safety, had been jammed by the violence of the explosion and all night long attempts continued, by the light of underwater projectors, to get it open. It was only at daybreak that, with a heave of the trawler's windlass, the stubborn hatch was uprooted and a way of escape thereby opened for the imprisoned men. But the divers were confronted by a horrible vision: in the manhole the corpses of the two petty officers were found stiffened in death. During the night they had tried to force an exit but had been unable to open the hatch.

Meanwhile, the position of the seven survivors had been rendered awkward, despite the fact that it was now possible, by means of hoses, to supply them with fresh air. Symptoms of mental derangement began to appear; faith in the work of the rescuers wavered, while, as time passed, the supply of oxygen was giving out and the poisonous effect of the gas escaping from the accumulator batteries was increasing. The rescue party issued orders from outside: "You must open the watertight door and flood the whole compartment. Hold on tight so as not to be knocked over by the rush of water coming in. As soon as the compartment is flooded, swim underwater into the manhole and work your way up."

Inside the submarine the order was discussed and debated for a long time by men no longer in full possession of their faculties. They declined to obey the instructions, though the orders given represented the only possible solution. They seemed to prefer slow and certain death, caged in their steel coffin, to any attempt at resistance to the avalanche of water which could put them into communication with the outside world. Finally, stern methods had to be applied. "If you don't obey instructions within the next half-hour," the rescue party told the prisoners, "we shall leave you to your fate." As an indication that this was no empty threat, the entire party returned to the surface, abandoning the captives to their hesitations in the sepulchral silence of their underwater dungeon.

One of those present at this tragic scene will now take up the tale:

"From the little sailing vessel on which we have now been living for two days we stare fixedly at the blue waters and vainly try to avert our eyes from the point where we expect to see the eddy showing us that the hatch has been opened. For a long time nothing happens. The slow minutes pass and the agreed time of half an hour is now almost up. Suddenly, a column of water and turbid air spouts out of the sea for a few moments and falls again with a resounding splash: they have opened it! We get ready to dive again so as to give assistance if needed, while the surface of the sea slowly resumes its tranquil aspect.

The sound of a shrill cry and the sudden appearance of a man, waist-deep in the water, abruptly disturb the barely restored equilibrium of the elements; it is the first of the shipwrecked men saving himself.

After 24 hours in a steel tomb, in complete darkness, on the verge of insanity, stifled by poison-laden air, a fugitive from excruciating agony, this man, at the sight of the sunlit sea, of the world, and of Nature, screams out his enormous shout in assertion of his right to live. It is the wail of a new-born child magnified a hundred times by the force of his 20 years. The others follow at brief intervals and the eyes of some of us are bright with unshed tears."[1]

[1] Toschi, *op. cit.*

In this way, one by one, they all emerged; the last man, the most obstinate of them, had to be literally dragged from his tomb by de la Penne, who had managed to get into the aft compartment of the *Iride*. Unfortunately, pulmonary lesions and the hæmorrhages due mainly to lack of experience in resisting pressure brought about the deaths of two of the rescued men, despite the efforts of our surgeons and the vigorous application of artificial respiration methods.

At last, after the operators had recovered their four torpedoes and the submarine's flag, which was still drifting at her stern, and saluted their fallen comrades in a sad submarine leave-taking, the unhappy trawler, with its cargo of death and bitterness, turned away.

Still aboard the *Calipso*, the men who had set out with such high hopes a month before returned to the Serchio. They had sustained a defeat the causes of which had to be analysed to prevent its recurrence; but it acted as a stimulus to the assault craft operators; and the same men who had experienced that appalling disappointment, who had been constrained to expend their energies up to the limit of human resistance, not in striking a blow at the enemy but in saving their imperilled comrades, immediately resumed work in order to put themselves, as soon as possible, in a position to repeat the experiment.

The assault craft officers, the commanding officer Giorgini, the officers of the *Iride* and the commander of the *Calipso* received, in connection with the events narrated above, the silver medal; those who lay beneath the waters, almost the entire crew of my old command, the *Iride*, were decorated posthumously with the war cross; two of the survivors from the torpedo compartment aft, who had kept the internal situation in hand during the dramatic hours spent at the bottom of the sea in the wreck of the submarine, received the bronze medal.

So ended, with the loss of a submarine, a steamer and many human lives, the first tentative, improvised and inadequate experiment in the use of the new naval arm; it was evident from the superficial and casual way in which the material had been got ready and the preliminary moves organized that there had been no real probability of any better luck, even if the enemy's torpedo had not put a stop to the operation at the start.

It had been ordered by Admiral de Courten, who was at that time responsible for the employment of the assault craft.

CHAPTER IV

SEPTEMBER 1940: OPERATIONS OF THE SUBMARINES *GONDAR* AND *SCIRÈ*

The leaky Vettor Pisani—*In the Baltic*—*I am appointed to command the submarine* Scirè—*The* Gondar *on her way to Alexandria: she is sunk*—*The* Scirè *moves on Gibraltar: an empty harbour*—*Espionage?*

THE beginning of the war had found me a Lieutenant in command of the submarine *Vettor Pisani*, a unit of the Augusta Flotilla. She was an old ship, with many wheezy whims, and leaking all over the place; to take her on war missions was quite a feat.

I undertook three of them with the *Pisani*, one being on the occasion of the battle of Punta Stilo. In order to deal with the infiltration of water through the hull, a reserve stock of rubber hose was kept in every compartment of the submarine and used for conveying the water, as it entered, direct to one of the trimming tanks, with the result that, after some hours of submersion, the interior of the submarine assumed the aspect of a virgin forest, through which it was difficult to make one's way among the elastic liana tangle of reddish-coloured rubber climbing up in every direction. In response to repeated reports of this state of affairs, the Ministry, after some slight delay, classified the *Pisani* as 'unfit for active war service', and detached her to the submarine personnel school at Pola.

In August 1940, I was sent, with two other officers (Lieutenant-Commanders Masi and Buonamici), to attend a special training course for submarine warfare against Atlantic convoys, which had been organized by the German submarine personnel school at Memel on the Baltic. The course, which was essentially practical, consisted in an interesting cruise of about ten days, in which I participated aboard the parent ship and some of the *U*-boats. I was on that occasion able to observe that the German submarine personnel, from commanders to crews, were neither individually nor collectively in any way superior to the Italians; but they had the advantage of a prolonged and first-rate

39

theoretical and practical apprenticeship, which gave the Germans, while they were still in training, an experience and skill which our own commanders and crews only acquired on actual war missions, to the benefit, of course, of the survivors of such drastic training.

Since I was one of the three officers who had completed their training for service in the Atlantic, I expected, on my return to Italy, to be appointed to the command of one of our ocean-going submarines, which in those days moved to join our new naval base at Bordeaux. I was, however, summoned to the Ministry, where Admiral de Courten, of the Naval Staff, offered me the command of the submarine *Scirè*, held at the disposal of the Assault Craft Department of the Navy. I accepted this offer with enthusiasm.

I joined my ship forthwith, at La Spezia. I found the *Scirè* in dock under repair. She was a small submarine of 620 tons, Mediterranean type, thoroughly up to date and belonging to a class which had always passed its tests excellently and which I knew well, for it was that of the *Iride*.

After the unlucky attempt against Alexandria in August, during which the submarine *Iride* had been torpedoed and sunk in the Gulf of Bomba, active preparations were going forward for a new mission; two submarines, the *Gondar* and the *Scirè*, were being thoroughly transformed into 'assault craft transports'. With this object three steel cylinders had been placed on deck (two aft and one forward), having the same pressure resistance as the submarines themselves, and designed for carrying the two-man torpedoes; the gun was removed, since there was now no room for it; further modifications were introduced in connection with the ventilation of the batteries of the two-man torpedoes and the flooding and exhaust systems of the cylinders themselves. I had other improvements, which my experience suggested, carried out on the conning tower, which became smaller and more slender, so as to render the unit less conspicuous when surfaced; with the same object, after prolonged comparative tests to discover which colour was least visible at night, I decided upon a pale, greenish tint, which proved to be the most suitable for camouflaging the submarine by blending its appearance with that of the night sky.

The command of the *Gondar* was entrusted to Lieutenant Brunetti in deference to his request to be allowed to carry the mission, which had been so suddenly interrupted, to a successful conclusion; my own appointment to the *Scirè* had been suggested, perhaps, by the fact that, as a diver, I had been engaged for a long time in underwater training and research.

In compliance with Admiral de Courten's order, a plan of operations was drawn up for attacking simultaneously, during the favourable moon nights of September, the two great British military harbours in the Mediterranean. The *Gondar*, under the command of Brunetti, was to renew the attack on Alexandria which he had attempted shortly before when the *Iride* was engulfed tragically by the sea, under his very feet. The *Scirè* was to attempt to strike a blow at the ships of the Gibraltar force. The two actions were to be carried out at the same time, in order to profit by the element of surprise. No attack had hitherto in fact been made upon the enemy with the new secret weapons of the Italian Navy: they were formidable weapons, but their employment was difficult and hazardous; it was logical to suppose that many chances of success would be lost as soon as the enemy, as a result of the first mission brought to a conclusion, became aware of the threat to his ships, since he would immediately spread the alarm and new expedients would be studied and applied to the defence of the harbours; it would have then been a much more arduous business to renew the undertaking, if it did not indeed prove, as some feared, impossible.

On the evening of the 21st of September the *Gondar* left La Spezia with its two-man torpedoes safe in their cylinders; at Villa San Giovanni, in the Straits of Messina, she took the operators aboard in order to make their stay on the submarine as short as possible. For the atmosphere on board a submarine is far from suitable for keeping, at the desired ideal pitch of physical condition, men who are about to make an exceptional effort and from whom a maximum performance is expected. Apart from Commander Mario Giorgini, the commander-in-chief at sea, the following pilots embarked:

Lieutenant Alberto Franzini, Midshipman Alberto Cacioppo; Naval Engineer Lieutenant Gustavo Stefanini, P.O./diver Alessandro Scappino; Naval Engineer Lieutenant Elios Toschi, P.O./diver Umberto Rugnati; also, Midshipman Aristide Calcagno, P.O./diver Giovanni Lazzaroni (reserve crew).

The approach to Alexandria was uneventful; on the evening of the 29th the *Gondar* surfaced and ran in at full speed for the pre-arranged point of launching. This bold advance, as well as the impatience of the operators, as zero hour approached, was cut short by a radio message from Rome: "British fleet has left harbour: return to Tobruk."

Bitter disappointment and helpless rage filled the hearts of the operators as the *Gondar* turned back, leaving behind the zone of Alexandria which, like all approaches to naval bases, was undoubtedly kept under strict watch. But no more than a few minutes had passed —it was half-past eight on the evening of the 29th—when a piercing whistle sounded through all the compartments of the submarine: the signal for emergency crash submersion. A few seconds later the conning tower hatch, the only one remaining open at sea in war-time, was closed; the submarine, obeying the rapidly carried out measures, began its swift plunge. "Enemy less than 800 metres off," shouted Brunetti, dropping down from the conning tower. Had they been seen? Or heard? Scientifically perfect detecting instruments were now in use on all British warships.

The whole crew was in suspense as they stood in silence at their posts and the steel spindle enclosing them sank swiftly to the normal maximum depth of 80 metres. The sound of propellers, clearly audible by the naked ear, and passing directly overheard, was not very encouraging. A few seconds later all doubt was at an end: five terrible explosions sent everything rocking, men and materials alike. The submarine, at the mercy of tremendous pressure, behaved like a leaf caught in a hurricane, while the men inside were plunged into utter darkness. The crew, with the utmost calmness, at this dramatic moment, set themselves, with every resource of energy and technical skill, to face what they knew would be a long and desperate struggle. The emergency lights were switched on, some of the instruments damaged by the smashing explosions fixed up; all hands fell in at their action stations, at their instruments: gauges, air panel, control levers; the fight in progress was not one of men against men, but of men against the convulsions of nature due to the frightful effects of underwater explosions.

The submarine was brought down to 125 metres and all machinery aboard was stopped, in order to prevent the issue of any sound which might facilitate the detection work of the enemy. The silence within became absolute, uncanny. The men, seated or squatting at their stations, scarcely breathed; with calm and measured gestures, they made the minimum movements necessary to perform the tasks they were ordered to carry out, and waited; it was a nerve-wracking game of patience, normal for submarine personnel in war-time; silence and immobility being the only weapons that they could use, underwater, in any attempt to evade enemy pursuit. The foe was himself traced, as he proceeded with his efforts at detection, by the voice of the hydrophonist aboard the submarine, which broke, from time to time, the icy silence: "Turbine approaching at 320 . . . drawing closer. . . . No. 2 strength . . . closer still. . . . No. 4 strength . . . dead overhead . . ."; the terrible explosions started again, with a tremendous roar, which seemed to be irresistible; trickles of water began to appear between the plate-fastenings and the rivets strained under the impact of sudden and enormous pressures.

So it went on for hours and hours, all night. There were three enemy ships engaged in the work of detection; every hour the submarine was attacked with depth-charges. The crew held out with admirable tranquillity, continuing to oppose the resources of technical skill to the onsets of unfettered force; they plugged leaks with improvised means, pumped out the water which was now pushing in on all sides. But the struggle was an unequal one; the submarine lost its trim, reared, dived, buoyed up and sank again, progressively less obedient to the controls, with the gradual exhaustion of the vital powers, compressed air and electrical energy, by which a submarine is governed.

At last, about eight o'clock in the morning, after some 12 hours of pursuit and a night of horror, the *Gondar*, now completely out of control, began to drop like a lump of lead, down and down: it seemed as though she were never going to stop and that the end had come. There was a rapid consultation among the officers: to sacrifice human lives would be useless; they had, if possible, to be rescued. All the air left was immediately rushed into the tanks. Would it be enough to stop the fall and to surface the vessel? All eyes were glued to the needle of the depth gauge: at 155 metres the falling stopped. At first very slowly, then more and more rapidly, the submarine rose from the depths until, like an air-bubble, it broke the surface.

Aboard, everything was ready to scuttle the ship; in a moment all the hatches were thrown open, the men hurled themselves into the sea, just before the submarine, with the air whistling out from everywhere, went to the bottom in a few seconds, and was never seen again.

Thus the men who, apparently, had been condemned to eternal darkness, were suddenly restored to sunlit seas, under blue skies. They filled their lungs with the pure, salt air, marvellously bracing after the acid and oily vapours they had been inhaling for so many hours. At last they had come back to life; it did not matter that the two destroyers, the *Stuart* and the *H 22*, and the corvette, continued to fire, and that a *Sunderland*, diving down to 50 metres, dropped a number of depth-charges on the submarine while the crew were still in the water; it was better to die in the open air, with the sun in one's face. In the end the shipwrecked men were rescued by the *Stuart* and the corvette. With the capture of Toschi, Franzini, Stefanini, the commanding officer Giorgini, Brunetti and all the crew (except the electrician Luigi Longobardo, who disappeared) and the loss of the *Gondar*, the second attempt of the assault craft against the British fleet based at Alexandria came to an end.

Meanwhile, on the 24th of September, the *Scirè*, too, had left La Spezia with three human torpedoes ready for action and the following operators: Naval Engineer Lieutenant Teseo Tesei, P.O./diver Alcide Pedretti; Lieutenant Gino Birindelli, P.O./diver Damos Paccagnini; Sub-Lieutenant Luigi de la Penne, P.O./diver Emilio Bianchi. Reserves: Naval Engineer Sub-Lieutenant Giangastone Bertozzi, P.O./diver Ario Lazzari.

The plan of operations was that the submarine, on arrival at the Straits of Gibraltar, should enter the Bay of Algeciras, on which the British base lies; the commander of the submarine was then to select a suitable point for the launching of the operators. They were to approach the harbour, negotiate the defences and penetrate; then attack such targets as the commander of the submarine had indicated in accordance with the wireless information received at the last moment from Rome as to the positions of the vessels. The order of precedence in selecting the targets would be: battleships, aircraft-carriers, cruisers and the gates of any occupied docks. After having fixed the charge to the target, the operators would have to try to leave the harbour. By exploiting the favourable geographical position of the Spanish coast, being a few thousand metres from Gibraltar, the operators should attempt to reach that neutral territory. Their rapid passage through Spain and return to Italy by air would be organized in advance.

The mission was a useful test for the transformations on board the *Scirè*. The submarine, with the three bulky, cylindrical cases on deck and her background of pale-green paint against which, in a darker shade, had been outlined the shape of a trawler, with its bows pointing in a direction opposite to that of the course of the submarine (so as to mislead the eye of a sighting enemy), was the strangest thing afloat; it would not have been possible to conceive a clumsier or less seaman-like 'line'. At a certain distance she looked neither like a submarine nor even like a ship; she might have been mistaken for a lighter or a barge. But we soon got accustomed to her and for me she was destined to become the finest submarine in the Italian Navy, as had been, one after the other, the nine submarines aboard which I had formerly served.

During the approach I got to know my crew better. They were all veteran submarine personnel who had acquired the fundamental traits of character developed by this specialized service: coolness, the ability to keep calm under all conditions, patience, perpetual readiness for self-sacrifice raised to the level of a principle of behaviour, a deep and quiet devotion to duty, modesty and reserve, a certain deliberate, assured, methodical way of performing all professional tasks, and, finally, unwavering faith in their commanding officer, the one ruling deity at sea, only second (perforce) to the God of the heavens.

Lieutenant Antonio Ursano, a Neapolitan, was my second-in-command and an expert in the organization of life aboard; Sub-Lieutenant Remigio Benini, from the merchant navy, short in stature, invariably calm and cheerful, a very fine seaman and pilot, was my excellent navigation officer; Midshipman Armando Olcese, from Liguria, also called up from the merchant navy, was the torpedo officer, another quick, courageous and expert seaman. The chief engineer was Sub-Lieutenant Bonzi, later replaced by Naval Engineer Lieutenant Antonio Tajer, a handsome young man with an honest, reliable look about him, professionally first-rate. Then there were the petty officers, the backbone of the ship, all old submarine sea-dogs, with years and years of service: Ravera, a splendid and loyal chief mechanic; Rapetti, our chief electrician, a well-educated man, suitable in every way for promotion to the rank of officer; Farina, chief torpedo-gunner, modest and efficient, and the rest, the subordinate petty officers and the seamen, all good and plucky fellows and all professionally reliable. A wonderful crew, composed not of exceptional, hand-picked men, but of ordinary sailors serving together aboard the *Scirè* by mere chance and proving by their lives as seamen at war, as well as by their deaths, the heroism of which Italians are capable when properly led, with due attention paid to their physical and spiritual needs. It is to

45

you, seamen whom I shall never forget, who sleep for ever in our *Scirè*, lying somewhere at the bottom of the Eastern Mediterranean, that I dedicate these lines, so that Italians may know of your silent service and your even more silent disappearance into the depths of the sea and may render you the tribute you deserve of gratitude and imperishable remembrance.

After an undisturbed and normal approach we had arrived, on the 29th of September, at a point 50 miles from Gibraltar, when a radio message from the Supreme Naval Command ordered us to return to La Maddalena, as information had been received that the Gibraltar fleet had left harbour. On the 3rd of October the *Scirè* cast anchor at La Maddalena.

As already mentioned, a similar order, on the same date of the 29th, had been despatched to the *Gondar*, since the Alexandria fleet had also unexpectedly left that harbour a few hours before the date specified for the attack. Were the British warned? Espionage? Intelligence Service? Or was it simply the pure coincidence of some operation by their naval forces which had nothing to do with our planned attacks? The mystery is one which I am not in a position to clear up.

But various aspects of the matter and in particular the fact that later assault craft actions found the British ships wholly unprepared for the fate awaiting them, quietly anchored at their usual mooring stations, incline me to the theory of the normal incidence of unfavourable circumstances alternating, as is natural in human affairs, with favourable ones; men are by nature prone to fix responsibility in certain directions, though events are often merely dependent upon the caprices of destiny.

Our duty is neither to yield, nor to resign ourselves, nor to renounce effort. "Patience and perseverance can do a great deal," Nelson used to say.

CHAPTER V

MOCCAGATTA ORGANIZES THE TENTH LIGHT FLOTILLA

Moccagatta in command—Name of the Tenth Light Flotilla—
Problems of organization—Underwater and surface divisions—
Total mobilization—Relations between officers and seamen—
Training—The radio-directed vessel San Marco—*Life on the*
Serchio—Our sailors—Admirals de Courten, Giartosio,
Varoli Piazza—Increasing activity of the Tenth—Moccagatta's
cool head.

OUR commanding officer, Giorgini, was succeeded by Commander Vittorio Moccagatta, an officer of great talent and high professional qualifications, tenacious and resolute in pursuit of his aims. As he had mostly served on capital ships, he was without specific technical knowledge of the new weapons; but he was tirelessly industrious, endowed with an inexhaustible capacity for work and exceptionally energetic. He soon acquired the necessary knowledge. His gifts for organization resulted in his giving the assault craft department a settled framework which was to make it a highly efficient instrument of war, specializing in the study, construction, training in and employment of all weapons having as their object 'to strike at the enemy wherever he might be found'.

The Department was detached from the First Light Flotilla of which it had been a branch since 1938; the new Command thus constituted was given, as from the 15th of March, 1941, at Moccagatta's suggestion, the cover name 'Tenth Light Flotilla'. The Command was organized into a planning office, a section of research and materials and a secretariat; the latter was headed by a petty officer of great intelligence and splendid character, Ottavio Morbelli, who, from 1939, throughout the whole course of the war, discharged his important duties with much ability, conscientiousness and regularity. The special weapons department had two divisions: the underwater division, to the command of which I was appointed, and the surface division, entrusted to Lieutenant-Commander Giorgio Giobbe.

The underwater division consisted of: the pioneer training centre at Leghorn, the piloted torpedo centre at the mouth of the Serchio, the transport submarines, and lastly the sabotage groups. The surface division controlled the explosive assault boats which had their training centre at La Spezia (the Cottrau artillery testing station at Varignano) together with the various groups of other motorboats which were gradually put into use, as the exigencies of the war required their adoption; such were the MTS, which subsequently became, first MTSM, and finally SMA, these being various types of improved torpedo craft, miniature light vessels for insidious warfare; then there was the E-boat MTR, an explosive motorboat of dimensions enabling it to be carried in the submarine-mounted cylinders for storing the two-man torpedoes; and there were other floating devices which we shall describe in due course (MTL, MTG, etc.).

Recruiting facilities were considerably extended. Special instructions were sent by the Ministry to all Naval authorities, to allow their personnel freedom to volunteer for 'special war missions', thus providing a wider field for selection; health services for the pilots were overhauled and developed by the institution of a suitable 'Biological Centre', attended by the highest authorities in Italy in various specialized branches of medicine, deputed to assist the Flotilla Command in the vital sphere of the specific physiological needs of the operators.

Commanding Officer Belloni was put in charge of a 'Subaquatic Research Centre' for the study of all subjects connected with the technical problems of human life under water. Further funds were obtained from the Ministry and, what was even more important, greater independence in their appropriate disposal within the frame of the terms of reference drawn up by the Naval Staff. Closer and more direct contact was contrived with the underwater weapons division of the dockyard at La Spezia; a brilliant technician, Naval Engineer Major Mario Masciulli, was appointed to take charge of the secret weapons works, which issued a continuous supply, in ever-growing perfection, of piloted torpedoes for employment in war, and other arms which were continually being elaborated. The Flotilla was, furthermore, authorized to correspond directly with private firms for the delivery of the necessary material; there was a particularly close collaboration with the firm of Pirelli, which made breathing sets and underwater material for the pioneers, and with that of Cabi, which built special parts of the assault craft. One of the latter's managers,

COMMANDER J. VALERIO BORGHESE—the author.

COMMANDER BORGHESE (the author) on the turret-deck of the submarine *Scirè*.

the engineer Cattaneo, called up with the rank of Naval Lieutenant, joined the technical staff of the Flotilla.

There was thus brought about, in this small branch of the Navy, a fusion between its professional and civilian staff and that co-operation between medical, scientific, inventive, engineering, maritime and industrial producers which is indispensable for achieving maximum results in military effort; it would have been desirable to extend such a collaboration to the entire organization of the armed forces; yet in Italy the Tenth was an exceptional, perhaps a unique, example of it. Other countries, better provided than Italy with natural resources and industrial power, mobilized all their reserves of energy in the conduct of the war and directed to a single aim the concerted activity of the whole scientific and productive strength of the nation.

In the sphere of planning, too, the authorities, who were now at last becoming convinced of the great possibilities of the new weapons and were acquiring more faith in the seriousness of the intentions of the Tenth Light Flotilla and in its ability to achieve positive results, gave the latter an increasingly free hand. The innovation, contrary to the usual practice in the Italian Navy (for it was a decentralization as opposed to the centralizing policy maintained by the Supreme Command), yielded excellent results; the initiative of individuals was stimulated, the interval between the presentation of an idea and its execution was shortened, and military secrecy was more strictly maintained.

The Tenth lived a retired life of its own, resistant to every kind of interference from outside. Politics, the illusory idea of a short war, sudden fits of exaltation consequent upon a success or of depression following a reverse, did not enter into our calculations and did not distract us from our work. A single thought, a single spur, a single activity inspired us: it was to keep our men and weapons up to the mark and sharpen our wits to discover ways of striking at the enemy as hard as possible: nothing else interested us.

From the commander to the officers, from the petty officers to the seamen, such was our sole concern, such the sole objective of our labours: in silence, in cheerfulness, in concord. We were all linked to one another by a tie infinitely more binding than that imposed by formal discipline: it was the respect we had for one another's qualities: the seaman 'felt' in the officer his natural superior, and the officers, in their turn, behaved on all occasions and especially in the presence of

D   49 the enemy, in such a way as to deserve such recognition and to lead their seamen, by example more than by giving orders, to compete with enthusiasm in a rivalry of skill and courage; the reciprocal attachment thus engendered was very strong and the services rendered by crews whose members were imbued with such sentiments were of the highest order.

In order to maintain military secrecy, which was always essential and grew more and more difficult to keep as the Flotilla extended its activities and increased its personnel, the system of division into cells was adopted and gave excellent results. Each special branch was sealed off from the others; consequently the members of the different groups knew nothing of the activities which were being developed in the Flotilla as a whole, under a unifying command, beyond the spheres with which they themselves were concerned. Thus two seamen, both members of the Tenth but employed in different divisions of it, would on meeting throw dust in each other's eyes, one saying, "I'm in the Light," and the other, "So am I," neither of them revealing their identical secret of membership of the special weapons department.

Training became highly intensified, this being the key to secure the greatest possible efficiency in the men and materials composing the unit. The pilots of the human torpedoes, who had finished their course of training on the Serchio, travelled to La Spezia twice a week and were there dropped off from a boat or, in all-round tests, from one of the transport submarines, and then performed a complete assault exercise, naturally at night; this consisted of getting near the harbour, negotiating the net-defences, advancing stealthily within the harbour, approaching the target, attacking the hull, applying the warhead and, finally, withdrawing. The vessel placed at our disposal for this purpose was the old cruiser *San Marco*, formerly under wireless control for gunnery practice; she was anchored in Varignano Bay and surrounded by anti-torpedo nets which, in addition to an actual protection of the cruiser against enemy attacks, gave an entirely realistic character to the exercises. Sometimes an attack was carried out, instead of against the *San Marco*, against any of the battle squadron units that happened to put in at La Spezia. I remember in particular an assault made on the battleship *Giulio Cesare* when, although of course the officers and sentries aboard had been warned and consequently the element of surprise was lacking, the warheads were applied without anyone aboard being aware of it; just when those on the *Cesare*, after having attentively watched the sea for some hours, had sceptically come to the conclusion that "they can't do it!", six black heads emerged a short distance from the vessel, two by two; whereupon the operators, with a brief wave of the hand, as much as to say, "Service, gentlemen!" disappeared into the darkness of the night.

During these exercises I escorted the operators aboard a small electric launch; its silent engine enabled me to hear any sound made by the submerged navigators and especially possible appeals from anyone in trouble. Such appeals were, of course, inevitably made fairly often; one has to remember the conditions under which a human body has to work when immersed in water for hours and hours, with its respiration rendered unnatural either by pressure or owing to the mask and also through the inhalation of pure oxygen, the gas with which the bottles were filled to obtain a greater range of action.

Damage to materials also occurred, just as inevitably; and the sudden accesses of physical indisposition felt by the operators for one reason or another, as well as the effects of cold, against which the use of wool and special greases is no more than a palliative, were all accidents calling for prompt intervention by myself or by the doctor who always accompanied us.

After the practice, at about four o'clock in the morning, everyone assembled aboard the *San Marco*, where a substantial hot meal awaited us, its first item always being a tasty dish of macaroni. I have a vivid memory of the scene, repeated so many times, when these suppers took place in the scantily furnished mess-room; there was a single table, at which officers, petty officers and seamen sat side by side, straight from their gruelling work, their faces still furrowed with the marks made by the mask; they were magnificent fellows, great-hearted, steel-muscled, with lungs that could stand anything; their hands were red and swollen from arrested circulation due to the elastic wrist-bands of the pioneer's overall, the finger-tips wrinkled from long immersion. And among them sat the doctor, Falcomatà, whom I shall never forget, watching them closely, one after another, in all their attitudes, ready to note at once the least sign of excessive fatigue or any preliminary symptom of disablement.

"How did it go today, boss?" de la Penne would ask, with his slight Ligurian drawl, his big fair head, with its ruffled curls, emerging, above his mighty form, from behind a mountainous heap of macaroni. And Birindelli, the Tuscan, a man of indomitable pluck, iron will and

51

few words, would answer: "We'll have to do better!" "Yes, but at Malta, fusing at zero and being blown sky-high," Tesei, the man from Elba, told him sternly, while Marceglia, the athletic Engineer Lieutenant from Trieste, nodded in silence. The talk would turn to women or to sport, until Martellotta, the Engineer Lieutenant from Taranto, would sum up our state of mind with a seraphic "Peace and good will . . ." By crack of dawn the lads, with their hunger appeased and half asleep, would be on the way back to the Serchio in their bus, ready to stretch out, at last, in the deep slumbers of recuperation.

Life on the Serchio was the most natural, healthy and primitive imaginable; after the practices were over the men were free to do as they pleased: open-air sports, interminable and fiercely contested volley-ball matches, sea-bathing, rambles through the pine-woods, wild-boar hunts (benevolently ignored by the owners of the game reserves), a great abundance of health-giving food, permanent tranquillity of mind, gaiety and good-fellowship. A certain amount of reading and discussing ranging over the most various fields of human knowledge; also some choral singing of old sailors' shanties varied by a few new ones composed on the spur of the moment during walks through the pine-woods, for example:

> "Hello! Jack Tar, what a beautiful day!
> We frogmen are coming to teach you to swim,
> so we hope you're all right and we hope you are trim.
> We dive, but you go down to stay.
> Drop your bombs, drop them galore,
> drop them from aft and drop them from fore!
> We dive, but you go down to stay.
> . . . ."

No newspapers, no talk about politics and no women, who were not allowed on the premises in any circumstances. The favourite topic discussed was that of war missions; everyone had his own idea where he would like to go, how he would deal with certain difficulties or how he would dispose of a given unexpected snag; their desks, to the detriment of the inevitable pictures of pin-up girls, were covered with aerial photographs and maps of various enemy harbours, mainly those of Alexandria, Malta and Gibraltar, daily examined under a magnifying glass and annotated from the latest intelligence and air reconnaissance reports; those harbours, with their moles, obstacles, wharfs, docks, mooring-places and defences, were no mysteries to the pilots, who perfectly knew their configuration, orientation and depths, so that they, astride the 'pigs', could make their way about them at night, just as easily as a man in his own room.

Many dreams were brought into being simply by turning over the leaves of naval year-books; the outlines of the large enemy vessels forming part of the Mediterranean Fleet became impressed upon the memory. Would it ever be possible to see those ships themselves some night?

When would the next mission be? Whose turn would come? And what would be the objective? No one could say and no one pretended to worry much about it, but everyone knew how to hold himself in readiness; everyone hoped, in his heart, that he would be chosen; all had faith in themselves and in their training.

Certain gaps which already existed in their ranks caused them sorrow, but no depression; they had all voluntarily taken the risk; tomorrow, perhaps, it would be their turn, and they were not nervous. What was the secret power that kept them fresh and keen? What was it that made these men so different from the majority of their fellows, so indifferent to personal and material interests, so superior in their mentality to the common run of mankind? It was not ambition: they evaded, even in their hearts, all personal distinction and were embarrassed by decorations and praise; it was not the hope of wealth: they had no reward for what they did; it was not professional promotion, which was easier to achieve from a desk in the Ministry than on active service; and it was not even the common human vanity to which the distinction of being pointed out as the heroes of such exceptional undertakings might appeal, for death stood across the chosen path, and what was the use of being pointed at after death? It was one faith alone that inspired them; their strength came from but a single source; it was one quite innocent of hidden or transcendental motives. As Italian seamen, they felt it to be their duty to devote themselves entirely to the service of their country, without any kind of reservation; their offering was comprehensive and absolute, arising solely from an instinctive sentiment, part of their very essence: the sentiment of patriotism.

The surface craft department, to which, in particular, our commander, Moccagatta, devoted his concentrated and thoroughly practical activities, was also very considerably enlarged under the

53

guidance of so talented and open-hearted an officer as Lieutenant-Commander Giobbe. While technical studies and constant experiments at sea brought innovations and continual improvements in materials, the personnel proceeded with their training most conscientiously and earnestly: long nocturnal training with prescribed courses off the blacked-out Ligurian coasts, with landings at certain points in such conditions of silence and concealment as would not alarm our coastal defences, which as a rule were not notified beforehand; the alarm given by some vigilant sentry and the fire of machine-gun posts and riflemen were the price paid by the clumsy for allowing themselves to be seen. Exercises approximating more closely to actual fighting conditions would have been impossible; at one and the same time the pilots were thus trained not only in the precautionary measures required for the exploitation of surprise tactics but also, if discovered, to continue the attack without flinching under enemy fire, as both the nature of the weapon employed and the method of its employment demanded.

These exercises, as indispensable as they were undoubtedly perilous, cost the lives of some of the volunteers: an E-boat pilot was drowned during a practice at the mouth of the River Magra when his craft was capsized in a high sea which suddenly arose; Sub-Lieutenant Francesco Regnoni was also drowned when, in company with a group of assault swimmers, he was carrying out a sham attack on the light cruiser *Quarto*, in harbour at Leghorn. These men and others fell at their action-stations; their lives were not laid down in vain: no goal is achieved without sacrifice.

In order to co-ordinate and incorporate the activities of the Tenth Flotilla in the general plan of war operations and to maintain liaison of the Tenth with the other sections of the Navy, with the rest of the armed forces and with our German allies, three admirals were appointed in succession: they were de Courten, Giartosio and Varoli Piazza. These men were the link between the Tenth and the other military authorities; for us they represented the concrete personification of that vague and elusive abstraction, 'the Ministry'; they were the champions and defenders, before the Supreme Naval Command, of our pleas and requirements. They were, finally, the sole sharers of many of our secrets, especially in connection with the employment of our weapons, and sometimes assumed responsibility for the authorization of actions we proposed, only bringing them to the notice of other interested authorities at a time when possible indiscretions could no longer injure the due execution of the project.

Collaboration with these admirals, whose characters were all entirely different from one another, always remained good; it was strengthened as time went on and as the Tenth came to assume more and more importance in comparison with the other operational divisions of the Navy.

It was Moccagatta's very great achievement to have created, almost out of nothing and with much breadth of vision, the organization of the Tenth Flotilla in such a way that, even after his time, it was always able to meet the regularly increasing demands made upon it.

In his war diary, under the date of the 29th of November, 1940, he wrote: "I am now giving up the whole of my time to organizing the special weapons division: I have stopped reading and working on my own account, but have been more than glad to do so. I shall have to keep a cool head for the future in order to obtain positive results."

Moccagatta was very soon to give the best possible proof that he possessed that cool head.

CHAPTER VI

SECOND MISSION OF THE *SCIRÈ* AGAINST GIBRALTAR: OCTOBER 1940

The beginning of a three years' war between the Tenth and Gibraltar—The Scirè *again at sea—Choice of launching point —Currents of the Straits—The* Scirè *in the Bay of Algeciras— Tough life on the* Scirè*—Missions of Tesei and de la Penne— Birindelli inside the actual harbour—Discovery of our secret by the British—Submarine crews in the mountains—Gold medals for Borghese and Birindelli—Report to Palazzo Venezia.*

WITH the sinking of the *Gondar* and the lack of success which had attended the mission of the *Scirè*, the first serious and co-ordinated attempt to strike at the enemy with the new weapon had failed. But that was no reason for confidence in the special arms to weaken in those who believed in them and devoted all their energies to them; the recent defeat even proved a spur to pride, a stimulus to action and a reinforcement to determination; iron tenacity in the pursuit of the objective, splendid by reason of its very danger, to strike at enemy vessels within their safest harbours, despite and in the face of all difficulties, became the chief characteristic of the assault seamen.

So, with the next new moon, that of October, the *Scirè* returned to the attack on Gibraltar. This mission was the first to be concluded of a long series of actions performed by the Tenth Light Flotilla in the course of the war, against the stronghold of Gibraltar. All these attacks required inexhaustible tenacity and indomitable courage in order to carry the offensive into the distant and in all other ways inaccessible base of the British Western Mediterranean Fleet.

A British Naval Intelligence officer who served at Gibraltar during the war says:

"The *Scirè*, commanded by Prince Valerio Borghese, transported three assault craft crews to attack the British battleships at Gibraltar. Such was the commencement of a three years' war fought out silently below the surface of the bay of Gibraltar. At the cost of three men killed and three captured, Italian naval assault units sank or damaged fourteen Allied ships of a total tonnage of 73,000.

The constant threat of silent attack in the night demanded tens of thousands of hours of vigilance by Naval and Army personnel.

The inner story of that 'war within a war' is a long chronicle of deception and intrigue. . . . Each one of its seven operations demanded of the attackers physical daring and endurance which would have won respect in any navy of the world."[1]

The same operators who had taken part in the previous attempt wished to try their luck again (P.O./diver Viglioli replaced Lazzari, who was sick).

On the 21st of October the *Scirè* left La Spezia. Aboard her everyone was cheerful and confident, though no one under-estimated the difficulties of the task. The operators remained in their bunks during the greater part of the approach, to avoid loss of energy and to feel as little as possible the inevitable inconveniences due to the cramped conditions of life aboard a submarine, especially caused by the foul air. They ate abundant meals and remained in the highest spirits. Their job would begin in a few days' time; for the present the crew of the submarine had to work: the task was to bring the operators safe and sound as close as possible to the enemy ships. And this task was carried out well. The passage provided the usual war-time entertainments: on the 22nd a drifting mine was sighted and sent to the bottom with a few bursts of machine-gun fire; on the 23rd a very high sea got up; on the 26th enemy aircraft obliged us to proceed submerged. Finally, on the 27th, we reached the entrance to the Straits. I attempted that night, and again on the night of the 28th, to approach Gibraltar while surfaced, but could not manage it; we were disturbed by enemy destroyers, which gave chase. At last, on the 29th, we succeeded in slipping into the Straits, taking a course towards the Atlantic, submerged and against the current, till we had passed beyond the entrance of the Bay of Algeciras.

We had long considered which would be the best point from which to effect the delicate manœuvre of dropping the operators. This point would have to be one which met a number of requirements, mostly contradictory: it would have to be as close as possible

[1] Frank Goldsworthy in the *Sunday Express*, 25th December, 1949.

to the harbour, to prevent the operators becoming fatigued, losing time and running excessive risks in their preliminary approach; it would have to be over a depth of about 15 metres, so as to permit the submarine to lie on the bottom while the operators went through the business of pulling their 'pigs' out of the cylinders, and yet it would have to be in a zone as far as possible from the normal course of patrol-boats, which might otherwise, even if inadvertently, ram the submarine, deprived as it would be of the chance of manœuvre while on the sea-bed.

The most suitable zone for the purpose was found to be the stretch of coastal waters at the far end of the Bay of Algeciras, where the River Guadarranque discharges into the sea (see map opposite).

This was the point which, in complete agreement with the operators, I chose; it had also the advantage that, owing to a play of currents characteristic of the Bay, the approach of the 'pigs' to the harbour would be facilitated by a light current in the same direction. In order to reach the point in question the submarine would have to slip cautiously and laboriously into the gulf, going right into the lion's mouth while it was still light, in the afternoon, so that the manœuvre of dropping could be begun immediately after sunset and the operators would have the whole night at their disposal for concluding their delicate and arduous mission.

The difficulties of the manœuvre would be increased by the well-known Straits current, of considerable strength, which flows permanently inwards, i.e. direct from the Atlantic to the Mediterranean. To traverse the Straits while submerged, with the current head-on or astern, was easy enough, though whirlpools and eddies are often encountered there which require great care in negotiating; but to cross the breadth, as opposed to the length, of the Straits, with the current abeam, is a really arduous business, above all on account of the speed of the current, about 1.5 knots or half the average speed of a submarine while submerged. Consequently, the manœuvre which I considered the most suitable to attempt (there were no precedents, no Italian submarine having ever entered the Bay of Algeciras before while submerged, either in time of war or, so far as I know, in time of peace) was to proceed against the current to begin with, so that I could then have it in a favourable direction for entering the Bay. Accordingly, at noon on the 29th, the *Scirè* found herself in the Straits of Gibraltar, having passed the entrance to the Bay of Algeciras while

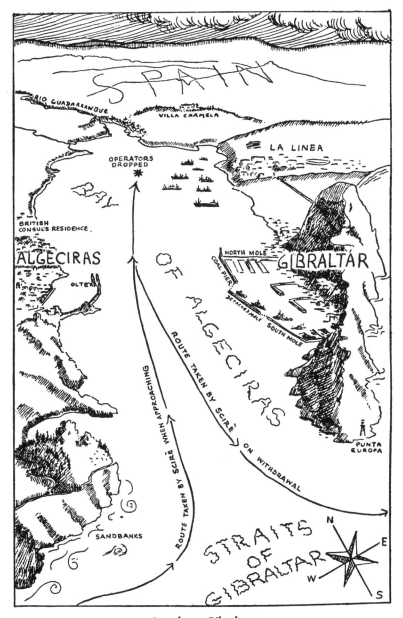

Attack on Gibraltar.

submerged, hugging the steep, rocky bottom of the Spanish coast and waiting for the evening. The whole day was spent in this position, clinging to reefs at a depth of 70 metres; every now and then, owing to eddying motions of the subaqueous current, the submarine took a leap forward and banged on an underlying rock with hollow booming noises which re-echoed ominously in the sounding-box formed by the steel spindle we were in, to our great concern lest the submarine should be damaged or the enemy detect her presence with their hydrophones.

At last evening came; we surfaced. The sea was calm, the wind in the west, visibility excellent; I took our bearings: we were 500 metres off the coast of the Bay of Tolmo; I steered, still surfaced, towards Gibraltar, clearly perceptible on my port bow due to it being brightly lit. At nine o'clock, while we were approaching Gibraltar, we were picked up by the beam of a searchlight; we submerged and, steering sometimes by depth measurement and sometimes by the intermittent flashes of the Spanish lighthouses visible in our periscope (for these were all, of course, functioning), we entered Algeciras Bay. The current was strong and troublesome; at the very point of entry there is a series of reefs and sandbanks (Las Bajas) which are extremely dangerous (a slight shock may be fatal) and all round them the water eddies in all directions, throwing the unfortunate *Scirè* about like a dry leaf before the wind; sometimes she dived, sometimes she made a powerful effort to reach the surface, sometimes she veered at her own sweet will, ignoring the helm (which was in any case extremely slug-gish at such low speeds); in order to counter the tendency to drift, due to the current, I had sometimes to steer for a point 40 degrees off my objective; at last we succeeded in breaking in our rearing steed and holding him in check while we proceeded slowly but steadily towards our destination.

What was the enemy doing? We were approaching his base, we were now a few thousand metres from Gibraltar. Traffic in the road-stead could be heard, and its progress followed, by our hydrophones: there were destroyers on patrol, motorboats were scouting about in front of the estuary, engines could be heard thudding in practically all directions (perhaps they were Spanish trawlers from Algeciras): everything that moved on the surface of the water was reported by our listening apparatus; on the basis of these noises, from their character, intensity and direction, we 'reconstructed' whatever might be happening up there, over our heads, and we regulated our actions accordingly.

How many sounds are heard under water in time of war when, blind as one is in a submerged submarine, attention is concentrated only on the acoustic instruments!

We heard the sound of a turbine . . . it was a destroyer; as it came nearer we could clearly distinguish, with the naked ear, the sound of the propeller cutting the water; it passed right over us. We all listened intently, holding our breath; then it moved on. Our courses had met by mere chance, the destroyer's on the surface, headed for the Straits, and our own down below, as we silently slipped into the interior of the Bay. Odd things do happen. . . .

The silence aboard became absolute; we were now at our closest to Gibraltar, only about two miles off. Everyone was wearing rope soles, the metal switch-keys of our instruments were wrapped in cloth, all machinery aboard not essential to the progress of the submarine was stopped; every possible precaution was taken to prevent the watchful enemy, so close now, from becoming aware of our presence. The operators kept perfectly cool, ready for their coming mission; in the keenness of their desire to be off they looked as though they would like to speed up the *Scirè's* progress and the time schedule; Birindelli, commander of the group, gave me useful help in the business of navigation.

Steadily and warily, the *Scirè* continued on her way; depths began to diminish, we were creeping up the slope of the coast. An engine thudding above our heads suddenly stopped. We stared at one another. Was she after us? Did she have hydrophones? Had she depth-charges in tow? A term of abuse in the Roman dialect, addressed by me to that invader of our nocturnal quiet, broke the perplexed silence that prevailed within the submarine, a smile appeared on all the faces; the moment of doubt had passed. And there we were, at half-past one on the morning of the 30th of October, at the point agreed upon, in a depth of 15 metres, at the very mouth of the Guadarranque. Our first difficulty, that of approaching the point in question, had been overcome. We began to speed up our work; the operators put on their diving gear and went about their final preparations, while the wireless operator took down the expected message from the Supreme Naval Command: it was confirmation that two battleships were in the harbour. I assigned targets and, at two o'clock, surfaced to drop the six operators, taking affectionate leave of them and wishing them good luck. Immediately afterwards I submerged; a few minutes later I heard on the hydrophones the characteristic sound of two-man torpedoes in motion, dying away in the distance; their mission had begun. The *Scirè*, with her task completed, inverted her course; very slowly, still submerged, she slipped along the bottom, so as not to cause any alarm which might prove fatal to the success of the pilots' raid, and re-traced her route, in the opposite direction, through the Bay of Algeciras; at seven o'clock we were clear of it and, taking advantage of the current, we progressed all day, heading for Italy. Submersion was necessary because we still remained within the range of action of the British patrols, but it was a trying business to maintain it so long; our electric power began to dwindle, for the batteries were almost empty, though we had travelled throughout at the lowest speed possible; compressed air had been practically exhausted, which meant that we had little possibility of controlling buoyancy; the air we had to breathe had lost so much oxygen and was so charged with carbon dioxide that respiration became troublesome; we all had thick heads and a tremendous desire for a mouthful of pure, fresh air.

But that was out of the question, for we were still within range of the enemy patrols: to surface would mean catastrophe. This painful situation continued all day; towards six in the evening the first case of fainting occurred; we were now at the extreme limit of physical endurance. An hour later, at seven o'clock, though the sun was still above the horizon, I decided to surface: the submarine had been submerged for exactly 40 hours. The sudden influx of pure air, full of oxygen, increased by the violent suction of the Diesel engines, gave us a feeling of intoxication, a kind of inebriate happiness. I climbed out of the conning tower and filled my lungs with the bracing evening air. The sun, flaming in an intensely clear blue sky, was about to set behind Gibraltar; the great rock, crouching like a lion on the sea, was now far away, sharply outlined over the horizon against the reddish glow of the fading light.

In the evening of the 3rd of November, running before a stiff north-wester, we made the harbour of La Spezia.

According to the message which reached us by wireless from Rome, two battleships had been in harbour at Gibraltar. I had therefore assigned the following targets to the operators, before dropping them: Birindelli was to attack the nearest battleship; Tesei, whose craft had the longer range of the two, would attend to the vessel further in; while de la Penne was to carry out reconnaissance among the buoys, and see if he could find aircraft-carriers or cruisers; if he did not succeed in doing so, he was to act against the battleship in the outer position, attacking it aft, above the propeller shafts, in the hope of thus being able to cause damage, as well, to the bows of the adjoining battleship occupying the interior position.

I had, moreover, given the following instructions to all three operators: if there were no large vessels, they were to attack destroyers and harbour works (the commercial harbour viaduct, the guardship on barrier observation duty, the dry-dock gates, etc.). In any case, they were not to allow any trace of their raid to fall into the hands of the enemy.

We will now see how things went with the three teams we left 350 metres from the Spanish coast and precisely three miles from Gibraltar harbour; with the men we left in the sea, some hundreds of kilograms of explosive between their legs, to be carried, by means of a fragile little engine, inside the enemy harbour and fastened under the hulls of those great 35,000-ton monsters, half asleep and at ease under the protection of the harbour defences.

DE LA PENNE—BIANCHI. On leaving the hatch of the submarine they went to the cylinder on the port quarter, opened its main door, got out their 'pig' and began to check it over. Finding everything in order, they surfaced on it. They then experienced their first disagreeable surprise: the compass was jammed and did not function. This trouble, however, would not be of much importance so long as they kept on the surface and set a course straight to a perfectly visible target, such as the town of Gibraltar, which was all lit up and clearly distinguishable against the darkness of the rock behind it. De la Penne, with his head above water, aimed resolutely at this objective.

"After about 20 minutes' navigation an anti-submarine motorboat with four powerful searchlights picked me out clearly. I submerged and went on at a depth of 15 metres. After about 10 minutes I felt an explosion and found directly afterwards that the motor had stopped. The craft was losing level and I could not prevent it from dropping further. At a depth I calculated to be about 40 metres I touched bottom and found my torpedo being squashed by the pressure. I again attempted, by exhausting the surfacing-tank, to get refloated, but, on checking the 'pig' after I had done so and finding its weight excessive, I concluded that it must have been stove in and flooded. I tried to get the motor and the exhaust pumps going, but without success. I then abandoned the torpedo-craft, which was now unserviceable, and regained the surface, where I found that Bianchi had preceded me and was afloat. We got rid of our breathing gears and sank them, then we swam in the direction of the shore, which I calculated to be about two miles off.

During this phase a motorboat with powerful searchlights came very near us several times, on occasion within less than 30 metres of us; we managed to avoid it and, after about two hours, got ashore a mile north of Algeciras about 5.30 a.m., local time.

We took off our divers' suits and set out to meet the agent N., whom we found on the road at 7.30 a.m." (De la Penne's report.)

TESEI—PEDRETTI.

"At about 2.30 a.m. on the 30th October I got out of the submarine *Scirè* and went to the forward cylinder. I pulled out and checked over my two-man torpedo, aided by Petty Officer Divers Viglioli and Pedretti. I found: (1) much cloudiness on the instrument panel, affecting the compass; (2) irregular functioning of the trimming pump. I got astride, with Pedretti, of the 'pig', left the submarine and steered east. After about five minutes I reduced speed to wait for the other operators. The coast was about 500 metres away; the sound of the surf breaking on the shore could be clearly heard. A fast boat equipped with searchlights (probably an anti-submarine craft), and also a trawler, made straight for us. I submerged rapidly to about 15 metres to avoid being spotted by the phosphorescence in the water, which was very bright. From that moment I lost contact with the other operators. The town of Gibraltar was lit up; the dockyard in complete darkness. Adjoining the North Mole I saw a green light with a white light above it. I set course towards it. After about an hour, when I was close up to this light, I perceived that it came from a lighted steamer with sentries aboard. Leaving it starboard, I steered east, crossing a wide area occupied by dozens of partially lighted steamers, with personnel moving about on them; there were also some escort ships (it was

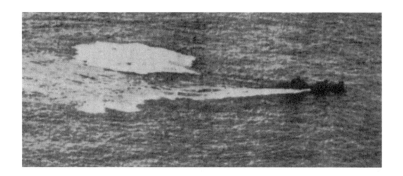

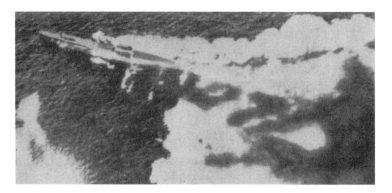

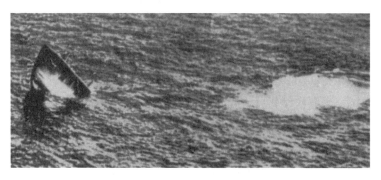

Sinking of the submarine *Gondar* as photographed by Allied aircraft. The top photograph shows the cylinders containing the two-man piloted torpedoes.

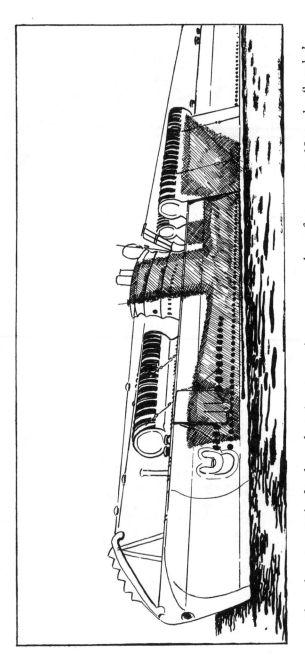

The submarine *Scirè* after her adaptation to service as an assault craft transport. Note the 'bunchy' appearance given by the cylinders, and the absence of the gun—which had to be removed. The camouflage represented a steam-trawler on a course *opposite* to that of the submarine.

obviously a convoy assembling). This situation obliged me to deviate continually from my course and to proceed for long stretches under water.

At about five o'clock I identified the North Mole starboard. I reached the northern entrance to the harbour and when I began to use my breathing set to negotiate the obstructions I found that it had been flooded. While getting the reserve breathing-gear out of its container, I circled around with my 'pig' in front of the harbour entrance. But the reserve gear turned out to be unserviceable, having been loaded ten days before, and had an emetic effect.

The second operator also had a breathing set which functioned badly. Since (1) I was deprived of my breathing gear and could not, therefore, submerge; (2) the torpedo was listing heavily aft and assuming great weight; (3) phosphorescence was very strong; and (4) an attempt to proceed surfaced would be doomed to failure and in particular could prejudice the other operators, I decided to give up the attack and make for the Spanish coast. After about 15 minutes I detached the warhead and sank it. I steered north, for the western lights of La Linea, and made land at 7.10 a.m. I destroyed the breathing gears and opened the flooding-tank of the torpedo, sending it off in a southerly direction.

After getting ashore and removing our divers' suits we took to the road, which we followed, avoiding the police control, until we met the agent N." (Tesei's report.)

Thus the second crew also, owing to faulty working of its equipment, failed to achieve the success to which it had, however, come very near.

Let us now follow the third team on their more dramatic adventures.

BIRINDELLI—PACCAGNINI. They emerged in the normal way, like the rest; they found difficulty in getting their torpedo out of the cylinder, losing about 40 minutes in consequence. At last they got afloat: but at once Birindelli realized that something was wrong: the trimming pump was not working and the 'pig' felt very heavy; it only remained afloat with difficulty. The second operator, Paccagnini, discovered, moreover, that his breathing gear leaked and was therefore unserviceable: he threw it into the sea and replaced it with the spare

E

one. It was next found that the torpedo was only developing a very low speed: most probably water had got into the batteries, a circumstance which would also explain the increased weight of the 'pig'.

"It had no buoyancy and could hardly be kept afloat with empty tanks; it would sink like a stone if the surfacing-tank was flooded. I decided, nevertheless, to go on with my mission, considering that, if I succeeded in forcing an entrance to the harbour while surfaced, I should then find such a depth as would enable me to proceed on the bottom while attacking the target assigned to me, which was the battleship *Barham*. I therefore began my approach by aiming at the lights of the town. After about an hour I found myself between two steamers, the first of two long rows of other ships. As I passed between the rows of steamers I heard the sentries talking. . . . As the torpedo was so heavy, only my head and a very small part of the bows of the 'pig' appeared above water. I continued on my course among the steamers for about another two hours till I found myself practically opposite the head of the commercial mole. I proceeded alongside the coal-pier at a distance of about 100 metres, aiming at the entrance. About three hours and 40 minutes after leaving the submarine I reached the obstructions. These were composed of large quadrangular floats moored at intervals of 5 metres and with heavy iron bars connecting them. These bars were each fitted with three great iron spikes, about 20 cm. in length, set at intervals of a metre and a half. I could hear the voices of the sentries on the piers and see their shadows, but no one spotted us as, with our torpedo *surfaced*, we passed the first and second obstructions. I had just cleared the second when I realized that I was now abeam of the *Barham* at a distance of about 250 metres. I spent some time laying a course for her, so as to get the exact direction with the compass, then flooded the surfacing-tank and submerged to the bottom at a depth of 14 metres. I had no sooner touched bottom than Paccagnini notified me that he had no more oxygen in his bottles. This circumstance was due to the low capacity of the breathing gear itself and to the fact that my assistant had been permanently under water even during our progress on the surface. Realizing that his breathing set was now unserviceable, I ordered him to swim to the surface and remain there without moving so as not to attract the attention of those on board the *Barham*. Left to myself, I proceeded slowly along the bottom, which was strewn in every direction with small, sharp rocks that bumped the torpedo considerably. After about 10 minutes' progress it suddenly ceased to move. I stopped the motor and, supposing that something had got caught in the propeller, went to have a look. The propeller was perfectly clear. I started the motor again several times and found that it was functioning regularly enough so far as I could make out from the sound, but the 'pig' still would not move. Finding that every attempt to get it going proved useless, I went to the surface, paying out a rope ('lift'), to see how far I was from the target. The distance was about 70 metres. I returned to the bottom, intending to pull the torpedo underneath the target myself. After about 30 minutes of strenuous effort during which I had very little oxygen to breathe, I experienced the first symptoms of collapse due to excess of carbon-dioxide and consequently decided to give up. I set the time-fuse going and returned to the surface. When I emerged I found that I was about the same distance away from the target as before but now nearer to the bows. There was nothing for it but to attempt to escape from the harbour and reach the Spanish coast by swimming. Moving very slowly, I reached the first, then the second obstruction. At the latter I climbed on to a buoy and removed my underwater suit and breathing gear. While I was doing this a searchlight shone out from the head of the mole, investigated the obstruction for a few moments and then went out. I sank the breathing set. . . . I dived down by the buoy and tied the suit to its chain so that it should not float, then I swam off. I had meanwhile been looking for Paccagnini but could not see him. After swimming about 200 metres alongside the coal-pier, I began to suffer from cramp. The pains gradually increased until I felt that I could not keep afloat much longer. I therefore approached the mole with the intention of climbing on to it, reaching the commercial mole on foot and then resuming my swim to the Spanish coast. I hoisted myself on to the mole by means of a steel cable and remained there about 20 minutes. Then I began to move in the direction of the commercial mole. By concealing myself behind sacks of coal and passing over two gates I eluded the observation of the sentries until I was half-way along the North Mole, where there is a very narrow bridge and a sentry-post. Here

I climbed down on to the net which closes the arches of the bridge and thus got past the sentry-post. Meanwhile the first traces of dawn had begun to appear. As I considered that I should be unable to remain unobserved any longer, I turned up the sleeves of my working-kit so as to hide the stripes and mingled with the labourers and soldiers who were now moving about the mole. Both sailors and soldiers stared suspiciously at me in my dirty and soaked condition, but no one stopped me. A number of steam-ferries and British motor-launches were moored at the outer side of the commercial mole and since it had become broad daylight I realized that it would now be impossible to get away by swimming. I went over to the inner side of the mole and saw a small ship there called the *Sant' Anna*. Thinking she might be Spanish, I boarded her and tried to hide under the fo'c's'le, where I proposed to wait until it was night. I was seen and questioned by the crew. I managed to make them understand that I wished to remain aboard; they answered that the vessel was under control and that no one could board it or leave it without British permission. I offered them 200 pesetas and they were just going to take the money when a British sailor came on board and asked if I were one of the crew. The men hesitated, not giving an affirmative reply. The sailor went ashore and came back shortly afterwards with two policemen who took me to a naval inspection office where a lieutenant asked me who I was. I showed my identity card. The officer, evidently in great astonishment, telephoned, and shortly afterwards a Commander arrived. Meanwhile the warhead of my torpedo exploded. Much excitement and running about followed. Immediately afterwards a number of destroyers left their berths and hurried out of the harbour. The Commander asked me who I was and by way of reply I showed him my identity card. He then informed me in French: 'If you are the man I think you are, you're three days late. Your friends have been hanging about La Linea beach for three nights. One has been staying at the Principe Alfonso hotel.' I made no reply and was taken to the gaol in Gibraltar. At eight o'clock that evening I was called out and a group of six officers of the Navy, Army and Air Force started questioning me. I answered that I could give them no information except concerning my name and rank. They went on putting every kind of question to me until five o'clock in the morning, when they sent me back to my cell, telling me that as I would not say how I had got to Gibraltar and with what purpose, they would consider me a saboteur. The following evening I was again called out and told that I would be considered a prisoner of war. My assistant Paccagnini was discovered in the sea the morning after the action and captured. He behaved perfectly throughout." (Birindelli's report.)

Such was Birindelli's account of his extraordinary adventure, which cost him three years of hard imprisonment, faced by him as a war operation, with exceptional courage, dignity and pride.

This mission, too, had failed to achieve success, despite the tenacious determination of the operators, owing, obviously, to defective materials, not yet developed to full efficiency. But it proved a notable advance on previous operations, since for the first time human torpedoes had been launched at the prearranged point, after remarkable natural obstacles and the defensive equipment of the enemy had been overcome; and one of the crews had succeeded in getting inside the harbour, arriving within 70 metres of his target.

We were not without information as to the result of the mission: the two crews of de la Penne and Tesei, thanks to the ingenious arrangements made in advance on the Spanish coast by Italians in the service of the Navy, were able to return at once to Italy; we learned from them the technical reasons which had forced them to give up the undertaking. Even Birindelli, though a prisoner, soon gave us news of himself. Every operator had been presented, before the mission, with a short secret cipher to memorize (each man had a different one); when prisoners of war wrote home, therefore, giving the ordinary information allowed, in conventional words and phrases, they could give a brief summary of the results of the operation, with information regarding the enemy harbour and what difficulties might be encountered there, and expressing an opinion as to the chances of repeating the attempt.

"Tell my brother that he ought to have another try for his degree," Birindelli wrote to his family. "If at first you don't succeed, try, try again; if one makes the proper preparations, one finds that the difficulties are not insuperable." The meaning was clear enough and the Command of the Tenth took it well to heart.

As always, there was a reverse side to the medal. For the first time Italian assault seamen had entered a British base, taking their new weapon to within a very short distance from the target and disclosing the secret of the existence of a new threat; it was logical to expect that measures would be thought out by the enemy to prevent any such attempts succeeding in the future.

At first, the British thought that the explosion due to the warhead of the human torpedo had been caused by air bombing; but after the capture of Birindelli and Paccagnini they had no further doubts about the nature of the attack delivered against their base; moreover, the 'pig' which Tesei had sent off went wandering about the bay, and then found nothing better to do than lodge in the sands of the Spanish coast in the immediate neighbourhood of Gibraltar. It is true that the Spaniards instantly took possession of it and carried it off to one of their torpedo works. But the British knew what had happened, especially as the matter was mentioned in the Spanish Press. The newspaper *Informaciones* of the 31st of October printed an article under the headline 'Italian Submarine Near Gibraltar?' which ran:

"La Linea, 31st. Persistent rumours among the inhabitants here assert that on the morning of the 30th an Italian submarine succeeded in approaching at night the entrance to the harbour of Gibraltar and in firing a torpedo which damaged the anti-submarine net guarding the harbour."

And the Madrid *A.B.C.* of the 2nd of November reported:

"Algeciras, 1st November 1940, 2300 hours. The apparatus found on Espigon Beach at La Linea passed through this city on its way to San Fernando for examination in the La Carraca works. The contrivance is 5 metres long and is shaped like an ordinary torpedo but new features are a couple of small seats of identical form and some hand-levers. Nothing is known of the crew, but it is supposed that the apparatus, like that which exploded against the defence net of the harbour at Gibraltar, must have been launched by some secret process from a submarine, a ship or an aircraft. When it was found on the beach at La Linea, the propeller was still in motion."

The Command of the British naval base at Gibraltar released the following news item on the 31st of October:

"An unsuccessful attempt was made this morning by officers of the Italian Navy to blow up vessels in harbour by means of a special contrivance. One charge exploded, without doing any damage, in the entrance to the harbour and another was stranded on a beach in Spanish territory."

And that the attempt had troubled the waters and alarmed the British found a prompt confirmation. In fact, on the 6th of November, the following report came from an agent:

"During the last few days several ships in harbour suddenly started dropping depth-charges; the action is attributed to the nervousness prevalent aboard the ships since the piloted torpedoes affair. . . . Public opinion in Gibraltar is alarmed by the appearance of the mysterious new weapon. The rumour is gaining ground that the submarine which launched the torpedoes may have done so from the Straits. It is probably a rumour which has been deliberately set going to discount the notion that a submarine could ever get into the bay without being discovered; the crews of merchant ships, which are always anchored outside the harbour proper, are much concerned about the matter."

Finally, the operation provided valuable experience for future actions: to approach a submarine to a point off the enemy base close enough for the range of the human torpedo had been proved to be practicable; our underwater materials ('pigs' and breathing sets) were not yet fully efficient; the Gibraltar defences could be negotiated; the operators would have been physically capable of carrying out their tasks if their materials had functioned properly; the operators had been considerably affected by having to remain for some days in the submarine where conditions were wholly adverse to the exceptional effort required by the mission; the enemy, finally, had been put on his guard by discovery of the danger represented by the new arm and had, in consequence, undoubtedly taken new measures to deal with it. On the other hand, a feeling of insecurity was arising among the crews of enemy ships, even when moored in the interior of the harbours; this fact constituted in itself a success, as did also the expenditure of energy and ingenuity forced upon the enemy by his need to counteract this hidden threat even within harbours hitherto considered inaccessible to our offensive.

On my return to base, I was ordered to report to the Under Secretary of the Navy and Chief of the Naval Staff, Admiral Cavagnari. He was pleased with the operation we had carried out and, during the interview, asked me if I had any particular wish that he could fulfil. "Yes, sir," I answered. "I should like to send my whole crew on leave to the mountains where they could stay in good hotels and feel like tourists, beyond the restrictions of discipline; where they could recuperate and relax, with a view, naturally, to putting themselves in the pink of condition for their next operation. The cost of this holiday should, of course, be borne by naval funds." The Admiral at once assented. A few days later half the crew of the *Scirè* were transferred to Ortisei in Val Gardena. Nothing could have pleased me better than to know that my brave lads were enjoying a well-merited period of relaxation and rest in that charming spot. They woke up in downy beds at whatever time they liked, rang for the chambermaid and asked for "chocolate with lots of cream; I'll take breakfast in bed". Later on, summarily rigged out as ski-ers, they hurled themselves with all the recklessness of the inexperienced down the steepest of the snowy slopes, often going head over heels in harmless tumbles which caused them the greatest merriment. In the evening, being regular ladies' men, as all sailors are, they were welcome company for the pretty girls among the tourists and the village beauties. To have obtained this reward for my crew was an almost greater satisfaction to me than the gold medal (the Italian equivalent of the V.C.) awarded to me for leading the operation.

Later on, I persuaded my colleagues in command of submarines to claim similar privileges for their own crews, so that the concession I obtained for the crew of the *Scirè* was eventually extended till it became a rule for the whole of the Italian submarine personnel.

Birindelli, on his return from prison, was awarded the gold medal. Paccagnini and the four members of the other two crews obtained the silver medal.

In November, accompanied by Admiral Cavagnari, I was received by the Duce in his capacity as Head of the Armed Forces at War. For the first and last time I crossed the famous Globe Hall at the Palazzo Venezia. Tesei and Pedretti, de la Penne and Bianchi, were with me.

The Duce stood behind his desk (nor did he once sit down) with his hands at his sides. Exceptionally, he was not in uniform; he wore striped trousers and a black jacket. He looked tired and worried. (He had just received General Soddu, who had been inspecting troops in Albania, where the war with Greece was taking a tragic turn.)

The audience was a short one; after Admiral Cavagnari had introduced us, the Duce wished to hear an account of our operation. I gave him a concise summary of it, illustrated by the charts I had brought with me. He seemed particularly interested in the fact that Gibraltar was lit up as in time of peace; he encouraged us to persevere and congratulated us "in the name of all Italians".

With a curt "You may now withdraw" the audience ended.

I had already had the opportunity of getting to know Mussolini personally, a few years before, at the Armed Forces Club, during a luncheon given by the Navy to its officers who had been decorated for services in the Spanish war; I was not to see him again till three years later, in September 1943, at Rocca delle Caminate, when the destinies of my country were undergoing a dramatic development.

CHAPTER VII

FIRST SUCCESS OF THE ASSAULT CRAFT: VICTORY OF SUDA BAY: MARCH 1941

Greece enters the war—Operations against Santi Quaranta and Corfu—Establishment of a British base at Suda (Crete)— E-boats in ambush at Leros—Vain efforts in January and February—At last conditions are favourable—The E-boats attack—Reports of Lieutenant Faggioni and Sub-Lieutenant Cabrini—Sinking of H.M.S. York (10,000 ton cruiser)— Six gold medals—The Germans' mistake and the obstinacy of the British Admiralty—Two documents by the Commanding Officer of the York.

WHEN Greece became involved in the war (28th of October, 1940), the British at once made use of the numerous anchorages with which the coasts of that country and especially its islands are very well provided; among others they made use of those in the southern Adriatic to serve as supply stations for the units detached to intercept our communications with Albania: the south Adriatic roadsteads were open gulfs and bays, relatively close to our own shores and with defence works of a somewhat sketchy character, particularly vulnerable to attack by our surface craft.

A small operation was therefore organized against the ports of Santi Quaranta and Corfu, to take place at the beginning of April 1941.

"The operation is not one of any particular importance," wrote our commander, Moccagatta, in his war diary, "since there is unlikely to be anything much in harbour at Port Edda and Corfu, but the idea is to test the craft and give the pilots some experience. We shall then be able to undertake more weighty tasks. . . ."

On the 3rd of April a few E-boats, which had previously been detached to Brindisi, were towed by a motorboat to the islet of Saseno, which had been selected as the operative base in view of its proximity to the objectives.

The action took place on the evening of the 4th.

"The night was almost windless, the moon a little clouded," writes Moccagatta, who was on board the motorboat as the senior commander at sea. "The E-boats went off at full speed in the direction of Port Edda; but they made rather too much noise that calm night. When they got to within two or three hundred metres of Porto Ferruccio (Port Edda) a searchlight was switched on and heavy machine-gun fire was opened. Only Giobbe's E-boat was hit twice, while Massarini's remained untouched. I started looking for them through the night with the motorboat and found one of them; the other one I found next morning at Saseno. I was satisfied, because I realized what the E-boats could do and I had data to go on for future operations. It would be unfair not to mention the personnel in these notes of mine; they worked *ceaselessly*, did not know the meaning of rest, knocking off or sitting down to meals, etc., yet remained perpetually keen and asked for nothing better than to work and fight. I had to take two supplementary men on this operation, as I didn't have the heart to leave them ashore, after they had begged so hard to be allowed to come. One could really go to the end of the world with people like that behind one."

The operation against Corfu, also carried out by Lieutenant-Commander Giobbe and Sub-Lieutenant Massarini and under the command of Moccagatta, failed to achieve the success hoped for owing to an unexpected raid by our own aircraft which occurred at the same time, putting the defence on the alert; but it constituted a further test of materials and organization and gave the pilots practice in operating under fire.

Meanwhile, at Suda, a wide and deep bay situated on the north shore of the island of Crete, a naval base of considerable importance had been established for sheltering and supplying British units; this base threatened our islands in the Dodecanese and endangered communication by sea between Italy and that important possession, representing our most advanced post in the eastern Mediterranean.

Ever since December 1940, as part of the operational framework set up to counter reinforcement traffic between Egypt and Greece, a flotilla of E-boats had been detached to the Dodecanese and was actually posted in Parteni Bay at the island of Leros, being intended for action against the enemy units ascertained by air reconnaissance to be in Suda Bay.

Commander Moccagatta had been busy at Leros for nearly a month, completing the organization of this complex operation and putting the finishing touches to the special training required; it was a characteristic, in fact, of the use of the assault craft that, for each type of weapon, harbour or tactical and geographical situation, the most meticulous study was necessary so as to be able to overcome the various, often mutually contrasting, difficulties.

Two destroyers were selected as transports: the *Crispi* (Commander Ferruta) and the *Sella* (Lieutenant-Commander Redaelli); they were adapted to carry six E-boats each and also equipped with electric davits for hoisting up and lowering them. During the many tests carried out at Leros under the directions of our tireless and determined commander, Moccagatta, the six E-boats aboard each destroyer had been successfully dropped, simultaneously, in 35 seconds; an excellent result, due to the ingenuity of the novel installations and the thorough training of the crews.

On the 20th of January Moccagatta was recalled to Italy to resume charge of the Flotilla; he left at the disposal of the Aegean Naval Command (Admiral Biancheri) a most effective instrument of war, ready to be hurled against the enemy at the very first opportunity.

With every new moon, from about the 23rd to the beginning of the following month, the E-boat flotilla, under the command of their group leader, Lieutenant Faggioni, was kept ready for action aboard the *Crispi* and the *Sella*, while the Aegean Air Force carried out daily photographic reconnaissance over Suda in order to make sure of the strength and the position of the enemy ships anchored there and provide information as to the existing obstructions.

But neither in January nor in February (in the months, that is to say, when the long nights would be the most suitable for the attack) did a favourable opportunity occur; either the Suda anchorage contained no important warships or else seagoing conditions were not such as to permit transport and approach of the E-boats.

Once in January and once again in February the *Crispi* and the *Sella* set out on mission, but on each occasion they were recalled after some hours; the first time because air reconnaissance at sunset had ascertained that the British ships were leaving harbour and the second time because the strength of the enemy ships did not appear to be such as to render the action worth while.

How many factors had to coincide for the success of an operation! During the few days when the moon was favourable, the weather had to be good enough and the sky clear enough to permit air reconnaissance; the sea such as to enable the tiny craft to get through it; the destroyers had to be available; the E-boats as well as their pilots had to be ready for action and, of course, some enemy warships had to be in harbour.

During the long and nerve-racking period of waiting Faggioni's flotilla trained methodically, always in the best of good spirits, despite the January and February postponements and the isolated station at Parteni, where there were no facilities of any kind.

On the 20th of January two of the pilots were seriously wounded by the explosion of a bomb dropped by enemy aircraft: both, from the very first day, asked not to be removed from their post; they recovered with extraordinary rapidity, so as to be able to take part in the mission. In March air reconnaissance over Suda grew more hazardous, as anti-aircraft defences were improved and owing to the frequent intervention of numerous enemy fighters.

On the 25th of March the *Crispi* and the *Sella* were ready for action at Stampalia with the MTs aboard, when they were bombed by enemy aircraft. The *Crispi* had one man killed and three wounded. In the afternoon of the same day favourable conditions for the attack had, at last, come: the weather was fine and the sea calm; air reconnaissance had spotted two destroyers, five large steamers, seven smaller ones and a cruiser of some 10,000 tons in Suda Bay. The order was given to start. The night was dark, starry and somewhat overcast; after an uneventful passage, the two destroyers reached the assigned point, 10 miles off the enemy coast, at half-past eleven. The E-boats were dropped and affectionate and cordial leave taken of the pilots; the destroyers then turned back.

The six pilots were Lieutenant Luigi Faggioni, in command of the operation, Sub-Lieutenant Angelo Cabrini, P.O. Alessio De Vito, P.O. Tullio Tedeschi, P.O. Lino Beccati and Sergeant Emilio Barberi. They reached the entrance to the bay in orderly formation and unobserved.

The most arduous part of the mission now began: the E-boats had to negotiate, for about six miles, a long and narrow arm of the sea, the coasts of which were under enemy control, and to overcome successive barriers of net defences without being discovered or heard, till they reached the end of the bay, where the ships were safely anchored (*see* map facing page 80).

An extract from Faggioni's report follows:

"Weather and visibility good, a light, steady south-wester blowing. On reaching the entrance to the bay, speed was reduced to prevent the enemy from hearing our engines. I set course to pass the first barrier at the middle of the strait between Point Suda and Fort Suda. I slipped between two buoys and got through easily and the others followed me without trouble. A few minutes later I saw the second barrier and set course to pass it closer to the islet with the fort, where there were rocks above water which might easily be mistaken for MT's. I got through easily. But Barberi, behind me, remained stuck. So as not to lose touch, I shut off my engine and waited in the zone of the shadow cast by the islet. Shortly afterwards I saw all five of them again; once more I took the lead and continued mv approach, keeping to the middle of the bay. It was then about 2.45 a.m. on the 26th March: day would begin to break at 5.18; I increased speed in case I might lose time over the passage of the third barrier. After 10 minutes two searchlights swept the middle of the bay without spotting us."

At 4.30 the pilots reached the third barrier; as it was not possible to negotiate it, they went round it and passed through a gap between the barrier and the coast.

"I then reached the middle of the bay and after a few minutes signalled to the others to stop their engines and gather round me. It was then 4.46: we were too early for more favourable conditions of light. I decided to wait. The cruiser was anchored about 200 metres inside the barrier, while the steamers were scattered further back; one of them was about 100 metres to windward of us. I took an accurate look all around with my binoculars in order to select the largest targets, then I handed the glasses to Cabrini and the rest to give them a good idea of the position of their targets. It was then about five o'clock. Meanwhile reveille was being sounded aboard the cruiser, whistles could be heard and a lantern could be seen carried along the deck; smoke began to rise from the forward funnel; and shortly afterwards I saw red and green lights go on intermittently at the barrier-gate. I sent off Cabrini and Tedeschi to attack the cruiser. The MT's dashed away at full speed and after a few seconds, which seemed very long, there was a single explosion, immediately followed by anti-aircraft fire from the batteries against imaginary aircraft. Suddenly I heard a second explosion to my right, which I guessed came from Barberi's attack. Beccati was on my left and asked to go and attack the large tanker I had pointed out to him. I ordered him to wait and we approached the tanker. As soon as he could see it clearly, off he went; the explosion took place aft. The cruiser had a heavy list to starboard and was enveloped in a cloud of smoke. But she was slow in sinking and I therefore decided to go for her. Before putting on speed I had a look round with the binoculars and in directing them upon Beccati's tanker I discovered a camouflaged vessel behind her, a warship. I veered to starboard, whipped up to full speed and aimed at her. . . . I took an approximate sighting angle, jammed the rudder and, a few seconds later, threw myself overboard. For some seconds I heard the sound of the engine, then the explosion. But in view of its distance and the course I had set, it took place, as I suppose, against some obstacles within the harbour. I swam as hard as I could towards the north shore. Shortly afterwards it grew lighter and shouts came from the bows of a near-by steamer. A boat came off to capture me and brought me aboard. I gave my name and rank. I was searched and taken below where practically the entire crew were assembled, wearing their life-belts. I was asked if I had been shot down with my 'plane and whether mates of mine were in the sea, which I denied. I was not allowed to approach the port-hole to look out; I was offered whisky, tea and cigarettes and helped out of my rubber suit. After about half an hour I was escorted ashore by marines, who protected me from a rather hostile group of Greek porters and stood guard over me at the Port Command office. I saw a seaman with his head bandaged and "H.M.S. *York*" on his cap. Towards 10 o'clock, escorted by a naval officer armed with a revolver and two sentries, I was taken across to the opposite coast in a boat. We passed close to the tanker, which was losing oil from a leak. I saw the cruiser, down by the bows; her stern was at sea level, the after turret with its guns in top inclination, the crew busy aboard her and a tanker alongside her starboard quarter. A hydroplane was flying very low, searching the bay from end to end.

We made fast at a small pier and I saw, a little way off, one of our explosive-boats, undamaged, with a crowd of soldiers round it. The officer took me up to it and, levelling his revolver, asked me whether it was dangerous to touch it. In the hope that the explosion might still take place I replied that it was dangerous and added that 'it would be as well to send the soldiers away'. He asked me if I could tell him how to render it safe and how the explosive device worked. I answered that I knew nothing about it. The officer threatened me and insisted upon a reply. I said nothing. After a time he gave it up, dismissed the men and took me back to the place we had started from. . . .

In the afternoon of the following day, in prison at the Castle of Paleocastro, I found the other five operators. . . .

The forcing of the bay had been duly carried out; it was effected in accordance with the training we had and in compliance with the orders given by Commander Vittorio Moccagatta, who had timed that action to take place in the best possible conditions of visibility (i.e. at the first signs of daybreak) and had wanted the leader of the group to assign targets and await the result of attacks on the most important objective in such a way that he would still have reserve forces to call upon. Approach, passage of the barriers and assaults were executed with coolness and determination by all concerned. All the operators gave proof of great firmness in the fulfilment of their duty. On the 27th I requested permission to write to my family and notified, in the cipher arranged, the enemy's capture of an unexploded MT. After a considerable time I learned through a letter from home that my communication had reached the Command of the Tenth in June 1941." (From the report of Lieutenant Luigi Faggioni, drawn up on his release from prison.)

And here is Cabrini's account of his attack on the cruiser *York*:

"In accordance with the orders given by Lieutenant Faggioni, we shut off our engines and gathered round him. We could see the dark, massive shapes of a number of ships and, at some distance,

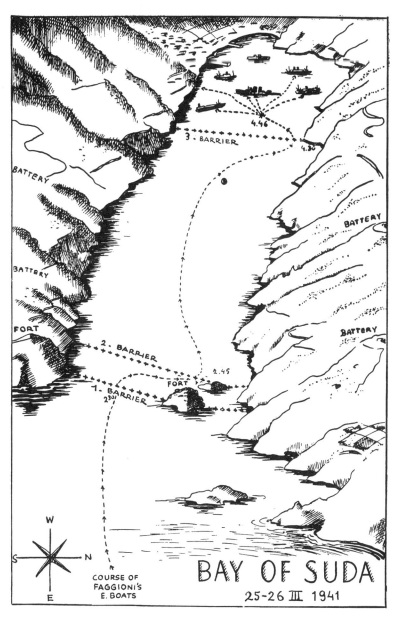

The attack in the Bay of Suda.

(S 150) Wt 27646 1770   400M. Pds. 9/39   B. & B. Ltd 51-4818   Revised December, 1935.
S. 1320b.

NAVAL MESSAGE.

For use in Signal Department only		

Originators Instructions (Indication of Priority, Intercept Group, etc.)	Codress/Plaindress	No. of Groups :

TO · Comr (E)		FROM · Capt

Write Across

Release take statements from all men who 5

were on RR's & ER's when the ship was 10

struck on 26ᵗʰ — also from any men who 15

can bear witness to the LRA's, who were 20

lost, being in the Engine Room. 25

30

I wd. like you also to make rough notes 35

now, whilst events are fresh in your mind, 40

of sequence of damage reports & appreciations as 45

time went on. Also a log of events since we 50

System	P/L Code or Cypher	Time of Receipt	Despatch	Operator	P.O.O.W.	Date
started pumping out.				RS		27/3

R.N. message from Captain of H.M.S. *York.* 27th April 1941.

we could hear the hum of turbo-ventilators. In the direction of this sound we could distinguish the dark mass of a cruiser which we later learned to be the *York*.

Faggioni gave us directions: two MT's would be detailed to attack the cruiser; this task was assigned to Tedeschi and myself, and was to be carried out the moment visibility conditions allowed it. The other operators, to each of whom a target was assigned, would attack as soon as they heard the first explosions.

I left Faggioni's group and began to approach the cruiser at minimum speed with Tedeschi, who was very close to me. The darkness was intense, partly owing to the height of the coast. The cruiser was camouflaged and difficult to make out. We continued to approach until we could see the vessel clearly, then we stopped, waiting for the first signs of daybreak; we were at a distance of about 300 metres from the ship. We remained there for a quarter of an hour. At five-thirty I made sure that Tedeschi had a good view of the target; I was afraid that if we waited any longer the enemy would catch sight of us or our companions. I therefore gave the order to attack. We proceeded for a fair distance side by side at full speed; when we were about 80 metres away I jammed the rudder, released the safety catch and dropped into the water; at the moment of abandoning, the MT was aimed at a point amidships of the vessel.

Before I could climb on to the raft I distinctly heard the two MT's strike the hull of the ship. I also clearly heard the explosions of the severing charges of the boats and, a few seconds later, a simultaneous and violent explosion under water, very near. Immediately afterwards I saw the cruiser take a heavy list. I could hear the engines of other MT's, then a whole series of explosions, some close by, others at a distance. . . .

I found that my rubber suit had got torn; I got rid of it with considerable effort and began swimming towards the coast in the hope of reaching the landing-place. Some 15 metres from land I saw a ship's boat coming towards me; an officer ordered me to put up my hands, levelling a revolver at me; I did not obey, partly because of my bad physical condition; I was hauled on board as a dead weight and had difficulty in keeping on my feet. I was taken ashore to a battery and put in charge of a couple of sentries.

F

I found Tedeschi, Beccati and Barberi there also." (From the report of Sub-Lieutenant Angelo Cabrini, drawn up on his release from prison.)

At the same time, the others had attacked their targets: De Vito a steamer and Barberi a tanker, which received a direct hit and sank; Beccati another big, fully loaded tanker of about 18,000 tons, which sprang an enormous leak and went to the bottom.

For some minutes the bay re-echoed with explosions of all kinds, while the numerous batteries opened intense anti-aircraft fire.

Then, as day broke, calm returned; in amazement and wonder, the British realized that they had been taken by surprise and assaulted by Italian seamen with a new, unexpected and unknown weapon. These Italians, although now prisoners, had the satisfaction of being aware that their operation was a success. Beccati, in his report, states:

"From the battery we could see a cruiser with a heavy list and tugs attempting to tow it ashore. We noticed that the bay was full of oil, which was coming to the surface at the spot where the tanker had gone down, and we observed another tanker listing in such a way as to give the impression that she was about to sink."

The conduct of the pilots had been perfect: they had gone far into enemy waters and overcome three separate barriers; after penetrating the enemy's safety zone to within a few hundred metres of the ships, they had assembled for consultation and coolly summed up the situation, passing the commanding officer's binoculars from craft to craft. In these circumstances, surrounded by sentries, searchlights and guns, they had calmly waited for more light, so as to be certain of their targets, till at the word 'Go!' they threw themselves, with careful aim and intent determination, upon the targets assigned to them; they had acted as coolly and steadily as if they had been taking part in normal practice, in friendly waters. It was an exhibition of self-control based on moral qualities of a high order, which had been strengthened by continuous and drastic training under difficulties even harder than those expected in action against the enemy.

The six gallant men who penetrated Suda Bay were awarded gold medals at the end of the war and their return from imprisonment.

The close, but still inadequate, collaboration between Air Force and Navy, rendered more effective by the unified command of the Armed Forces of the Aegean, the high efficiency with which the little boats, so ingeniously planned, had performed their tasks, the excellent organization and intensive training, due primarily to Commander Moccagatta, and, above all, the great valour of the pilots, led to a victory which, in turn, began the series of successes achieved by the Tenth Light Flotilla: the 10,000 ton cruiser *York* and three merchant vessels in the British service, amounting between them to 32,000 tons, had been sunk or put out of commission for the duration of the war.

When, in May 1941, the German troops occupied Crete, they found the partly emerging hulk of the *York* in Suda Bay and, supposing her to have been sunk as a result of the heavy air-raids they had made upon the island before occupying it, they included the destruction of this vessel in the list of their successes. But the incontrovertible facts related above leave no doubt whatever to whom this naval victory is to be attributed. Should any doubts remain they may be disposed of by documents found on the *York* herself by the Italian naval officers who were the first to board the ship immediately after the occupation. An order in manuscript exists, addressed by the Commanding Officer of the unit to the Chief Engineer Officer on the 27th of March. The text runs:

NAVAL MESSAGE
Commander (E)
from
Captain (by hand)
Please take statements from all men who were in boiler and engine-rooms when the ship was struck on the 26th, also from any men who can bear witness as to the R.A.s who were lost, being in the engine-room.

I would like you also to make rough notes now, while events are fresh in your mind, of sequence of damage reports and appreciations as time went on. Also a log of events since we started pumping out.

R.P.

27/3.

The second document is a typed Service Order:

H.M.S. York
28th *March,* 1941.

No. 37.

INTERIM MEMORANDUM BY CAPTAIN

To:

Heads of Departments.

1. *Heads of Departments are requested to compile reports as soon as possible on the following subjects in connection with the recent torpedoing of H.M.S.* York:

(a) *damage done;*

(b) *any items of special interest;*

(c) *names of officers and men whose conduct they consider deserving of special mention.*

2. *References to Admiralty Fleet Orders which may be necessary in this connection can be obtained from my office.*

(*signed*) *Reginald Portal,*

Captain.

It was further ascertained that the damage done to the deck of the ship was not caused by air bombing but by charges which the British had themselves exploded in the interior of the cruiser, hastily and at certain points only, before abandoning Suda.

In spite of these clear facts and although the British knew better than anyone else the true story of the sinking of the *York,* the British Admiralty, persisting in its usual line of conduct of trying to minimize admission of the damage inflicted on the Fleet by the Italian Navy, attributed, in its official list published after the war, the loss of the *York* to German air bombings.

CHAPTER VIII

THIRD MISSION OF THE *SCIRÈ* AGAINST
GIBRALTAR: MAY 1941

The Scirè *now plies regularly on the route from La Spezia to
Gibraltar—Christmas 1937—An innovation: the tanker* Fulgor
*—New operators—Once more at the mouth of the Guadarranque
—Harbour empty!—Reports of Catalano and Visintini—
Marceglia's sudden illness—Further disappointment.*

IN concert with an action planned against Malta in May 1941 the
Scirè, still under my command, made her third attempt to force the
harbour of Gibraltar. The shortcomings which had been brought to
light during the previous operation in October had been assessed and
sifted and we had done our best to eliminate them. The assault craft
materials had been improved and subjected to stricter tests; the
operators had undergone a more thorough training. To prevent them,
during their prolonged period of transport in the submarine, from
feeling the effects of the cramped environment, arrangements had been
made to take them to Spain by air, furnishing them with the papers
necessary to obviate suspicion on the part of the Spanish authorities
or anyone else who might be interested in keeping an eye on the
movements of travellers. The pilots were to be taken from the airport
by means of quick and independent methods previously arranged by
naval intelligence agents operating in Spain and brought aboard the
Italian tanker *Fulgor*, which had been interned in harbour at Cadiz
since the beginning of the war. The *Scirè*, after traversing the Straits
and reaching the Atlantic, would enter the harbour of Cadiz at night,
unobserved by the Spaniards, bring up alongside the *Fulgor*, take the
operators and the necessary supplies on board and then leave the
harbour before dawn; she would enter the Straits from the west and
go on into Algeciras Bay. The methods arranged for the dropping of
the operators were similar to those tried out in the previous mission,
when they had proved perfectly adequate for the purpose in view.

While we were working, the enemy had not gone to sleep. We
knew, for we had concrete proof of it, that in consequence of the

repeated operations of Italian assault craft, the British had set up a vast organization, with a staff of specialists and a wealth of contrivances and vessels, with the object of preventing attacks by the Tenth and taking defence measures against them. Appropriate underwater defence divisions had been created in all the Mediterranean bases; it was a regular 'anti-Tenth Flotilla' organization.

On the 15th of May, for the third time, the *Scirè* resumed her old course. She seemed to have become a commercial vessel plying regularly, with 'pigs' on board, between La Spezia and Gibraltar.

The heavy seas encountered off the Spanish coasts caused a delay of 24 hours in our approach to the Straits. The crossing from the Mediterranean to the Atlantic was accomplished without incident, along a course through the middle of the Straits, at a depth of 60 metres, submersion beginning at four in the morning, six miles from Europe Point, till we surfaced beyond Cape Tarifa at eleven o'clock at night. At daybreak on the 23rd of May we were off Cadiz. I submerged in front of the harbour and came to rest on the bottom at 40 metres; an entire day of repose for the whole crew ensued.

It is difficult to imagine surroundings more conducive to sleep than the interior of a submarine at rest on the bottom of the sea: the usual silence of submersion is reinforced by the cessation of all mechanical noises aboard; one feels safe from any intrusion on account of the layer of water above. After days and days at sea, which entail a continuous nervous and physical strain, while one is wearied and deafened by the sound of the waves, the wind and the engines, one has the sensation of being out of the war and even out of the world, since at such depths one is beyond the reach even of radio transmission waves; one is left entirely alone with oneself.

I remember another day spent at the bottom of the sea; on that occasion also we were off the Spanish coast. It was Christmas Eve 1937, the Spanish war was going on; the submarine was the *Iride*, forming part of the Legion, and the waters were those of Tarragona. For the midnight celebrations the crew had prepared, unknown to myself, a marvellous Christmas tree, made of materials found aboard (a broom-handle, straw painted green, coloured electric bulbs); there was also a manger which was a real work of art, with the figures cut out of the tin of our ration-boxes and the Infant Jesus modelled out of kneaded biscuits. Touched by this performance, I, for my part, suspended hostilities for a few hours on Christmas Day. I went, submerged, very near to the harbour of Tarragona and made everyone take it in turns to look through the periscope, which was directed towards the beautiful cathedral of that town; after this 'religious' ceremony had been concluded, I wished the seamen the compliments of the season and, after our thoughts had dwelt for a moment on our distant families, we came to rest on the bottom again, where we celebrated the glad occasion in peace with an unexpectedly magnificent feast (it had also been prepared by the collaboration of nearly everyone aboard, unknown to the commanding officer, since it was to be a surprise for him) followed by well-merited repose for all of us.

But this is a digression: the operational report by the commanding officer of the *Scirè* does not mention all that, but simply reads:

"23rd May, 6 a.m. Submersion 8 miles, 90° bearing from the lighthouse at Cadiz. Remained at bottom, depth 40 metres, till night-fall. Assembled crew. Informed them first phase of operation (voyage) now over and prepared them for the second phase (attack on Gibraltar). After this, all rested."

In the evening the *Scirè* surfaced and slipped warily and silently into Cadiz harbour, ascending the River Guadalete, the current of which, as it flowed down, met the incoming tide, forming strange eddies of wildly agitated, foam-crested little waves; she passed unobserved between the steamers at anchor in the harbour (a few British vessels among them) and after identifying the *Fulgor*, a tanker of 6000 tons, came alongside the latter, keeping only just above water, so as to remain as inconspicuous as possible. Our meeting with the ship's officers, especially with the Chief Engineer Di Dio and the operators, who had arrived a few days previously without having given rise to the least suspicion of their identity or the true object of their voyage, was a most cordial one.

The operators were Lieutenant Decio Catalano (leader of the group) with P.O./diver Giannoni; Lieutenant Amedeo Vesco with Diver Franchi, Sub-Lieutenant Licio Visintini with P.O./diver Magro. The reserves were Engineer Sub-Lieutenant Antonio Marceglia and P.O./diver Schergat. The Surgeon-Captain of the Tenth, Bruno Falcomatà, accompanied them aboard the *Scirè*, in order to attend the crews up to the last moment in the severe test they were about to undergo.

It was enough for me to shake hands with the boys to be assured of their physical and mental fitness; they were glad the passage had turned out so well and they were confident of success.

I took advantage of the installations aboard the *Fulgor* to get the crew refreshing hot showers, an amenity not available aboard the *Scirè*, and replenished our stock of fresh green vegetables, so as to break the monotony of dried victuals and provide the crew and especially the operators with vitamins.

The assistance rendered by the *Fulgor* was very welcome and much appreciated; it does not often happen that, right in the middle of a war operation by submarine, one can spend a night stretched out in a comfortable armchair in an officers' mess, feeling fit after a good bath and even a shave, in an atmosphere of cheerful gossip, sipping excellent sherry and smoking fragrant Havana cigars.

I used this opportunity to bring myself up to date regarding the situation of enemy vessels in Gibraltar harbour. The information was given me by a keen young diplomat who came of his own accord to be of service to us, having just returned from a reconnaissance in person and thus primed with the latest and most accurate intelligence. Meanwhile the operators got out their 'pigs' and gave their precious appliances a final and detailed check-over.

Before daybreak the *Scirè*, accompanied by the good wishes of the crew of the *Fulgor* and profiting by the current of the river, unmoored and left the harbour; with the first light of dawn, as soon as we were oustide, we submerged.

On the 25th of May, after evading, by repeated crash submersion, the destroyers patrolling the Straits, the *Scirè* entered upon her submerged approach to the Bay of Algeciras. Cautiously and prudently as ever (for we were going to put our heads in the lion's mouth without his becoming aware of it) and favoured by the inflowing current, we went ahead; but in consequence of the wildly eddying current I found myself behind schedule and decided to postpone aggressive action till the following night.

So I left the Straits, heading west, and resumed the attempt to enter the Bay at dawn of the 26th. This time I succeeded, for when, at half-past ten in the evening, I surfaced to get my bearings after a day of blind navigation, I found we were inside Algeciras Bay, exactly two and a half miles west of Gibraltar harbour. The town lay before us, brightly illuminated; the night was ideal: the sea was calm, there was

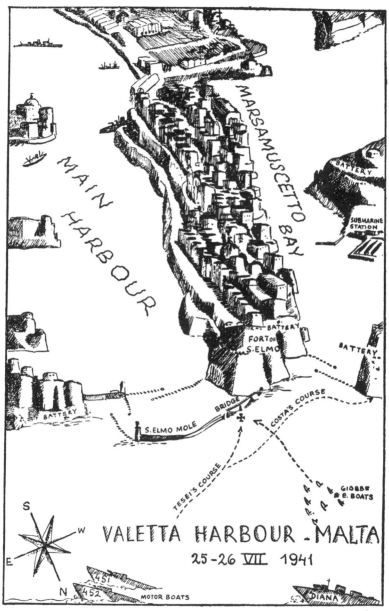

MAIN HARBOUR

MARSAMUSCETTO BAY

BATTERY

SUBMARINE STATION

BATTERY
FORT OF S.ELMO

BATTERY

BATTERY

S.ELMO MOLE

BRIDGE

COSTA'S COURSE

TESEI'S COURSE

GIOBBE & E. BOATS

S
W
E
N

VALETTA HARBOUR - MALTA
25-26 VII 1941

451
452
MOTOR BOATS

DIANA

no wind, the sky was overcast and it was pitch-dark; the omens were first-rate; perhaps this was to be our great chance.

I went ahead submerged, proceeding further into the Bay till I reached the off-shore point to which we were now accustomed. My operational report reads:

"2320 hours: at the agreed spot, mouth of the River Guadarranque, submerged to bottom in 10 metres of water. Operators got ready to leave and were given a last examination by the surgeon accompanying the expedition, Captain Falcomatà." But at half-past eleven the report goes on: "Supreme Command message that harbour is empty, all vessels having left during the evening; operators will have to attack steamers in the roadstead." I went on: "This was a great disappointment, but no one is discouraged. Gave final orders, at 2358 hours surfaced, operators left."

Marceglia replaced Diver Franchi in Vesco's crew, Franchi being sick.

The *Scirè*, with the reserve operators aboard, resumed her slow underwater withdrawal, taking the usual precautions to avoid giving the enemy any cause for alarm which would endanger the fate of the men who were meanwhile bravely facing their difficult enterprise. On the 31st of May the *Scirè*, after an uneventful passage, reached the base of La Spezia.

We will now follow the adventures of the three crews, guided by their reports; they had been given the order, since targets inside the harbour were lacking, to attack the steamers anchored in the roadstead, a very much less difficult and risky task, for approach would be shorter, the difficulties of negotiating the barriers would be avoided, and there would be no danger from sentry-posts on the piers.

CATALANO, MARCEGLIA and GIANNONI. Smeared with lanoline, with three tablets of Simpamine and a spoonful of Dextropur inside him, as well as an injection of kidney tissue, Catalano waited calmly for the order to leave.

His comment, on the arrival of the message from the Supreme Command, is as follows:

"The disappointment at not being able to operate inside the

harbour was only partially relieved by the satisfaction of being able at last, after months of arduous preparations, to take action. The morale of my companions on the operation was extremely high. Our departure took place in the order I had arranged, while we exchanged parting salutations with the submarine personnel. We were all sure of success . . ." (From the report by Lieutenant Decio Catalano.)

As soon as the 'pig' had been pulled out, checked over, and surfaced

"I made visual contact with the two craft of Vesco and Visintini. The latter was towing Vesco's two-man torpedo, the engine of which had not started. . . . I arranged for the craft to be sunk at a considerable depth after detaching its warhead and transferring it to Visintini's 'pig'; Marceglia was to come with me, as third operator, and Vesco would accompany Visintini. We went ahead on an easterly course. At about 1.40 a.m. we sighted to our left an anchor light very high above sea-level, about 600 metres away. I gave orders for breaking away, having assigned to Visintini the targets in the direction of Gibraltar Rock. We exchanged good wishes and separated. . . . I set course for the anchor light. The target was hard to make out against the dark background of the land; it seemed to be a steamer of medium tonnage. I placed myself between the vessel and Gibraltar; against the background of the lights of Algeciras I identified the vessel as a modern motorship. . . ."

Having decided to attack, Catalano went astern of the vessel with the intention of fastening the charge to the screw. While he, surfaced and astride his torpedo, held the rudder of the target vessel with both hands, Marceglia and Giannoni proceeded to detach the warhead and undertake the operation of attaching it to the propeller-shaft.

"While this work was going on Marceglia unexpectedly started struggling in the water, breathing hard and fast as though he had been suddenly deprived of air. I heard Giannoni ask him what was the matter and Marceglia reply 'I'm all right'. I realized that my third operator had overtired himself; I called him to my side and told him to take over my station, while I went forward to prevent the warhead coming in contact with the vessel's hull. Marceglia took up my position, astride the craft . . . I kept my eye on Giannoni, who had meanwhile dived. I lifted my head above water from time to time; in one of these intervals I observed that Marceglia was lying face downwards, motionless, with his head turned slightly aft; I went to him and found that his arms and legs were spread; he did not answer when I called him."

Catalano immediately went to Marceglia's assistance; during this moment of confusion the 'pig', left to itself, went to the bottom; Giannoni dived after it, but in vain; it was lost at a great depth. There was nothing more to be done about it.

Catalano and Giannoni then went to work on Marceglia, who had fainted and was a dead weight; they turned him on his back, the current meanwhile increasing their distance from the vessel.

"I pumped oxygen into Marceglia's artificial lung to keep him well afloat and started calling to him again, while Giannoni, at my orders, took off and destroyed both his own and my breathing gear. I got him to do the same for Marceglia.

Marceglia continued to remain motionless.

Our voices had been heard aboard the ship. A seaman on guard duty came aft and examined the sea in our direction with a powerful torch without catching us in its beam. We went on swimming towards the shore, ignoring a new and better directed attempt to find us by the said seaman. In a few minutes Marceglia, whose face I had been slapping, started wheezing very loudly, thus drawing the attention of the personnel of the vessel to us for the third time. . . . He began to recover consciousness and after vomiting copiously became well enough to swim.

At four a.m., after avoiding a sentry-post, we got ashore (in Spain); we took off our rubber suits and reached the agreed spot." (From Catalano's report.)

Marceglia's sudden collapse had been the indirect cause of the loss of Catalano's two-man torpedo; the latter's attack therefore failed just when he had already made contact with his target and success seemed assured.

VISINTINI, VESCO and MAGRO. Their departure was without incident. Visintini came alongside Vesco, who had serious trouble with his 'pig'; after taking orders from Catalano, who had meanwhile joined them above water, Visintini took the warhead of the damaged human torpedo in tow, the craft itself being sunk. Vesco coming aboard the other craft as third man, they began to approach the anchorage of the steamers. The addition of the metallic mass of Vesco's warhead made the compass unreliable, so that it was no longer possible to keep on the course while submerged. But in view of the position of the targets, which made submersion unnecessary, the roadstead being an open one, and owing to the illumination of Gibraltar and Algeciras, which made direction-finding perfectly easy, this trouble scarcely mattered. Visintini, on arrival in the vicinity of the steamers which had been assigned to him, made straight for one of them, but at once desisted from the attack on perceiving two large white crosses painted on her quarter; she was a hospital ship. He approached a second vessel but gave it up on seeing the name *Switzerland* on her bulwarks; a third was left alone because

"it was of barely 1000 tons displacement and had a very antiquated appearance; I approached a fourth but only, unfortunately, to find that she was a dismasted tanker of 600–800 tons. I turned down this target also, and looked at my watch: it was 2.20 a.m. and I reflected that I had very little time left to spend on looking round; I therefore decided to attack without further ado the vessel I was now approaching. From its outline I took it for a tanker, but I then found that it was only a storage tanker."

He went astern of her and ordered his Number Two, Magro, to begin the operation of attaching the warhead to the vessel with a rope.

"Some minutes went by and I thought that Magro might require assistance, so I left my post and, following the rope, I rejoined him and spoke to him, but he did not reply; I could only see that his hands were not moving and that he seemed to be making a tremendous effort. I noticed, in fact, that the rope was stretched ominously tight; then I dived, and, before reaching my torpedo, called out 'Amedeo, air, air!'

93

1 had scarcely reached the warhead before the rope suddenly slackened and the torpedo, Vesco and myself began to sink at a great rate. The craft was heavily down astern. I tried to get to the steering seat but failed because I had to keep supplying myself with oxygen. We went on sinking fast. I felt a strong pressure through my suit and after a time I had a strange sensation of well-being, with red, yellow and blue sparks before my eyes. We must have been more than 30 metres down and were still sinking; I realized, to my intense distress, that all was lost. I slackened my grip when I felt that the strange sensation of well-being was about to turn to loss of consciousness. In order to succeed in making an upward movement I had to take in more oxygen and swim as hard as I could. At last I reached the surface and the few seconds which elapsed before I could see Vesco come up seemed interminable.

In the end he too reached the surface; he looked as though he had had a bad time of it and I gave him all the help I could. Meanwhile Magro, alarmed at our absence, was calling us from the stern of the vessel. I told him to rejoin us and keep absolutely silent; we got rid of our breathing sets and sank them after making sure that our suits were retaining the dilation we had given them through the appropriate valves.

I learned from Magro that he had tied the rope to the hinge of the rudder but that the rope had snapped. Vesco told me that he had heard my shout and had pumped air into the tanks for surfacing but in vain.

I took to a very effective system of group swimming on the back, in which we were all three linked together and struck out rhythmically.

We swam from 2.40 to 4.15 a.m., by which time we had landed at the spot indicated by operational orders.

Petty Officer/diver Giovanni Magro distinguished himself by his daring, dash and the high order of professional ability which he in particular displayed in this operation. I hope he will be rewarded by being permitted to take part in further operations with two-man torpedoes."

So ends Visintini's report. He, too, had been the victim of a cruel trick of fate, an unlucky accident similar to that which had caused Catalano's attack to fail; during the execution of the manœuvres necessary for attaching the warhead to the target, the torpedo, subjected to a sudden increase of weight, broke its mooring rope and yielded to gravitation, sinking with its full weight and disappearing into great depth of water, despite the attempts of Visintini and Vesco to stop its downward plunge.

The operation failed, therefore, to accomplish its task; the harbour had been found to be empty of warships; one of the two-man torpedoes had proved to be hopelessly damaged immediately after launching from the submarine; the other two were lost during the phase of attack, owing to unforeseen difficulties caused by having to manœuvre in the deep waters of the roadstead instead of in the harbour.

On the other hand the expedition could be regarded as 'realistic' training for the operators; no lives had been lost; the new system had been tried out of getting the pilots to the objective *via* the *Fulgor* and its organization by Italian Naval Intelligence agents had been so perfect that the arrival of the six pilots in Spain, their sojourn there, the successive meetings with them on the coast, their immediate departure for Seville by car and their boarding of a LATI aircraft bound for Italy had been carried through without leaving a trace or arousing any suspicions on the part of either Spaniards or British. And since the latter were altogether ignorant of the risk they had run on the night of the 26th of May, the possibility of a renewed attempt to take them by surprise still remained open.

Finally, it had again been confirmed that the *Scirè* and her crew could be relied on to carry out any type of operation, whatever fighting risk or nautical difficulties might be involved.

The six pilots were awarded the silver medal for their gallant conduct in this mission.

CHAPTER IX

THE GLORIOUS FAILURE AT MALTA:
25TH–26TH JULY, 1941

Malta a constant menace to Italy—Tesei's fixed idea—The attempt in May—Renewed in June: bitter, terrible disappointment!—Tesei's request and Moccagatta's decision—Final plan —Action of the 25th–26th July—Giobbe's doubts—Tesei and Carabelli sacrifice themselves—Annihilation of the assailants —'A few seconds were enough for all movement on the water to cease'—The British secret: radar—The Governor of Malta's opinion of our sailors—The spiritual testament of Tesei.

THE idea of forcing La Valletta, the harbour of Malta, the chief stronghold of the British Navy in the Mediterranean, the possession of which by foreigners is a constant threat to Italy, had been considered as long ago as 1935, when the human torpedo was taking shape; Malta was the objective for which the weapon had been planned and built. For reasons we have already in part indicated, the resort to large-scale, lightning surprise attacks at the commencement of the war did not take place; since that time methods of warfare had developed in such a way that conditions had changed completely from those of 1935. Owing to the greatly increased danger by air raids and the proximity of the Sicilian airfields (15 minutes' flight away), Malta had lost, since Italy entered the war, its value as a permanent base for fleets; it only remained a refitting point for vessels in transit and an advanced base for smaller naval units employed in the interception of Italian traffic with Africa. As a logical consequence, the British battle fleet was divided up between Alexandria and Gibraltar, which were both so far from Italy that Italian aircraft could reach them only after long flights without fighter escort, thus giving the enemy the necessary time for alerts. Alexandria and Gibraltar had therefore become the principal targets of attacks by the Tenth Light Flotilla.

But the victorious result of the operation against Suda had led us to reconsider the original plan to raid Malta. Tesei was a convinced supporter of the idea; in his opinion the use of the human torpedo

H.M.S. *Barham* firing broadside. Picture
taken from H.M.S. *Valiant.*

The battle-cruiser H.M.S. *York.*

The tanker *Fulgor* in the roadstead at Cadiz. She was adapted as parent ship for the submarine.

should be regarded as having more of a moral effect than a physical one, the infliction of losses on the enemy:

"The whole world ought to realize," he used to say, "that there are Italians ready to reach Malta in the most daring way: whether we sink any ships there or not does not matter much; what does matter is that we should be able to blow up with our craft under the very noses of the enemy: we should thus have shown our sons and Italy's future generations at the price of what sacrifices we live up to our ideals and how success is to be achieved."

The general plan of the operation began to be developed, following an order by Admiral de Courten, on the 25th of April, 1941. Our commander, Moccagatta, who threw himself into the undertaking with all the resolution and pugnacity of his generous nature, had a number of interviews in Rome with the authorities charged with the supervision of the operations; but those responsible did not show themselves, at any rate in principle, very favourably inclined to the project. Moccagatta wrote in his diary on the 10th of May:

"To-day the memorandum was drawn up about the operation against Malta; but this evening it seemed to me that Admiral Campioni (Deputy Chief of the Naval Staff) was still somewhat dubious about the opportuneness of the operation. We shall have an answer to-morrow, but it's heavy going. . . ."

On the 22nd of May he continues:

"On the morning of the 20th I was received by the Under Secretary but he would not give us a free hand for the Malta operation. As I had suggested that, before embarking upon the operation itself, we should have a stab at the outer defences with two motorboats, the Under Secretary told me to make two of these thrusts and then report about them. If I could conscientiously advise him that the operation was practicable, he said, he would consider giving a definite order to proceed. . . . Here (at Augusta) crews are very keen and want to get into action at any price. But we have to keep a cool head and preparations must be carried out with attention to every detail."

G   97

Malta is an island difficult to get at for most of its coastline: its high cliffs rise steeply from the sea. There is a single large harbour, La Valletta, which forms an ideal natural anchorage, perfected by the work of human ingenuity. It resembles a ramified invasion of the sea into the interior of the island: bays, inlets of water and piers succeed one another for a number of kilometres along the two sides of a central peninsula on which the city stands and which divides the waters into two distinct havens, the Grand Harbour and Marsa Muscetto Bay. The channels of access by sea to La Valletta are hard to distinguish at night, being masked by massive coastal rocks which at a distance seem to be piled one on another. These natural obstacles are reinforced by defences due to well-designed works of military engineering accumulated for centuries by generations of warriors alternating in the possession of the island and by works added in very recent times as the result of experience gained during the war we were fighting: multiple net defences, alert systems equipped with radar and acoustic detectors and nests of light, quick-firing guns, enfilading the only possible entrance channels.

The information we possessed regarding the state of the defences of the island was very sketchy: it consisted almost entirely of what could be deduced from air reconnaissance; it was incredible, but true, that we had no agent at Malta who could furnish us with intelligence! In particular, we were quite unaware of the new defensive expedients the British had put into operation, following the experiences they had undergone when the Tenth Light Flotilla carried out the first daring attacks against Gibraltar in October 1940 and Suda in March 1941.

A group of E-boats was detached to Augusta; the preparation of the men and their weapons was being completed; they were ready for action at the May new moon.

Preliminary reconnaissance was undertaken with the object of probing the chances of approaching the island unperceived and testing the standard of alertness of the defence, as well as ascertaining the visibility conditions for reconnoitring the coast and the entrances to La Valletta harbour; all these elements were indispensable before we could risk an attack.

Moccagatta, who took part, himself, in the reconnaissances made by two motorboats, refers to them as follows:

"Augusta, 25th May. Put out to sea. After doubling Cape

Passero, the weather became so bad that I had to reduce speed from 30 to 18 knots. Consequently we arrived at our post, four miles off La Valletta, nearly two hours late. A dark war-time night; I remained on the look-out for about two hours, without sighting anything of interest: a few searchlights flashed and a British aircraft landed, but that was all. At 7.30 a.m. I was back in harbour at Augusta. I was very satisfied with the two motorboat commanders; the vessels themselves and their engines also behaved very well.

28th May. To-night I went out with two motorboats and again went to the look-out off La Valletta; the night was dark and overcast, a long swell running. There was nothing to see; only three air raids between 3.30 and 4.30, the last of which gave a clear illumination of the entire zone for some seconds."

But on the 30th of May Moccagatta writes:

"This morning Admiral de Courten informed me by telephone that in view of the few targets present in Malta harbour the Supreme Command does not consider it a good opportunity to take action. So this moon, too, has been wasted."

At the end of June, when the next moon would favour operations, the whole outfit returned to Augusta; a new start was to be made. Moccagatta thus describes the new venture, in his usual laconic style:

"Augusta, 23rd June, 1941. I arrived here after stopping two days in Rome. I finally have executive orders for the Malta operation. Perhaps this will be the great chance; we go into action on the 27th or at the latest the 28th.

24th June. This morning at 4 a.m. full scale forcing rehearsal with the E-boats. At 6, general sea-borne towing exercise.

26th June. Reconnaissance to-night in front of Malta; it was most useful, for we were able to observe the coast at close quarters due to over 30 searchlights being switched on for an air raid. We got within less than 3000 metres and could distinguish the houses. The operators I had brought with me to reconnoitre the coast returned to port satisfied. We shall start to-morrow evening.

28th June. Yesterday evening I left Augusta with the whole outfit to go into action against Malta, but a rather troublesome sea (a fresh south-easterly breeze) worried the E-boats and they all started having damage which made me lose time. Then one of them sank; I insisted on going ahead, but after two further cases of trouble had been reported I tacked about and returned to Augusta. A bad business: but we try again to-morrow. My mind is made up. . . .

30th June. Bitter, terrible disappointment! At 3 in the afternoon I was at sea with the whole outfit; auxiliary engines, speed six knots, usual breeze from the SE. Everything was going well, but at 4 I had to order everyone to lay to, as an E-boat on tow had sprung a leak and was in danger of sinking. After investigation of the trouble, not wanting to lose time, I took in tow, with my own motorboat, the sound E-boat which had been towed with the one that was sinking, and sent the other motorboat back to Augusta towing the damaged E-boat. I resumed my course, the SE breeze freshened off Cape Murro di Porco; I was sure that none of my subordinates considered it practicable to go on. But I was convinced that the wind would drop at sunset and I carried on grimly until 8 p.m. Finally, I was right and, at 2010 hours, off Cape Passero, with wind and sea quiet, I ordered all boats to lay to and had the E-boats checked over, their water pumped out and their engines tested. I was never a believer in bad luck but now I had 99 reasons out of 100 for believing in it; when all the E-boats were ready and *all* had given their engines a thorough overhaul, I again set out, at 9 p.m., for Malta. The sea and the wind had both fallen. I was now certain of success. But as soon as we got going an E-boat snapped her towing-line and could not start her engine so as to close the gap; I sent my best mechanics aboard her, but lost an hour and failed to get the engine going. It was a pity, for this was the E-boat I had detailed to blow a way through the net defences; but at 10 o'clock I decided to proceed without her. Giobbe warned me he was dead against it. After another five minutes one of the motorboats had engine trouble and stopped; this made me lose another 20 minutes. At that point I gave in; the E-boats would by then have arrived off Malta too late, i.e. at dawn, when there would be no more chance of surprise action. I veered and set course for Augusta: we had two hours and a half without any trouble; at 1.30 a.m. we reached harbour. There was one comic detail: a pilot who had gone to sleep in his E-boat did not

notice that we had tacked about and when we stopped and he saw
land at close quarters he got ready to attack, supposing himself
to be facing Malta. This was that excellent fellow Carabelli,
Engineer Sub-Lieutenant and first-rate pilot in every respect."

So ended, in failure, the second attempt against Malta. Once more
the tenacity and will-power of men had not been equal to the inherent
difficulties of this undertaking. But this was no reason for yielding to
adverse fate.

With unshakable determination the operation was decided for
the next favourable moon phase in July. These successive postponements, due to causes which we have already described in the words of
Moccagatta, led to very serious consequences.

The previous operational orders had provided for the employment
of E-boats alone. But the further delay of a month gave Tesei an
opportunity to have his own views adopted. In conformity with the
theories he had expressed all along he maintained that the piloted
torpedoes, and with them, of course, he himself, should share in the
attack on Malta.

The idea of employing, contemporaneously and in support of one
another, weapons so different in their nature and mode of employ,
was from a purely technical point of view an extremely hazardous
one; the obstinacy with which Tesei insisted on taking part in the
expedition was simply a sublime and patriotic way of committing
suicide.

From my knowledge of Tesei, his theories and his force of character,
and the meaning he gave to death on active service in the waters of
Malta, which he considered his particular duty, I am inclined to
conclude that Tesei's insistence in wanting to take part in 'Operation
Malta' arose from his firm resolve not to miss the chance of carrying
out his purpose of hurling himself with his torpedo against the enemy's
defences. Tesei had already done, in his former activity in war, more
than could reasonably have been expected from a man. As a volunteer
in the first operation against Alexandria he had, for 20 hours, lavished
a tireless energy in the attempt, which ultimately succeeded, to save
the survivors of the *Iride*, imprisoned at the bottom of the sea in the
wreck of that submarine. The efforts he then made had further
affected his heart, already weakened by many years of experiment and
training with the underwater breathing gear. He had also volunteered

for the *Scirè's* second mission to Gibraltar; on returning to base after this fresh effort, which had been made with a noble disregard of his state of health, Tesei was examined by our doctor, Falcomatà, and declared 'unfit for diving for six months, owing to serious cardiac weakness'.

In spite of this diagnosis, and although he knew perfectly well what would happen if he disobeyed the orders of the surgeon, he spent days and nights of indefatigable effort when he was called to Taranto because of his technical proficiency as engineer officer and as diver, at the time when the battleship *Cavour* was torpedoed by British aircraft. As a result of numerous and prolonged underwater inspections of the ship, he gave information which was of great value in preventing the loss of the vessel and enabled her to be salvaged. Such physical efforts, which would be exceptional for any normally healthy man, brought about an inevitable degeneration in his cardiac condition and general bodily fitness. He could therefore not have had many illusions left about his chances of future active service with assault craft. He had been sacrificing himself not in one sublime and fatal moment, as had been his dream, but bit by bit; he now sought to extinguish his remaining spark of life in a last gallant deed in favour of his companions, in the pursuit of a great victory. Such was Teseo Tesei's deliberate and conscious resolve. His proposals were put forward with such passionate ardour that he succeeded in overcoming the scruples and opposition of Moccagatta till the latter, at last, agreed to accept his offer.

The plan of operations assumed a new, more extended and complex aspect.

There were two possible ways of access to La Valletta harbour; the principal entrance, closed by four different orders of defences, and a narrow channel under the bridge between the Sant'Elmo mole and the mainland. This was a steel bridge, supported by three pillars, standing high enough above water to allow the passage of small vessels; but now, in time of war, a steel anti-torpedo net had been suspended from the bridge and probably reached down underwater to the bottom, so as to close this passage altogether. On the assumption, perhaps not entirely justified but certainly logical (it must be remembered that no reliable information was available), that the main entrance would be fully equipped with guard-posts, sentries, detecting apparatus, obstructions and other devices, and therefore practically impenetrable, it was decided to force the harbour by the subsidiary channel beneath the bridge. The method of taking the E-boats to Malta on tow by motor-boats had given much trouble in previous experiences and was abandoned. The *Diana*, a destroyer originally fitted out as a yacht for the Duce and by him placed at the disposal of the Navy for the duration of the war, was used instead. The plan was that the *Diana* should approach the island with the E-boats on board and with a special motorboat, the MTL, in tow. The MTL was to carry two piloted torpedoes within a very short distance from the harbour's entrance, thus sparing the operators the perilous and tiring approach on their own craft and also the difficulties of coastal reconnoitring. These last difficulties were aggravated by the limited range of vision of the operators who had only their heads above water.

One of the human torpedoes was to set course for the bridge: on contact with the anti-torpedo net suspended there, the charge was to be fastened and exploded. A gap would thus be blown in the net; through it the E-boats, launched from the *Diana*, and silently drawn close to the bridge, would make their way. Once in the interior of the harbour the pilots would go full speed ahead to attack the enemy ships. The other human torpedo would simultaneously enter the adjacent roadstead of Marsa Muscetto, where the submarine station was situated, and attach its charge to the hull of one of the submarines, in the hope of sinking more than one of them, since, as usual with the British Navy, they were moored alongside one another. After carrying out the attack the crews of the two piloted torpedoes would have to try to get back to the motorboats. The operation thus planned was obviously complicated; it required, in addition to extreme coolness and determination on the part of the operators (whose qualifications offered no doubts), perfect synchronization of the various elements of the scheme all directed to a single end. This synchronization is always difficult to achieve, especially at sea, and at night, and in time of war, since so many causes due to natural, human, war or merely fortuitous conditions may create the unforeseen and thus cause the failure of even the best-laid schemes.

We will avail ourselves of the notes left by Moccagatta, who was in command of the whole operation, to follow its development; in his military style he makes us live through the operators' days of action, sharing their hopes, their doubts, their splendid tenacity, will-power and resolution.

"9th July '41. La Spezia. I am hard at work getting the human torpedoes and their transport craft ready for the operation against Malta.

18th July '41. Rome. On the way to Augusta for the Malta action.

22nd July '41. Augusta. I arrived on the evening of the 19th. On the 20th, in the morning, the *Diana* pulled in and was placed at my disposal for transport of the *E*-boats. I am literally working day and night on the preparations for 'Operation Malta'; this evening the final rehearsals for launching at night from the *Diana* will take place and this will be the end of tests, experiments and exercises, unless something unforeseen happens. To-morrow evening I shall go and cruise off Malta with two motorboats, so that the pilots can become acquainted with the situation; on the evening of the 24th I shall give everyone a night off for rest and on the evening of the 25th I shall be ready for action. We shall see what happens; but meanwhile the weather seems to be fine and it worries me to see these days going by so quickly. Yet I cannot start without proper preparations and the human-torpedo pilots specially asked me to take them on that cruise off Malta. It was a reasonable request in the circumstances; the commander of the *Diana*, too, welcomed the opportunity of this rehearsal and the idea of coming along as my escort.

23rd July. Augusta. This evening I am taking the two motor-boats out to let the pilots take stock of the situation off Malta: there is a big British formation (a battleship, an aircraft-carrier, 14 destroyers and 14 steamers) making its way to Malta to-day. I wonder if there is any likelihood of our bumping into them? We certainly can't expect to do so with the big ships, but a few steamers may put in at Malta and, if they do, we shall have an interesting night of it.

24th July. Augusta. I got back this morning at 7.30; so far as the motorboats were concerned, everything went off very well, as I got to within about 2000 metres of Malta and identified the safety buoys marking the entrance channels. . . . But as for the operation with the *E*-boats, I came back feeling discouraged; the Malta coast is extremely difficult to reconnoitre in the dark, there is always a considerable current running east and, consequently, the assumed position for the start will always be subject to mis-calculation. Moreover, they must have heard me, for they switched on four powerful searchlights. . . . What can the E-boats do in these conditions? Wait for daybreak? It may be that these doubts of mine are due to my extreme fatigue; but to-night I shall rest and to-morrow, if the weather remains fine, I shall attempt the operation.

25th July. Augusta. All day yesterday Giobbe was telling me about his doubts and uneasiness; on the whole it was not a mistake to examine all the difficulties beforehand, and so yesterday I listened attentively and was ready to modify such arrangements as it might eventually prove necessary to modify. This morning, as soon as we met, Giobbe started telling me all over again that he was extremely dubious about the success of the operation. I answered that I had no doubts at all myself, that I was going to stick precisely to the operational plans drawn up two days before and already transmitted to the General Staff and that his job was to hurry up and get the detailed orders ready." (From the war diary of Commander Moccagatta.)

These are the last words of the diary. Moccagatta, always the first in operations, led his men in the glorious action from which they were never to return.

Under the command of Moccagatta the expedition left its base at Augusta on the 25th of July, at sunset. It consisted of the dispatch-boat *Diana* (Commander Di Muro) with nine E-boats aboard and towing the special motorboat transporting the piloted torpedoes, the MTL (steered by Paratore); the motorboats 451 and 452 (Lieutenant Parodi, in charge, and Sub-Lieutenant Sciolette) with Moccagatta aboard and towing, in their turn, a torpedo-motorboat, which Lieutenant-Commander Giobbe was to use to guide the E-boats to the entrance of the harbour and for picking up possible survivors.

The human-torpedo crews were Major Teseo Tesei, with Pedretti as his assistant, who were to blow up the net under the bridge, and Sub-Lieutenant Costa, with N.C.O./diver Barla, whose targets were the submarines at Marsa Muscetto. The Tenth Flotilla Command and the whole of the surface Division were therefore engaged in the operation. Surgeon-Captain Falcomatà had also wished to participate in the mission and he was aboard one of the motorboats.

The sea and the weather favoured the undertaking: it was a moon-less night, the water was calm and there was no wind. The vessels belonging to a British convoy coming from Gibraltar, which had been sighted at the time in the Malta Channel, had entered La Valletta; at this third attempt the best possible conditions for the success of the undertaking had finally been verified.

The approach proceeded without incident. On arrival at about 20 miles off Malta, the *Diana* launched her nine E-boats. One of the latter, which had not succeeded in getting its engine started, immediately sank: her pilot, P.O. Montanari, was taken aboard one of the escorting motorboats. The other eight E-boats, in line ahead formation, under Giobbe's orders and escorted by the two motorboats, proceeded at slow speed towards the Sant'Elmo bridge. At the same time the special motorboat carrying the piloted torpedoes was also towed close to its target. When the *Diana*, after fulfilling her task, started to return, the motorboats, the E-boats and the human-torpedoes transport went up to two miles off the harbour. The motorboats now stopped and the transport, aboard which were the crews of Tesei and Costa, made use of her silent electric engine during this final phase, to reach a point about 1000 metres from the Sant'Elmo bridge. Reconnoitring of the coast proceeded without incident, though the co-operation which the Air Force had been requested to provide turned out to be partial and ill-timed. To facilitate approach to the land and distract the attention of the defence it had been agreed with the Air Force that three raids should be carried out: a light one on La Valletta, at 1.45 a.m. to give us the direction; a heavier one on the same target at 2.30; and a third, still heavier, for distraction purposes, at 4.30 (zero hour for the sea attack), not against the coast at all but on the airfield at Mikabba in the interior of the island. The first raid did not take place, the second came at 2.45 with a single aircraft and the third at 4.20 with two.

At 3 a.m., on arrival at a short distance from the bridge, Tesei and Costa launched their human torpedoes from the transport. Costa's engine started missing; he and Tesei repaired it as well as they could. At 3.45 Tesei took leave of Costa. The latter remarked that they were about an hour behind schedule, so that Tesei would not have time to get away from the danger zone of the explosion after setting the time-fuse; should he, however, set the fuse for later, so as to be able to make good his escape back to the motorboats, waiting for him about 2000 metres from the bridge, the explosion would take place too late to enable the E-boats to force the entrance while it was still dark. When Costa, very reasonably, drew Tesei's attention to these considerations, the latter answered in the following words: "I presume that I shall not

106

have time to do anything but get my torpedo as far as the net. At 4.30 the net has to blow up and it will blow up. If I am late, I shall fire the charge straight away." (From Lieutenant Costa's report, drawn up after his release from prison.) Tesei's stoical determination could not have been more simply expressed.

Tesei and Pedretti, astride their 'pig', approached the net suspended from the bridge and which had to be blown up; meanwhile Costa, with his torpedo in poor condition, made for the entrance to Marsa Muscetto.

While this was going on, Giobbe, on his torpedo-motorboat, with P.O.s. Costantini and Zocchi aboard, led the explosive boat formation at slow speed, so as not to arouse the attention of the enemy, to within sight of the bridge. There he halted, collected his craft, counted them and pointed out to the pilots, in the darkness, the dimly seen outline of their target. Waiting began; the eight craft lay to with their engines shut off and the hearts of the eight men aboard them beat steadily as they held themselves in readiness to dash beyond the obstacle; they were black shadows in the night, resembling marine centaurs, their eyes fixed on the bridge below which they had to pass, their ears alert for the sound of the explosion of Tesei's charge, which would be the signal for them to start.

But these black shadows were men and each had a name: they were Frassetto, Carabelli, Bosio, Zaniboni, Pedrini, Follieri, Marchisio and Capriotti.

In their fragile boats, these Italian seamen were a few hundred metres from La Valletta, close to the threatening island, bristling with guns and defenders; in absolute silence the men waited for the event which would mean the beginning of their dash to victory or perhaps, as a result of some trifling incident (their being sighted, surprised by a patrolboat or a searchlight), to annihilation.

Time passed. In the east the darkness of night was already fading: in a very short time now they could be discovered; the discipline of self-control imposed by months of training had attained perfection in these young men: their strength of will had achieved complete ascendancy over their physique and its impulses, including even the most deep-seated of all, that of self-preservation. They were gathered around Giobbe, their commander, and watched, in the dim light, his familiar features; it was he who would give them the decisive order.

But Giobbe, for some minutes, had been silent: he seemed utterly absorbed, as though withdrawn into some inward conflict of his own.

It was his duty to make a decision: every minute which passed now might be fatal to the success of the operation and to the lives of his lads; if he were to hurl the *E*-boats against the net while it was still intact, the resulting explosion would kill Tesei and Pedretti, who would probably be somewhere underwater in the vicinity; if he went on waiting he would risk failure of the operation, since it would soon be daylight. But at last, at 4.30, they felt the shock of an underwater explosion. Tesei and Pedretti had accomplished their task.

The moment had come for Giobbe to give his men the signal to be off; but he still hesitated. Had the underwater explosion really torn a gap? To make sure, it would be better also to hurl an explosive boat against the net. But if Tesei and Pedretti, for some reason, should still be down there or only a short distance away, what would happen to them? The explosion of a boat would indubitably annihilate them. It was not Giorgio Giobbe, a man of flesh and blood, with a heart and human feelings, who had to decide the question, it was the commanding officer of the surface craft of the Tenth Light Flotilla; he was the leader of a handful of brave men whose lives had been entrusted to him with a single purpose, that of achieving success. And if he went on hesitating . . . dawn and the British defences would catch him there still hesitating; that would mean the failure of the mission and the loss of his men.

"Attention, lads!" Giobbe's cool, energetic voice was heard to break the silence. "We're off now. Frassetto will take the lead, then Carabelli; if the way through is still closed by the net, blow it up with your craft; the other six, Bosio leading, will slip under the bridge at intervals of a few seconds. And remember your orders: to enable one man to get inside the harbour all the rest will have to sacrifice themselves, if necessary, in clearing the way. Good hunting! Off you go!"

The decision had been taken; the men's tension, undefined but alert, the strain of their impatience and the over-long repression of their ardour were at last relaxed. After an instant of utter silence the eight *E*-boats, two some distance ahead, the rest following, dashed away at full speed, churning up the smooth sea as they whizzed along. Frassetto and Carabelli made straight for the bridge; the former threw himself into the sea 80 metres from the net but did not hear any explosion; Carabelli, transformed into a human projectile clinging to the framework bearing that terrible load of explosive, rushed of his own accord, hard as he could go, on his own death. A few seconds later the air was rent by a thunderous roar: the boat had blown up on contact, the pilot being instantly killed. But unluckily the explosion of Carabelli's boat had an unforeseen effect: down came the whole span of the bridge and completely obstructed the entrance channel so as to render it impenetrable. Simultaneously with the crash of its fall machine-gun fire broke out from every direction and innumerable searchlights swept the sea to identify the assailants. The scene was apocalyptic. The blinding beams of the searchlights picked out the six little craft led by Bosio, which were making for the bridge at full speed, in clouds of white spray; they could not know that the entrance was now barred by the tangled wreckage of the fallen mass of metal.

One after the other the six E-boats, as clearly visible as by day-light, came to a halt under the bursts of point-blank cross-fire. 'A few seconds were enough,' the British were to write, 'for all movement on the water to cease.' Immediately afterwards fighters, which had risen at once from the airfields, swooped over the water, machine-gunning boats and men incapable of any kind of defence, within a few metres of the Sant'Elmo mole. Bosio was killed; Frassetto, who was swimming when Carabelli's boat blew up, was seriously wounded; Capriotti, Pedrini and Marchisio were also hit by enemy fire. All the survivors, including Follieri and Zaniboni, were later picked up at sea and taken prisoner by the British.

But that tragic dawn had scarcely broken. Other disasters were still to happen and more blood to flow.

Costa had failed to penetrate the bay of Marsa Muscetto owing to engine trouble and the alarm given to the fortress; consequently the attack on the submarines could not be made, and both he and Barla were captured by the British. Giobbe, who had been witness from a short distance of the tragedy of the assault craft, returned to the motorboats as soon as silence had set in again.

The motorboats, finding that no one had come back although they had waited a long time, were now proceeding slowly northwards. Giobbe overtook them after about a quarter of an hour; his boat was taken in tow by motorboat 452, which he boarded in order to give Moccagatta a report on what had occurred. The two vessels, at as high a speed as the towed craft permitted, turned for home. But after about an hour, when it was already full day, they were spotted by fighters from Malta, which were all in the air as a result of the attack. The units were raked again and again by machine-gun fire; aboard the '452'

Moccagatta, Giobbe, Falcomatà, the pilot Montanari and the crew of Giobbe's craft, Costantini and Zocchi, fell at the first burst; at the next Parodi, the commanding officer, and a seaman dropped; the other 11 men aboard managed to escape on Giobbe's craft, in which they subsequently rejoined the *Diana*, already far on her homeward course.

Aboard the other motorboat, the petrol tanks caught fire as soon as the vessel came under enemy attack; one of the British aircraft was brought down by the machine-gun aboard; the crew then threw themselves into the sea just in time: the '451' blew up and disappeared into the water in flames and four seamen perished. The survivors (nine out of 13), most of them wounded, including the commander, Sciolette, were picked up six hours later by a British motorboat and taken prisoner; during the voyage to Malta they sighted the '452', crippled but still afloat, and aboard her the corpses of Moccagatta, Giobbe, Falcomatà, Parodi, Montanari and three of the crew, which were examined, but in vain, by a British naval surgeon in case any of them might still need his attention.

Nothing more was ever heard of Tesei or Pedretti: it appears that, in the water not far from the Sant'Elmo bridge, the British found the mask of a breathing set with tatters of flesh and tufts of hair. . . . But we now *know* how they met their end, for Tesei told Costa, as they parted, what it would be. On arrival at the bridge, they fastened the warhead to the net, glanced at the time—it was 4.30, the hour at which the E-boats were to get through—and then Tesei did not hesitate for a moment. He took leave for the last time, with a handclasp, or perhaps an embrace, of his faithful companion Pedretti, then switched the fuse to zero and the next moment their earthly bodies were annihilated: 'tatters of flesh and tufts of hair'. . . .

Thus, the only survivors of the tragic holocaust were the 11 men who were able to rejoin the *Diana* on Giobbe's boat.

Moccagatta, commander of the flotilla created by his own energy and enthusiasm; Giobbe, the brave chief of the surface Division; Falcomatà, our friend the surgeon; Parodi, commander of the '452'; Tesei and Pedretti, of imperishable memory; Carabelli, Bosio and Montanari, the E-boat pilots, had all perished; Costa and Barla had been captured at Marsa Muscetto; the other six pilots, almost all seriously wounded, Paratore, the helmsman of the boat which had been towing the human torpedoes and was sunk by the fighters, the majority of the crews of the '451' and '452', including Commanding

Officer Sciolette, were all prisoners of war; altogether, 15 had fallen and 18 were prisoners; one motorboat had been sunk and one captured; eight E-boats, a special towing craft and two human torpedoes had been lost; two of our fighter aircraft, which had valiantly come up to oppose the British fighters, had been shot down. In favour of our side, one enemy aircraft had been destroyed in addition to the damage, in any case of a secondary nature, done in the wrecking of the bridge.

"So ended the Malta failure, the cruellest and bloodiest of all the operations ever undertaken by the crews of the assault craft, but also the focal point of circumstances so extraordinary as to render it without doubt the most glorious of failures; so glorious that any navy in the world would be proud of it." (MARC' ANTONIO BRAGADIN: *What Did the Navy Do?* Published by Garzanti.)

The memories of Commanders Moccagatta and Giobbe were honoured by the award of the gold medal, as were those of Major Tesei and his companion P.O./diver Pedretti, of Surgeon-Captain Falcomatà, of Engineer Sub-Lieutenant Carabelli, who sacrificed himself to clear the gap, and of Sub-Lieutenant Bosio who lost his life in the attempt to get through it; also of P.O./Torpedo-Gunner Vincon, aboard one of the motorboats. Sub-Lieutenant Frassetto obtained the same decoration.

The Tenth Light Flotilla named its underwater Division after Teseo Tesei and its surface Division after Vittorio Moccagatta, so that the sacrifice of its best men might serve as an example and the remembrance of their deeds as an inspiration and guide for those who were to continue their work.

Today we know that, from midnight on, the assailants had been detected by the radar equipment of the island and had been under observation from that moment until the action began. We are so informed by an official British publication issued in 1944, *The Air Battle of Malta*. Here is an extract from it which, by telling the story from the standpoint of the other side, enables us to complete the picture of that tragic night:

"Malta had been using radiolocation (radar) ever since the beginning of the war. On the night of the 25th July, 1941, it became known, through radiolocation, that a surface force was approaching the island, interrupting the relative tranquillity which prevailed at that time. The alarm was given, the *Swordfish* aircraft were ordered to readiness and the *Hurricanes* stood by for first light.

The alarm was given just before midnight: an air raid had failed to take simultaneous action with the approaching units. The sound of motorboat engines was soon reported along the NE coast: the coastal defences, harbour batteries and searchlights waited on tip-toe. A convoy had just arrived in Grand Harbour, the submarines were at their usual berths, but the teeth of La Valletta were ready to bite as the unknown formation approached. A little before dawn a track was seen to be approaching Sant'Elmo, the fortress constituting one of the jawbones that close the mouth of Grand Harbour. At the very moment the wake was seen from Tigne (the other jaw) an explosion was observed on the breakwater viaduct, the first barrier of the harbour. At once the searchlights were switched on and illuminated a group of explosive motorboats (*E*-Boats) moving at full speed towards the place where the explosion had occurred. The lighted area instantly became the target at short range of devastating cross-fire by all arms in the neighbourhood: six-pounders from 500 to 2500 metres range, Bofors guns and machine-guns. The barrage lasted two minutes. Then silence ensued; there was nothing left to fire on. When day broke the guns found a further two targets and destroyed them. Meanwhile the *Hurricanes* had already taken off in search of the remaining units, which were withdrawing, and launched an attack on them. The whole of the attacking formation was destroyed. Twenty corpses were found and 18 men were made prisoners. In order to cover the retreat of their gallant but rash formation the Italians had sent *Macchi* fighters against the *Hurricanes* which were just finishing off the motorboats in the first light of day, but three *Macchi* were shot down. The prisoners were interrogated and a complete set of orders, captured with one of the *E*-boats, was scrutinized; the most remarkable fact about these most detailed and complicated orders was the almost complete absence of any reference to possible counter-action by ourselves in this connection; it is very noticeable that prior to the moment at which our defence action developed, i.e. when the viaduct was blown up and the fort opened fire, the

Assault swimmer at practice.

Assault swimmer at practice: note the webbed feet and the highly luminous dial of the swimmer's watch.

With the Augusta Light Flotilla prior to setting out for
Malta. Commanding Officer MOCCAGATTA in centre.

An explosive boat goes in to the attack.

whole plan had been carried out with great determination and the time schedule kept with admirable precision.

Within two minutes from the time of opening fire, however, the attack had been completely annihilated and all risk of the defences of the harbour being forced was at an end. The reconnaissance photography on which the attack had been based must have been at least four days old. In a desperate attempt to take photographs two bombers escorted by 30 fighters had been sent over Malta but thanks to our fighters the two reconnaissance planes were shot down together with three of the escorting fighters. The determined search for and destruction of every motorboat in retreat by our *Hurricanes* turned failure into disaster." (*These notes have been taken from the official report of the Vice-Admiral, Malta, Sir Wilbraham Ford.*)

The then Governor of the island, Sir Edward Jackson, expressed himself as follows:

"Malta was attacked once from the sea. Last July the Italians launched an assault conducted with great determination in order to penetrate the harbour, employing motorboats and piloted torpedoes belonging to *suicide squads* . . . this enterprise required displays of personal courage of the highest order." (*Daily Mail*, 4th of October, 1941.)

A letter dated the 17th of July, a few days before the mission, from Teseo Tesei to a friend reads:

"By the time you receive this letter I shall have attained the highest of all honours, that of giving my life for the King and the honour of the Flag. As you know this is the supreme desire of a soldier and the most sublime joy he can experience. . . ."

H

CHAPTER X

FIRST SUCCESS OF THE HUMAN TORPEDOES —GIBRALTAR: 20TH–21ST SEPTEMBER, 1941

Reconstruction work after the Malta losses—Commander Todaro—An innovation: the 'assault swimmer'—The 'bug' and the 'limpet'—Alpine swimmers—The Scirè *again heads for Gibraltar—Vesco and Catalano sink two steamers— Visintini's fine exploit: he enters the harbour and sinks a naval tanker—The enemy intensifies his defence measures—Royal audience.*

AFTER the death of Commanding Officer Moccagatta I was appointed to take temporary command of the Tenth Light Flotilla. It was a great honour, especially in view of my rank (I had only just been promoted Lieutenant-Commander), but the duties of the post had been rendered onerous for a number of reasons, including the heavy losses of men and materials undergone during the latest operations against Suda and Malta.

I put all my energy into the reconstruction work on the lines of the organization created by Moccagatta. To replace the gallant Giobbe, I entrusted the command of the surface Division to an officer of the highest personal and professional qualifications, a friend whose career had run parallel with my own, Lieutenant-Commander Salvatore Todaro, the hero of epic gun-fights in the Atlantic, when he had been in command of the submarine *Cappellini*. He was of middle height, but seemed shorter owing to his sloping and slightly rounded shoulders; he had flashing dark eyes and sharp features ending in a black, pointed beard. He was a keen psychologist, far-sighted and remarkably well versed in theosophy, and possessed a fund of cool and deliberate courage, together with exceptional determination and capacity for work; in addressing himself to his task he inspired his subordinates with his own great gifts. He was always on the spot wherever his men were employed and made the department committed to his charge an instrument of war wielded in the most combative of spirits. Todaro also devoted much attention to materials; many of the improvements in the assault craft were due to his activities and suggested by his experience and ingenuity, as was also the creation of the new torpedo-carrying motorboat, the SMA, which marked a distinct practical advance on the original model. He also arranged for the replacement of the lost craft; with his genius for getting things done, he obtained an acceleration of production in the factories where they were made, so that in a short time the Flotilla command was enabled to cope with the ever-growing demands.

At the same time certain conveyer ships were attached to the surface Division for taking the assault boats from La Spezia, the head-quarters of the command and of the pilots' school, to their action stations. The steam-trawlers *Cefalo*, *Sogliola* and *Costanza* were modi-fied to fit them for this purpose; they were units which, being emi-nently seaworthy and economical to run, were found extremely suitable for their new task.

As the reconstruction of the surface Division was now making good progress in the safe hands of Todaro, I devoted myself entirely to the underwater Division, the direction of which I kept in my own hands. I took advantage of the summer season, which was unsuitable for piloted torpedo operations owing to the shortness of the nights and the length of the hours of daylight, though favourable, on account of the mildness of the temperature of the sea, to intensive and pro-longed training. Therefore I subjected the veteran pilots of the Serchio, who were anxious to renew their former experiments with greater chances of success, and the recruits who had since been coming in, full of the enthusiasm of neophytes, to exercises of the most concentrated, thorough and rigorous description. The object was to put them in a condition to overcome the difficulties which had in the previous operations, especially the last one against Gibraltar, prevented successful action.

At the same time, I availed myself of the quiet, steady and effective work of a gifted technical officer, Naval Engineer Major Mario Masciulli, aided by Captain Travaglini, both members of the secret torpedo works put at the disposal of the Tenth by the underwater weapons Board of La Spezia dockyard. The existing piloted torpedoes were overhauled (these were still of the type initiated by the original blue-prints of Tesei and Toschi) by the removal of the causes of the many shortcomings which had been identified in the past. I also had research work done and, later, construction begun, of a new model of human torpedoes, similar to the previous one but with greatly superior practical characteristics, embodying the fruits of experience and advances made in scientific knowledge and industrial technology. Other weapons, suggested by particular plans of attack, were also projected and built: such were acoustic and incendiary mines for the pilots to lay in the interior of harbours penetrated.

Meanwhile Admiral de Courten, who had formerly been in charge of our supervision and was now at sea, had been replaced by Admiral Giartosio. He saw to it that the Ministry sent the Tenth Light Flotilla a new submarine to be turned into a transport, which could act in concert or alternation with the *Scirè*: it was the *Ambra*, commanded by Lieutenant Mario Arillo. Work was at once commenced upon it on the lines which had already proved successful in the case of the *Scirè*.

The Naval Staff issued instructions to the Tenth to redouble activities directed to the end of a closer siege of the enemy in his harbours, and to the object, if possible, of putting some of his warships out of action and molesting his supply traffic. These orders were complied with, not by extending the command organization, but by speeding up work; the numbers of operators, however, were increased. At the same time private industrial firms were induced to ensure supplies of materials, but only with very considerable difficulty, which had to be overcome by our entering into alliance with industry in opposing ministerial restrictions on war construction; the indispensable replenishment of weapons and technical implements was increased, thus also permitting the setting up of reserve stocks.

In order to make good our losses and meet future demands, the recruitment of volunteers was considerably enlarged, new schools were opened and selection and training methods were improved.

Meanwhile, the underwater Division was amplified: in addition to its previous specialities a new one was created, that of 'assault swimmers', which was camouflaged by the cover name of 'Gamma Group'.

In the previous missions against Gibraltar operators approaching the harbour in their craft, to attack big warships, had passed large numbers of steamers at anchor in the open roadstead, where convoys arrived, were formed and set out.

Since a merchant vessel is a primary objective in war, a way of attacking such ships had immediately been studied. The first idea was to launch a certain number of assault divers from the *Scirè* who would,

116

while the 'pigs', with their 300 kg. of explosive, made for the harbour in search of large warships, move along the bottom of the sea with a much smaller charge carried in a pouch on the shoulder (to use a charge of 300 kg. against a steamer would be like firing a heavy gun at a single man): these divers would come right up to the steamers and attack them, such targets being more accessible and vulnerable. After various difficulties had been overcome (clothing, trim and ballasting of the operators, direction-finding while progressing underwater at night, type of boots required, etc.), the first tests were carried out; squads of 'underwater infantry', marching along the bottom of the sea, covered distances up to 2000 metres in Indian file and in full war kit. Next, the original idea of Raffaele Paolucci was taken up again. It was found that results were far better if the approach were made by swimming; special precautions had however to be taken in order to ensure that the assailants should be practically invisible. It was also discovered that a single charge, cumbersome and inconvenient to carry, could be advantageously replaced, with equally deadly effects on the steamers, by three or four smaller charges, any of which would be enough to cause a leak at the hull of the target.

Thus a new weapon was born and, with it, a new method of use by a relatively new attack; it was called the 'bug'; it consisted of a small, circular casing of metal, bi-convex in shape and containing some 3 kg. of explosive; it was provided with a rubber ring inflated by a phial of compressed air with a breakable neck, thus ensuring its adherence to the bottom of the hull, and also equipped with a time-fuse for causing the explosion at any moment desired. Three or four of these weapons, the thrust of which was zero, fixed to a special belt, were taken under the target by a swimmer and were enough to sink an ordinary cargo-steamer.

The swimmer was clothed in an extremely close-fitting suit of rubber which kept him from direct contact with the water but did not impede his freedom of movement. On his feet he wore long rubber fins which gave him greater speed during approach and enabled him to swim and to dive without needing to work his arms. He approached the target at first rapidly, then more and more cautiously; on reaching it, he made use of the small breathing set provided, with an air container allowing him about 30 minutes' underwater breathing, and dived under the steamer; he then attached the charges to the hull, set the time-fuse and returned to the surface.

He had then, if it were possible, to escape to neutral territory or else land on enemy soil, where he would try to hide or, if he were unable to get away, give himself up.

Volunteers attained to the degree of 'water-worthiness' required by displaying great endurance in swimming and special ability in diving and direction-finding at sea both above and below water (the swimmers were equipped with a small luminous compass strapped to the wrist like a watch). To these talents the Gamma man had to add, as his training proceeded, a facility in camouflage which would render him almost completely invisible while he was approaching the enemy steamers, the protection of which by sentries, searchlights and other defensive measures became more and more efficient as time went on. With this object the swimmer's face was painted black and his head covered with a small net in which seaweed, tow or loose straw from the casing of an old bottle were entwined; consequently, with his eyes only just above water, his arms motionless and his legs moving only very slightly as he swam slowly along, the swimmer would have been taken, even by the most wary and wide awake of sentries, for nothing but some harmless piece of débris such as floats everywhere in harbours and frequented roadsteads.

The approach to a ship lying at anchor had to be made towards her bows; the current itself would then take the swimmer, while he remained practically inert, amidships of the vessel, on reaching which he would dive without visible movement or the formation of bubbles, to carry out the attack. He would make his getaway, still with the current in his favour, astern.

A long and disciplined apprenticeship was of course necessary before perfection in this difficult technique could be acquired.

The command of the group was entrusted to Lieutenant Eugenio Wolk, a splendid specimen of athlete and an extremely expert swimmer. The school was at Leghorn, on the premises of the Naval Academy, so that training could be carried out both with the equipment of the already existent pioneer school and with the advantage of the covered swimming-pool, which was essential to instruction in the perfecting of swimming technique.

This type of offensive action was used with good results, as we shall see later, in assault operations at Algiers and Gibraltar. In view of the diminutive size of the 'bug' and the slight equipment required for its use, it was also planned to employ it in sabotage work in neutral harbours against enemy vessels awaiting loading or unloading of their cargo; for this object it was necessary to make some modifications and improvements in the weapon. With the original 'bug' the explosion was meant to sink the vessel in harbour, where depths are generally slight; hence the result was not the total loss of the unit but its temporary disablement (in war one vessel sunk is worth five damaged). Actually, the ship which had been struck merely came to rest on the bottom with a good part of its structure above water, so that its cargo could be salvaged and any operations to refloat the ship could be carried out more easily. Moreover, since the act of war took place in neutral waters, awkward incidents and diplomatic complications might ensue.

These difficulties were removed by use of the 'limpet', an underwater weapon of the 'bug' type but with different characteristics. The weight of the charge was only slightly increased, but its destructive potential was greatly augmented by employing more powerful explosive. There were two fuses: one working by time and the other by distance. The latter consisted of a small propeller which only came into action when the steamer started to move (only at a speed exceeding five knots, otherwise the current in harbour might set the propeller going); after the propeller had completed a certain number of revolutions, corresponding, for example, with a run of 100 miles, the spindle connected with the propeller started the normal time-fuse. After a pre-arranged period, by which time the vessel would certainly be on the high seas, the explosion would occur, with high probability of total loss (in view of the considerable depths) and without the risk of any complications with neutral authorities, while leaving the enemy in doubt whether the cause of the explosion were a torpedo, a mine or some other direct event more probable than sabotage, with such long delayed action, in the harbour from which the ship had set out. This weapon, too, was used with success; we shall tell in due course the story of the mission carried out by the swimmer Luigi Ferraro at Alexandretta, a most brilliant performance which cost the British the loss of two steamers and damage to a third as the result of the work of a single operator.

In order to recruit the volunteers required for this special service we needed men who were both excellent swimmers and had a natural 'water-worthiness'. The list of members of the Italian Swimmers' League enabled us to find plenty of good men who were perfectly suitable and anxious to join the new service, for which they felt they had the right qualifications. We discovered with astonishment that the majority of swimmers in the Italian League were down for Army conscription and were consequently not serving in the Navy, as would have seemed more logical. The Ministry of War was approached by the Navy and, after circumventing bureaucratic objections and long-standing prejudices, complied promptly with our requests; it thus came about that the Tenth Light Flotilla received volunteers (not only for the 'Gamma Group') from all sections of the Army and from every theatre of war, from Africa to the Alps (some swimmers were actually in the alpine troops) and even from the far distant Russian front. Although the majority of the volunteers naturally came from the Navy (for certain special services it was essential that members should be actual sailors before they could be employed, for instance with piloted torpedoes), yet the influx of these new reinforcements was of great advantage to the schools in so far as it allowed stricter selection to be made. Moreover, it was, once more, characteristic of the Tenth that an extremely close collaboration was established between elements originating from the various other arms, forging bonds of brotherly comradeship between the soldiers of one country; such collaboration did not, unfortunately, always exist in other sectors, a circumstance which seriously prejudiced the service rendered by our armed forces as a whole.

A year after the commencement of hostilities, after the painful experiences consequent upon the lack of timely preparation and the disorganized nature of the first instructions given for employment of the Tenth Light Flotilla, the unit, with its weapons tempered and its personnel now trained to war, stood ready to face the struggle, which it was now obvious would be prolonged and of the sternest nature.

Meanwhile, basing my activities on the experience acquired in previous operations, I was preparing a new mission by the *Scirè* against Gibraltar; it took place in September, as soon as the longer nights made it feasible.

The *Scirè*, still under my command and with the same crew as before, received operational orders similar to the preceding ones, which the facts had proved to be perfectly practicable.

As the piloted torpedoes of the new model were still under construction, the usual ones were taken aboard, after being surveyed and overhauled to ensure that shortcomings which had come to light on former expeditions would not be repeated.

I left La Spezia on the 10th of September and on the 16th passed through the Straits of Gibraltar, submerged, without any trouble; the whole of the 17th was spent by the entire crew in resting, while the submarine lay on the bottom in front of Cadiz; I surfaced in the evening, entered the harbour and again went alongside the tanker *Fulgor*: a hot bath, fresh victuals, bananas and brandy.

The operators came aboard; except for a few changes they were the same as had been with us before, whose request to try again had been granted. Their names were:

Lieutenant Decio Catalano and P.O./diver Giuseppe Giannoni; Lieutenant Amedeo Vesco and P.O./diver Antonio Zozzoli; Lieutenant Licio Visintini and P.O./diver Giovanni Magro. Reserve crew: Engineer Captain Antonio Marceglia and Diver Spartaco Schergat. Surgeon of the expedition, Sub-Lieutenant Giorgio Spaccarelli, a volunteer for the assault craft and an apprentice pilot.

Before daybreak I collected the latest information as to the situation of the vessels at Gibraltar and left the mooring-place of the *Fulgor*; I got away from the harbour unobserved and started to approach our target.

That night I met a large British convoy coming from Gibraltar and headed for the Atlantic; it passed me at short range, escorted by no more than two destroyers and presented a series of excellent targets; it was a great chance for a submarine commander and one that seldom occurs! But our special task forbade me to carry out a torpedo attack and thus reveal my presence.

On the evening of the 19th I entered Algeciras Bay and ran up its whole length, ending, as usual, at the mouth of the Guadarranque. During this part of the approach we distinctly heard depth-charges exploding at intervals of half an hour. We had received intelligence that this was an innovation introduced by the British some time before as a defence measure against the danger we represented; a new and far from negligible obstacle to be dealt with by the pilots.

At 1 a.m. on the 20th of September, the operators had set out for the targets assigned to them according to the latest intelligence received from Rome, and I reversed my course. Delayed for a day by high seas, we reached La Spezia on the evening of the 25th. Admiral Goiran, Naval Chief of the North Tyrrhenian Sector, welcomed us on behalf of Admiral Riccardi, Under Secretary of the Navy.

.   .   .   .   .

The telegram received from the Naval Staff at 2330 hours on the evening of the 19th, an hour before the pilots left the submarine, reads as follows:

"Situation of vessels in harbour at 1200 hours on the 19th: at Mole I, battleship; at anchorage No. 27, aircraft-carrier; at anchorage No. 5, cruiser; at anchorage No. II, a second cruiser; in addition, seven tankers and three destroyers in harbour. One destroyer in dock. Convoy of 17 steamers in roadstead."

As a result of this information I assigned the pilots their targets as follows:

Lieutenants Catalano and Vesco both to attack the battleship of the *Nelson* class (35,000 tons) anchored at the South Mole; Lieutenant Visintini to attack the aircraft-carrier; if impracticable, the three crews to attack any other units, in decreasing order of importance; no clue to be left in the hands of the enemy, so that he may be left completely in the dark about the nature and origin of the explosions.

Descriptions of the operations of the three crews follow, compiled from their reports.

VESCO—ZOZZOLI. "At about 0030 hours on the 20th September, 1941, in accordance with Commanding Officer Borghese's orders, I left the submarine, followed by my Number Two, P.O./diver Antonio Zozzoli. The target assigned to me was a battleship of the *Nelson* class, moored inside the harbour, half-way along the south breakwater. Surface approach was normal, though impeded by wind and high seas. I removed my mask at intervals, so as to see with the naked eye, but on each occasion only for a few seconds, because, even when I was stationary, the waves breaking over my face were a great nuisance, especially to my eyes. After an emergency submersion to evade discovery by a patrolboat on duty I sighted the entrance to the harbour.

I was about 300 metres from the defences and slowed down so as to prevent my being heard by hydrophones and in order to have time to find out about the manœuvres of a boat which was shuttling, with her lights on, in front of the entrance . . . I set a bee-line course and submerged to the greatest possible depth, proceeding at low speed to prevent the phosphorescence of my wake from being detected from the surface.

At about 3.15 I got down to a depth of about 26 metres, just grazing the bottom, which was hard and smooth, and did not interfere in any way with my progress. At about 3.30, at a depth of 15 metres, I heard and felt against the cask of the 'pig' and against my own body three consecutive underwater explosions. As everything continued to function normally I decided to go on. At 3.40 I was at a depth of 13 metres when I heard two further explosions, slightly more subdued than the previous ones, but of greater volume."

The presence of a patrolboat and other considerations induced Vesco to renounce the attempt to force the entrance, and accordingly, "to my deep regret, while I was about 50 metres from the defences, I resolved to abandon the target assigned to me and turn my attention to a vessel in the roadstead."

Vesco surfaced and reached the steamers in the roadstead.

"At four a.m. I started to look for the most important target. A boat with its lights dimmed was moving about among the steamers. At last I sighted a vessel with a long, slender outline, lying low in the water and therefore heavily laden; I guessed her to be about 3 or 4 thousand tons displacement. I made my approach and performed the manœuvre of contacting: I submerged deeply beneath the ship, stopped and came up, exhausting the tanks, till I reached the hull. I managed to do this unseen and unheard, but owing to damage to my breathing set I could not avoid swallowing water containing soda-lime which caused painful burning to my mouth and throat."

He surfaced hurriedly, got rid of his damaged breathing set and fitted the spare one. He then went back underwater and, with the aid of his second man, fastened the charge to the hull in line with the funnel position. Finally, after setting the fuses, he disengaged and made for the pre-arranged landing point. He sank the torpedo after setting the fuses of the self-destructor charges every human torpedo had, and swam for the shore.

"We had a good deal of trouble owing to our bad physical condition and to the sea, which repeatedly broke over our heads. My second was very tired and feeling ill. We got ashore just before seven a.m., about 100 metres west of the prearranged point, where we were halted by two armed Spanish sentries. One of them instantly fired two rifle-shots into the air. We had just time to hide our two breathing sets in a secluded spot of the beach, as, for obvious reasons, I did not want the sentries to see them. I told the Spaniards we were shipwrecked Italians. . . . We were taken to the coastguard station, where we were met by the agent P., who took steps to recover our breathing sets."

Vesco and Zozzoli watched, from the station, the punctual explosion of the charge.

"The vessel split in two, slightly astern of the funnel. Her stern disappeared, the bows rising high out of the water." (From the report of Lieutenant Amedeo Vesco.)

So sank the British tanker *Fiona Shell*, 2444 tons.

CATALANO—GIANNONI. The operators left the submarine without a hitch.

"The night was extremely dark. At 1.25 a.m. approach was begun. Rough sea and an east wind impeded our progress considerably; we could hardly breathe while surfaced. The lights of La Linea, Gibraltar and Algeciras were a perfect guide for us. At 2.35 we sighted a motorboat, moving at slow speed, 70 metres to starboard. I stopped and took careful note of its course and speed, then turned larboard to get away from her. I waited for another few minutes, then proceeded towards the north entrance at slow speed. In spite of the wide detours I had made I did not succeed in shaking off the patrolboat, which was moving slowly and almost in silence, in such a way as to be inaudible at a distance of 50 metres. I guessed it to be fitted with entirely silent electric engines and hydrophone detectors.

I took a course between two steamers so as to cover up my tracks once and for all, but the patrolboat continued to follow me a short distance away. I decided to submerge and proceeded on a southerly course for about 15 minutes; I then surfaced, at about 3.30; I stopped: the patrolboat had lost track of me.

As time was now running very short and I was still a long way from the entrance to the port, I thought it best to attack the steamers in the roadstead.

I had seen three large steamers on my route. I made for them surfaced and in fourth gear.

On arriving near them, I took careful note of the position of a large, empty tanker, and resolved to attack it astern. I approached it slowly, surfaced; but at some metres from the stern I discovered a launch moored to the tanker; I stopped, but was unable, despite the short distance and an intense observation of the launch, to discover whether there were guards aboard her; in order to run no possible risk of alarming the whole base I decided to attack another ship."

The second man, Giannoni, had already attached the warhead to the propellers of the new target when Catalano managed to read the name on her stern: she was the *Pollenzo*, of Genoa. Though this was a captured vessel in the service of the enemy, Catalano did not wish to destroy an Italian ship. He therefore, with the help of that excellent fellow Giannoni, detached his warhead, found a large armed motorship and attacked her.

"The work proceeded in first-rate style, owing to the splendid conduct, both in skill and in enterprise, of my second operator. At 5.16 I set the fuses of the warhead. We left at high speed and I sank the 'pig' in $5\frac{1}{2}$ metres of water, after setting the fuses of her self-destructor charges: by that time it was 5.55. I surfaced with Giannoni; after removing our breathing sets and sinking them, we swam to the shore, landing at 7.15.

At 8.55 I saw, at the place where I had sunk the 'pig', a characteristic white spouting and then a number of gulls flying over the spot; the self-destructor charges of my human torpedo had done their job.

At 9.16 a violent explosion took place at the stern of the motorship I had attacked; a column of water rose to about 30 metres. The motorship settled slowly by the stern, the entire structure of her bows emerging from the water. Four powerful tugs came to her assistance and towed her ashore, with considerable trouble, at a point opposite the neutral zone.

I afterwards found out her name; she was the armed British motorship *Durham*, of 10,900 tons." (From the report of Lieutenant Decio Catalano.)

VISINTINI—MAGRO. After normal launching, they immediately began their approach.

"Magro and I removed our masks so as to obtain good visibility. But we had trouble from a high and persistent easterly sea which reduced our speed. However, we made good progress; by way of variety I noticed on two occasions the shock of a depth-charge against the cask.

. . . About 2.30 a.m. we sighted, almost starboard abeam, the dark outline of a patrolboat, not more than 100 metres away."

Visintini took evasive action. He continues:

". . . a little later I sighted the entrance to the port. At this stage I felt the shocks of two depth-charges, but did not worry as they seemed a long way off. But I now saw that a patrolboat, coming from the south, had just arrived at the north gate; she was going very slowly, at a speed of not more than two knots an hour. I held on my course, but found at one point, that the patrolboat was very close to me, patrolling the stretch of water between me and the defences and turning in my direction. I submerged at once . . . and felt an explosion take place not far off; but its effects were not alarming.

I surfaced . . . a rapid survey enabled me to see that the patrolboat was now proceeding towards the south gate and I was almost inclined to fancy myself clear of her; but I had no time to feel relief at this discovery, for I instantly sighted a smaller boat coming straight at me, in silence, with her lights on. I was afraid I had been seen, but I submerged all the same, much preferring death as the result of an explosion to capture on the surface without being able to defend myself; then there was the question of the craft, which *had* to be sunk. But they had not seen me.

I heard distinctly the hum of the propeller passing over me. From that moment, for a period of about 10 minutes, I played hide and seek with the enemy, now surfacing, now submerging, so as to avoid the effects of the depth-charges and reach waters where I should be less likely to be sighted.

Finally, the patrolboat moved away southwards and I got into position to negotiate the defences: it was then 3.45. I set my course carefully and submerged, proceeding in third gear at a depth of 11 metres. I stuck to my three components (course, speed and depth) with the greatest precision and at the time foreseen I perceived three steel cables, undoubtedly forming part of the gate defence nets, which grazed my cask as I slipped between them. Having thus penetrated the harbour I surfaced and took off my mask to see better. I sighted a cruiser of about 7000 tons ahead of me, and four large tankers at the Detached Mole.

It was now five minutes past four and I calculated that I had no time left for operating at the south end of the harbour where the targets assigned by our commander were anchored.

I also rejected the cruiser, for the following reasons:

(1) because she was too near the depth-charges which were being almost systematically dropped at the gate (in the immediate neighbourhood);

(2) because I hoped to be able to inflict greater damage by attacking the tanker (by setting the oil alight and so setting fire to the harbour).

I resolved, accordingly, to attack one of the four tankers, choosing the second from the north end, because she was fully loaded; I guessed her to be of about 8000 tons.

As we were carrying out the attack at seven metres depth we were knocked against the hull of the tanker by a violent explosion, which did not, however, do us any damage.

I proceeded with the work. At 4.40, after detaching the warhead, I set the fuses."

Visintini left the harbour, manœuvring in the same way as he did to enter it, avoided the two patrolboats cruising about the entrance, set course for the Spanish coast, sank his 'pig' and got safely ashore, with Magro, at 6.30 a.m, when he met the agent P., who was waiting for them.

"From the place where we were hiding we heard an explosion at 8.43, followed by four or five others a few minutes later."

At 8.43 a.m. the naval tanker *Denby Dale*, 15,893 tons, blew up and sank inside Gibraltar harbour. A small tanker, moored alongside her, also went to the bottom as a result of the explosion. Though the fire which Visintini had hoped to start did not take place, the operation performed was an extremely brilliant one.

At last, after so many disappointments, we had a positive result, though not of the importance we had desired. It was the first success of the piloted torpedoes; three vessels, including a large naval tanker and amounting in all to 30,000 tons, had been sunk.

The operation had proved highly instructive.

We had learnt that the enemy had adopted new precautions and defence methods against the daring of the Tenth Flotilla: noiseless patrolboats, shuttling slowly or rapidly at the entrance to the harbour; systematic dropping of depth-charges; intensified control by hydrophones.

But we had also discovered, thanks mainly to the brilliant operation of Visintini, that these defences were not insuperable, provided that a determined will to succeed were accompanied by a contempt for danger and perfect mastery of the means of assault and of the environment in which it took place, the sea itself.

A new name had been inscribed upon the roll of the brave, that of Visintini.

He was a young officer, highly trained professionally. Born and bred at Parenzo (near Trieste), he was brought up in the patriotic spirit typical of the Italian frontiers, where the inhabitants have had to struggle for centuries to preserve their independence and their nationality. He spoke little but was always cheerful; loyal, courageous, cool in danger, a first-rate and experienced seaman, he displayed, in his behaviour during the course of this operation, exceptional gifts.

The human torpedoes had at last met in full the demands made upon them by the operators. Engineer Lieutenant Bertozzi, a technician who had carried out tests at the outset of the expedition and collected the reports of operators on their return to the base, wrote in his definitive statement:

The bridge and the breakwater of the Grand Harbour, Malta, on the morning of July 15, 1941, after it had been blown up by CARABELLI's E-boat during a dawn attack. Net obstruction clearly visible under left span.

Another attack begins. . . . (*Note :* the British named these 'chariots'.)

TESEO TESEI (diver).

"In conclusion, it may be said without fear of contradiction that these craft, as constructed and modified by the Underwater Weapons Board at La Spezia, in consequence of the experience gained in previous operations, now constitute an absolutely efficient and trustworthy weapon, capable of achieving the most brilliant success in war."

In recognition of the deeds which have been described, the six operators all received the silver medal for gallantry in war.

The entire crew of the *Scirè*, as in previous missions, was also decorated. I was myself promoted to Commander for services rendered in war, with the following citation:

"As commander of a submarine detailed for special service, after having carried out a bold and extremely daring operation involving transport of assault craft to the proximity of a very heavily fortified enemy base, he repeated the same operation a second and a third time with deliberate courage and evident contempt of danger.

After assuming, in addition, command of the assault Division, he prepared, with great ability and assiduous attention to detail, both the men and the materials, successfully employed during the third operation in attacking three enemy units, of which one was seriously damaged and the other two sunk.

In every one of these operations he succeeded in bringing back his submarine and its crew to the base, despite the difficulties due to determined pursuit by the enemy and to navigation under water driven to the limit of human endurance, thus providing a splendid example of organizing capacity and leadership."

King Victor Emmanuel deigned to receive me in audience and accorded me a long and gracious interview. He was in the best of spirits. When I told him of the difficulties we had encountered in the Straits owing to the currents, he said: "I know them well. Once, many years ago, we happened to be fishing at Gibraltar and the currents were such a nuisance to us that neither I nor my wife managed to catch a single minnow!"

He then expressed his interest in the piloted torpedoes and wished to know what their characteristics were. He asked me where training took place. "In the waters of the Serchio, bordering the San Rossore estate of your Majesty." He expressed the greatest astonishment. "Well, I never knew that! You have really succeeded in keeping your secret in a most extraordinary manner!" He then asked me whether, as a special concession, he might be allowed to penetrate the closed circle of the Serchio Group in order to make the acquaintance of those "splendid fellows" and witness one of the exercises. "Of course," I answered. "But I would beg of your Majesty to be so kind as to make your suite a small one."

In fact, some days later the King, accompanied by only one attendant, and dressed in civilian clothing, crossed the Serchio in a small rowing-boat and paid a visit to the lads, whose acquaintance he wanted to make individually. He then stood on a raft in drenching rain and watched a submersion exercise of the human torpedoes by which he appeared to be very much impressed.

After taking leave of each man personally, with a handclasp, and presenting the sailors with a wild boar from his estate, he went back across the river in his rowing-boat.

This was the last time I saw the King.

CHAPTER XI

SINKINGS OF THE BATTLESHIPS *VALIANT* AND *QUEEN ELIZABETH*—ALEXANDRIA: 19TH DECEMBER, 1941

Ark Royal *and* Barham *sent to the bottom—Only* Valiant *and* Queen Elizabeth *left—Forza in command—The attack is organized—Intense preparations—Choice of crews—The* Scirè *again at sea—2000 metres from Alexandria—Christmas pies— Marceglia sinks the* Queen Elizabeth *and de la Penne the* Valiant—Martellotta's *task: total destruction—The missed strategic opportunities offered by the victory—Churchill's secret speech.*

DURING an operation in the waters of Gibraltar, the British aircraft-carrier *Ark Royal*, 22,000 tons, was hit on the 13th of November, 1941, by a single torpedo from a German submarine (Lieutenant Gugenberger of the German Navy) and sent to the bottom.

On the 25th of November, off Tobruk, the British Eastern Mediterranean Fleet, consisting of the three battleships *Barham* (flag-ship), *Queen Elizabeth* and *Valiant*, at sea with its usual escort, was attacked by another German submarine (Lieutenant von Tiesenhausen). This action deserves to be briefly related on account of the bravery displayed by the crew of the submarine, the deadly effects achieved and the fortunate and fortuitous circumstances that accompanied it.

It was broad daylight when von Tiesenhausen sighted the three battleships through his periscope, steaming in line ahead, at intervals of 500 metres. He came on at full speed, submerged, holding a collision course for the leading unit. He passed through the cordon of escorting destroyers in this way and went on still further, till he got within so short a range that the torpedo could not possibly miss.

He was actually only 400 metres from the *Barham* when he fired the four forward torpedoes. A few seconds later the battleship received a direct hit in her magazines and blew up; her wreckage was flung into the air like chaff and the battleship disappeared beneath the waves in less than five minutes, taking with her more than 800 men of the crew.

Aboard the submarine, however, conditions were far from ideal for celebrating the victory.

For some reason or other the U-boat had unexpectedly surfaced, owing probably to the sudden loss of the weight of four torpedoes, and was being carried by the momentum of her dash against the enemy to within a few metres of the bows of the *Valiant*, the second ship in the British line. The battleship was firing everything she had at the submarine, but the latter was so close under her quarter that the guns, even at maximum depression, could not score a hit! By a miracle of seamanship and also by good luck von Tiesenhausen succeeded in evading being rammed by a few metres, manœuvring to slip past the bows of the *Valiant*, and then in submerging again, with his vessel untouched, and finally reached his base without damage or casualties. (In his official report von Tiesenhausen stated that he had hit a battle-ship, but could not declare her to be sunk.)

This heavy loss reduced the British Fleet in the Mediterranean, by November 1941, to two battleships only, the *Queen Elizabeth* and the *Valiant*, at the very moment when, with the addition of the *Doria* to the *Vittorio Veneto* and the *Littorio*, the Italian battle fleet amounted to five battleships, three of which had been modernized, while two were new and extremely powerful units; this was a total which had never been exceeded in the past and never would be in the future.

In order to minimize the risk of loss of the two remaining British battleships, which had now become of great value, since they represented the whole of British naval strength in the eastern Mediterranean (the arrival of reinforcements was hindered by the situation in the Far East), they were surrounded and protected at the Alexandria anchorage by all the defensive measures and contrivances the British had adopted after the attacks by the Tenth at Suda, Malta and Gibraltar. Thus the battleships were kept waiting for a time when they might be able to risk exposure in favourable conditions.

This was the situation at the moment chosen by the Tenth to renew the attack on Alexandria.

Meanwhile, Commander Ernesto Forza had been appointed Chief of the Tenth Light Flotilla. He was an able and courageous officer, formerly in command of the Augusta Light Flotilla; he had received the gold medal for gallantry in war in recognition of a brilliant action carried out in the Malta Channel against a British convoy. In addition to this prestige he had recent experience of active service at sea with light units, most useful in the employment of special craft; he was also remarkable for efficiency, energy and impatience of red tape in the execution of his tasks and had the advantage of first-rate theoretical and practical training in naval aviation tactics, since he had been an Observer officer for a number of years and an instructor of young officers in this type of service.

Showing great intelligence in his work and always prompt in finding the best solutions to the problems which continually confronted us, this officer was an excellent colleague, always cheerful and accessible; he retained command of the Flotilla until the 1st of May, 1943; collaboration between us always worked smoothly, to the great advantage of the business in hand.

The operation against Alexandria was most carefully thought out. The most important requirement was the maintenance of absolute secrecy, that indispensable co-efficient of success in any action, and particularly in those where the vulnerability of a handful of half-naked men, plunged underwater in the dark depths of an enemy harbour, had to overcome armour-plates, barriers and a hundred methods of watching for and spotting them, and also thousands of people on dry land, operating from cover and behind defences on mole and ships, whose business it was to discover and destroy the assailant.

Wide use was made of air reconnaissance for the obtaining of information and photographs with a view to keeping us informed about the usual moorings of vessels and the nature of the protective measures employed (net obstructions, etc.). Great care was also taken in preparing materials: the human torpedoes, which were now in good shape, as had been verified during the last mission to Gibraltar, were brought to the highest level of efficiency.

The *Scirè* was again appointed to carry out the approach. Her gallant crew, now thoroughly accustomed to such experiences, remained unchanged. All its members, after their usual period of rest in the Alto Adige, were in excellent physical trim.

The senior group of pilots had been given a long training by myself in carrying out exercises similar to the performances they would have to accomplish at Alexandria (they were, however, not told the final object of the courses and defence negotiating they were ordered to do). In other words, practice took place at night in the actual conditions prevalent in the enemy harbour, their difficulties being, wherever possible, increased. Thus, while the operators were being trained to economize their strength in view of the prolonged and difficult nature of the assigned task, we ourselves were obtaining the data necessary for the study of the plan of operations and had the opportunity of verifying, as if we had made a survey on the spot, the methods to be adopted for the job, the periods required to complete the various stages and the precautions needed to circumvent difficulties and elude enemy detection, as well as, lastly, to check the degrees of skill acquired by individual operators.

One day we called them all together; Forza made the following very brief speech to them: "Now, boys, we want three crews for an operation in the very near future; all I can tell you about it is that it differs from the Gibraltar operations in the fact that return from it is extremely problematical. Is there anyone who would like to take part in it?" Without an instant's hesitation they all volunteered. Accordingly, we of the Command had the delicate task of making a selection. Finally, the crews were as follows: Lieutenant Luigi Durand de la Penne and P.O./diver Emilio Vianchi; Engineer Captain Antonio Marceglia and P.O./diver Spartaco Schergat; Gunner Captain Vincenzo Martellotta and P.O./diver Mario Marino.

These men were chosen because they were the pick of the bunch. De la Penne, leader of the group, was a veteran of the previous missions to Gibraltar and the rest were all equally vigorous, steady and resolute fellows, in mind as in body. It was pure chance that the three officers represented three different services of the Navy: deck, engines and guns.

The reserve crew consisted of Surgeon Sub-Lieutenant Spaccarelli and Engineer Lieutenant Feltrinelli, both belonging to a lower age group than the others but equally keen.

The usual instructions were given: absolute secrecy was to be maintained without exception for anyone, whether comrades, superior officers or, naturally, relatives; training, now openly designed for this particular operation, was to be intensified; each man's private affairs were to be settled in view of his imminent departure for a length of time which could not be foreseen; at worst, it might be for ever, at best there would be some years of imprisonment.

Meanwhile, all the wheels of the machine began to go round. This kind of operation, if it were to have any decent chance of success, had to be thought out to the last detail; the whole of an extensive organization had to be got ready; there were a thousand details to be studied and put into practice: from the collection of hydrographic and meteorological data to intelligence as to enemy vigilance; from the taking of aerial photographs of the harbour to the arrangement of safe and extremely rapid channels of radio liaison with the submarine, so that the latter could be informed, immediately before the operators were dropped, as to the number and disposition of units on the night of the operation; from the determination of suitable ciphers to getting materials ready for action; from composition of the series of operational orders to the training of operators so as to bring them to the maximum of physical efficiency by the pre-arranged day; from the study of navigation and the best routes of approach for the submarine and those for the forcing of the harbour by the pilots, to research on new devices for causing the enemy maximum damage should the occasion arise; in a word, the proceedings were exactly the opposite of what the phrase 'assault craft' might be supposed to mean; there was to be nothing in the nature of making a dash, nothing was to be left to chance, all impulsiveness was to be held in check; on the contrary, everything was to be coolly calculated and every technical and ingenious resource was to be exploited to the fullest extent possible.

During this preparatory phase, we were afflicted by the grievous loss of a valued collaborator; this was Lieutenant Sogos, belonging to the Command of the Tenth. While he was in transit to Athens for consultation with the military authorities there, his young and promising life was cut short by a wretched traffic accident.

At last the time came to start. On the 3rd of December the *Scirè* left La Spezia, ostensibly on an ordinary cruise, so as not to arouse curiosity among the crews of the other submarines at the base.

My gallant, steady and reliable crew neither knew nor wished to know where we were going, so as not to be burdened with a secret which, like all secrets, would be difficult to keep; they only knew that we were on another dangerous operation, perhaps as dangerous as the former ones, perhaps more so; they had confidence in their commander and in their vessel, to which each of them had devoted every care during the period of preparation, knowing well that it was on the proper functioning of the elements of which it was composed that the outcome of the venture, its success and the very lives of all aboard depended.

We had scarcely left harbour, at twilight, so as to elude any

135

indiscreet watchers, when a lighter approached us; it was carrying the human torpedoes 221, 222 and 223, which had just left the works at San Bartolomeo in the pink of condition, as well as the operators' clothing and breathing sets; such was the slight equipment necessary to transform three pairs of men into three engines of destruction.

The operators checked over their craft with a sort of tender solicitude. Each possessed his own; he had done his training with it and knew its good points, its shortcomings and its caprices; he placed it in the appropriate cylinder (de la Penne's was forward, those of Marceglia and Martellotta astern), settling it in such a way as to avoid risking shocks and injury to it. Finally, late at night, everything was fixed to rights; we took leave of the lads, who would rejoin us at the last moment by 'plane, and set out, hugging Tino Island, along the safety route through the minefields. It was 2300 hours on the 3rd of December, 1941. 'Operation EA 3', the third attempt of the Tenth Light Flotilla against Alexandria and the ships of the British Eastern Mediterranean Fleet, had begun.

We proceeded normally along the courses set until we made the Sicilian coast; here a curious episode occurred which is worth relating. The Cape Pelorias signal station sent out a Donath (nocturnal signalling lamp) message in clear: "Submarine *Scirè.*" A piece of madness! Did they want everyone to know that the *Scirè*, the only submarine in the Italian Navy equipped to carry assault craft, was at sea? Not much of a secret, apparently, though such trouble had been taken to keep it! Off the San Ranieri (Messina) lighthouse a launch belonging to the Naval Command approached us. I was handed an envelope; we immediately resumed navigation. The note was from the Supreme Naval Command informing me of the position of the allied vessels then at sea in case I met them. And the Messina Naval Command told me that an enemy submarine had been seen a few hours before close to Cape dell'Armi, firing torpedoes at one of our convoys.

I had, in fact, to pass near Cape dell'Armi; I decided to give it a wide berth and cruised along the coast of Sicily as far as Taormina. There I sighted a submarine which appeared to be motionless. I kept my bows turned towards it (one can never take too many precautions) and signalled it. I couldn't make head or tail of the answer: the vessel was clearly one of the enemy's. The situation being what it was, both of us being surfaced and visible to each other (it was a bright moonlight night), and considering my orders and my special task, as well,

136

finally, as the fact that my adversary had two guns and I had none, I sent a signal to the Messina Naval Command that I had seen an enemy vessel and continued straight on my course towards the Eastern Mediterranean. And the enemy submarine? Well, she started off on a course parallel to my own! We proceeded in this way, side by side, with about 3000 metres between us, like the best of friends, for about an hour; after this, the other submarine, as unexpectedly as it had joined me, left me to myself and turned back towards Taormina. Strange things happen at sea in time of war! The next day we encountered a melancholy spectacle. We were passing through waters strewn with wreckage and flotsam of every description, including many life-belts; one of our convoys had been surprised during the past few days. On the 9th we reached Leros and entered Port Lago, which I knew well, having made a long stay there, years before, while in charge of the *Iride*. It is a magnificent natural inlet, protected on three sides by high, rocky mountains, while on the other lies a pleasant little village, built entirely during the last few years, with its inn, church and town hall; it looked like a corner of Italy transferred to this Aegean island. I moored at the pier outside the submarine barracks; and was at once visited by Spigai, a career colleague of mine, in command of the 5th Submarine Flotilla at Leros. He put himself at my disposal with the affection of a good comrade. The first thing I did was to cover the *Scirè's* cylinders with enormous tarpaulins; we were ostensibly a submarine belonging to another base which had put in here on account of serious damage sustained while fighting and was in need of prolonged repairs. Leros was full of Greeks and no precaution could be excessive. Six technicians flown from Italy for the purpose proceeded, meanwhile, to give the 'pigs' a final check-over.

On the 12th, the 10 operators arrived, also by air. To keep them out of sight, they were given quarters in the transport *Asmara*, which was moored in the deserted bay of Parteni, at the opposite end of the island; the same anchorage had been used by Faggioni's detachment and the Suda E-boats. The lads spent the last few hours before their operation in the peace and quiet of that isolated roadstead, with nothing to distract them and no dangers to be encountered; on the 13th, I paid them a visit and we studied the operational plan in detail, also examining the latest aerial photographs of the harbour and the data I had been receiving (only very few messages up to now); we also gossiped a little, possibly to distract our minds for a while from the subject on which we had been concentrating our whole attention for the last month.

Admiral Biancheri, Commander-in-Chief of the Aegean naval sector, arrived at Leros from Rhodes. He wanted us to carry out exercises and tests in his presence, there and then, at Port Lago! I took advantage of my orders giving me full authority during the operation to decline the invitation. The admiral expressed his disappointment and his convinced opinion that "we shan't do any good if we cut training short".

I could not lose time. The favourable lunar phase had begun, the nights being absolutely dark; weather reports were good. I resolved to start on the 14th of December. I kept in continuous touch with Forza, who had gone to Athens on the 9th to take charge of and co-ordinate air reconnaissance services, intelligence reports, the issue of weather bulletins and radio liaison with the *Scirè*.

The plan of operations provided for the arrival of the *Scirè* on a certain evening, a few thousand metres from the entrance to Alexandria harbour; as it was assumed that everything would be in darkness (owing to the black-out), it had been arranged that, in order to facilitate the submarine's landfall, the coast being low-lying and without conspicuous features, and allow her to identify the harbour (for the success of the operators' raid would depend largely on the precision with which the point of their release was determined), on the evening before, and also on the one of the action, our aircraft would bomb the harbour. The submarine would then release the operators. The latter, proceeding on courses laid down beforehand, as soon as they arrived in front of the harbour, would have to overcome the obstructions and attack the targets previously assigned to them by the commander of the *Scirè*, who would base his orders on the latest data transmitted to him by radio. After attaching the charges to the hulls of the targets, the operators were to lay a certain number of floating incendiary bombs with which they had been supplied. These bombs would go off about an hour after the warheads had exploded and were intended to set alight the oil which would by then have spread from the ships which had been attacked; it was expected that this would cause fire to break out in the harbour, affecting all the vessels therein, together with the floating docks, the harbour installations and the warehouses . . . ; thus putting the chief enemy naval base in the Eastern Mediterranean utterly out of action.

The *Scirè*, directly the operators had been dropped, was to start back. The pilots had been told which zones of the interior of the harbour were considered the least vigilantly watched, where they were to land on conclusion of the operation and what routes they were to take to get clear of the harbour area in the shortest possible time. Plans had also been laid for their rescue: on the days following the action the submarine *Zaffiro* (commanded by Giovanni Lombardi) would shuttle for two consecutive nights 10 miles off Rosetta in the Nile delta; such operators as eluded immediate capture would be able to reach her by any boat they could find on the coast.

The *Scirè*, with the pilots aboard, left Leros on the morning of the 14th. She proceeded without incident and, so to speak, in secret; by day we submerged, surfacing only at night, to charge the batteries and freshen up the atmosphere aboard. The task of the *Scirè* was, as usual, to find a method of getting as close as possible to the enemy harbour, without arousing prohibitive alarm or allowing her presence to be suspected. Discovery would mean arousing anti-submarine measures; a remorseless pursuit would begin, which would prevent us from carrying out the operation. We therefore took the strictest precautions. And as we might be detected by hydrophones as a result of normal sounds aboard the submarine, we had to proceed noiselessly, muffling the machinery. The intelligence we had received on setting out was to the effect that Alexandria harbour was surrounded, like all other harbours in time of war, by minefields. To quote the report: "*Fixed and mobile defences ascertained*: (a) minefield 20 miles NW of harbour; (b) line of 'lobster-pots' arranged at a depth of 30 fathoms in a circle with a radius of about six miles; (c) line of detector cables closer in; (d) groups of 'lobster-pots' in known positions; (e) net barriers relatively easy to force; (f) advanced observation line beyond minefield."

How could all these dangers be circumvented? How could the minefields be evaded if we did not know the security routes? Or the 'lobster-pots'? Or the detector cables?

In order to reach the target we were obliged, after a certain stage, to trust to luck; there was nothing else to do. But luck can be 'assisted', especially when the matter in hand is a complex one. I had therefore decided that, as soon as we reached a depth of 400 metres (which would probably be where the minefields started), we would proceed at a depth of not less than 60 metres, since I assumed that the mines, even if they were anti-submarine, would be located at a higher level; if the submarine should then collide with one of the mooring cables, I felt sure that the latter would slide along her sides, which were accurately streamlined and carefully cleared of all adherent matter, without getting caught up anywhere, till it fell harmlessly astern. There was nothing else I could do to elude the peril of the mines, except, naturally, to trust to luck.

The other difficulty was that of taking the submarine to the *precise* point prearranged; in other words, to navigate with the exactitude of a draughtsman working with compass and ruler, despite the drifting caused by underwater currents, which are always difficult to deal with, and despite, above all, the impossibility of ascertaining one's position from the moment when, at dawn of the day appointed for the operation, the submarine would be obliged to submerge (so as not to be detected from the enemy base) and proceed at a great depth (to avoid mines), until the time came to release the operators.

The solution of this problem of underwater navigation cannot be reached without perfect control of the speed of the vessel; the course has to be laid and kept to with great precision (so as to eliminate errors due to faulty steering) and finally position has to be determined from variations in depth quota, the only hydrographic factor which can be ascertained in a submerged submarine; here we are in a sphere closer to that of art than to the science of navigation.

Everyone aboard gave me effective help, officers, petty officers and seamen. Each man, in his own special department, took care that his services should be regularly maintained and that his machinery should function in such a way as to prevent any unforeseen accident which might compromise the success of the operation.

Ursano, my second-in-command, had the general supervision of routine aboard; Benini and Olcese, the two efficient navigation officers, helped me in following the course and with the tricky business of dealing with codes and communication; while Tajer, the chief engineer, regulated the performance of the machinery (engines, electric batteries, air supply, etc.) and kept the respective services in order. The petty officers were first-rate: Ravera was chief mechanic, Farina chief torpedo-gunner, and Rapetti chief electrician; the wireless operators kept us in continuous touch with Rome and Athens; all were praiseworthy in the discharge of their various duties. Last but not least there was the cook (a seaman to whom this task had been allotted; he was

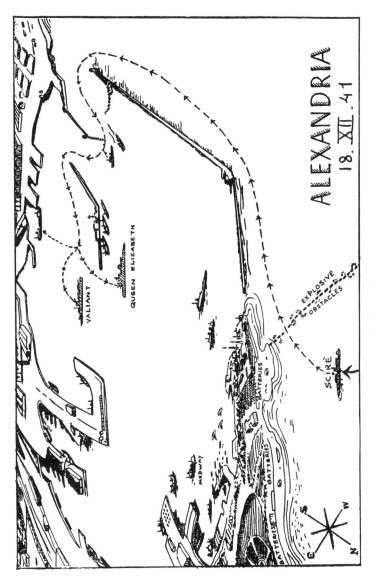

Map of Alexandria Harbour.

a mason in civil life) who became the martyr aboard; he was on his feet 24 hours out of 24 at the tiny, red-hot electric stoves, whatever the sea was like, concocting from dry rations dishes to satisfy the tastes and digestions of 60 people, as well as hot drinks for those on night watch and solid meals to keep up the spirits of the operators.

The latter, meanwhile, in perfect serenity (for the die was now cast) stored up their energy by resting. De la Penne, with his big fair head of rumpled hair, was generally to be found lying in his bunk asleep. Even as he slumbered he would every now and then stretch out an arm, put his hand into a drawer and extract a large fruit cake, which he ate up at a great rate. Then he would blissfully turn over and go back to his dreams.

Martellotta, permanently in good spirits, occupied another bunk. "Peace and good will!" was his invariable greeting; a heartening phrase. Marceglia, a giant of a man, with a tranquil temperament and something stately about him, was absorbed in study: his *basso profondo* tones were rarely heard and, when they were, it was to make some technical request or utter some comment on the operation. Feltrinelli, Bianchi, Marino, Schergat, Favale and Memoli all managed to find acceptable accommodation among the ship's equipment and spent their days in unbroken repose, only interrupted for the necessary more than substantial meals.

Public health was in the hands of Spaccarelli, surgeon, diver and reserve crew leader; every day he put the pilots through a thorough medical examination; it was essential to have them in the pink of condition on the day of the operation, which was now at hand.

The pilots remained very calm: the difficulties and dangers of which they were naturally well aware did not make them uneasy but merely increased their determination; anxiety and strain were inevitable, but did not find expression; talk went on at the ordinary level of cheerful tranquillity characteristic of life aboard; there were periods of gay hilarity, when facetious repartees were exchanged.

They were really extraordinary fellows, those lads; they were about to undertake action which would require the exploitation of their whole physical and moral energy and put their lives in peril at every moment, hour after hour; it would be a mission from which, *at best*, they could only hope to emerge as prisoners of war, and yet they preserved the attitude of a team of sportsmen off to play their customary Sunday game.

Meanwhile the *Scirè* encountered, on the 16th of December, a heavy storm.

"In order to avoid exposing materials, and above all our operators, to excessive strain, I remained submerged even at night, the moment our supplies of air and electricity had been taken in."

The same day I wrote:

"In consequence of the bad weather and the lack of exact information as to the number and size of the enemy units in harbour, I decided to postpone the operation for 24 hours from the night of the 17th/18th to that of the 18th/19th." (From my official report.)

On the 17th of December I added:

"In view of the ship's position and the favourable weather conditions I decided that the operation should take place on the evening of the 18th, hoping that I should meanwhile receive precise intelligence regarding the presence of vessels in harbour."

This was a hope that was soon realized. The same evening we obtained at last, to our great delight, confirmation from Athens that both the two battleships were at Alexandria.

The word was now: forward! Throughout the day, on the 18th, the *Scirè* proceeded through a zone which we presumed to be mined, at a depth of 60 metres, over bottoms which rose rapidly as we approached the coast, till we slipped over them like a silent and invisible tank, "continually regulating our movements in accordance with the rise of the sea-bed, till at 1840 hours we found ourselves at the prearranged point, 1.3 miles by 356° from the lighthouse at the west mole of the commercial harbour of Alexandria, at a depth of 15 metres". (*See* map facing p. 140.)

Preparations were made for release of the operators. As soon as I had discovered, by a survey taken through the periscope, that the darkness was complete, I surfaced just sufficiently to enable the trapdoor to be opened ('outcrop level', as it is technically known) and came out on the conning tower. The weather was perfect: it was pitch-dark; the sea very smooth and the sky unclouded. Alexandria was right

143

ahead of me, very close. I identified some of its characteristic buildings and determined my position; to my great satisfaction I found that we were within a metre of the pre-arranged point. This was an exceptional result after 16 hours of blind navigation! Immediately afterwards, with the pilots wrapped in their rubber suits and wearing their breathing sets, the ceremony of leave-taking began; we neither spoke nor embraced one another: "Commander," was all they said, "give us the good-luck kick, will you?" And with this strange rite, into which I put all I knew, so that my good wishes might be evident, the farewell ceremony terminated.

The first to go up were the two leaders of the reserve crews, Feltrinelli and Spaccarelli. Their job was to open the cylinder doors, to save the operators the fatigue of doing so.

One by one, de la Penne and Bianchi, Marceglia and Schergat, Martellotta and Marino, covered from head to foot in their black suits, their movements encumbered by their breathing gear, went up the ladder and disappeared into the darkness of the night and the sea. I submerged to the bottom.

A few minutes later the hydrophones told us that the three crews were on their way. "God be with them," I prayed, "and speed them well!"

Inside the submarine we waited for the sounds of blows struck against the deck, the agreed signal to be made when the doors of the cylinders, now empty, had been closed and the reserves were ready to be taken aboard again. When at last we heard them, I surfaced. Feltrinelli told me, in a voice broken by emotion, that as he could see no sign of Spaccarelli, he had gone astern to look for him: by pure chance he had stumbled against something soft on deck; he had discovered by groping (for we must not forget that the scene took place underwater at night) that it was the missing Spaccarelli, who seemed lifeless. I instantly sent up two other divers, who had been kept ready for any emergency; Spaccarelli was lifted up and lowered down the ladder into the interior of the submarine. I descended to the bottom again and began to head for home, following precisely the same course which had proved to be safe during my approach.

The unfortunate Spaccarelli was forthwith relieved of his mask, breathing set and diver's suit and put to bed; he was quite blue in the face, his pulse was imperceptible and he was not breathing; he showed every normal symptom of having been drowned.

What was to be done? The mission's surgeon was not much use to us in this extremity, for he himself was the victim. I arranged for two men to give him continuous artificial respiration; I rummaged in the medicine chest and had him injected with the contents of all the phials that, judging from the description of the ingredients, seemed capable of exercising a stimulating action on the heart and circulation; others gave him oxygen (the air aboard was emphatically unsuitable in this case); all the resources of our extremely slender store of medicaments and of our still slenderer knowledge of medicine were brought into play in the attempt to achieve what appeared to be an utter impossibility, the resuscitation of a dead man.

Meanwhile the *Scirè*, with this dramatic episode taking place aboard her, slipped along the sea-bed, further and further away from Alexandria. We took care not to reveal our presence in any way; discovery would have been fatal to the six adventurous lads who were at that very moment engaged in the crucial phase of the operation. But the submarine was not responding very well to my directions: the cylinder doors astern had been left open, a circumstance which made it difficult for me to keep my depth and maintain trim. As soon as we were some miles from the coast I surfaced to close them. I noticed that the Ras el Tin Lighthouse was functioning; a number of lights which I had not seen before showed at the entrance to the harbour; units were evidently going in or out; I hoped the operators would be able to take advantage of the fact. As for the cylinders, I found that they could not be closed on account of damage to one of the doors.

I continued on my course of withdrawal, remaining submerged, for the zone we were now crossing had been notified as constituting the minefield. After three and a half hours' continuous artificial respiration, a number of injections and some applications of oxygen, our surgeon, who had till then shown not the smallest sign of life, drew his first wheezing breath; it was a deep, hoarse sound, resembling a death-rattle. But it meant he was alive and we could save him! A few hours later, in fact, though his condition was still serious, he got back the use of his voice and was able to tell us that while he was making a terrific effort to close the starboard cylinder door, which stubbornly resisted every attempt he made, the effects of the oxygen he was breathing and those of water pressure at the depth involved had caused him to faint; luckily he fell on deck and did not slip overboard, as might very easily have happened, for there were no rails or bulwarks to the vessel (they had been removed to prevent the mine-cables from catching on them).

At last, on the evening of the 19th, since we were now presumably clear of the minefields, the *Scirè* surfaced, after 39 hours of submersion, and set course for Leros. On the evening of the 20th we received the following wireless communication from the Naval Supreme Command: "Photographic reconnaissance indicates two battleships hit." There was great enthusiasm aboard; no one had doubted it would be a success, but to have our expectations confirmed so soon gave us great satisfaction.

On the evening of the 21st, as soon as we had docked at Port Lago, we took Spaccarelli ashore to the local naval hospital. He was now out of danger but still required a good deal of attention in consequence of the severe shock he had experienced.

The return of the *Scirè* from Leros to La Spezia proceeded without any notable incidents, except that on Christmas Day, while the submarine was off Bengazi and the crew were listening to the Pope's speech on the loudspeaker, an aircraft of unidentified nationality came a little too close to the vessel and got within range of our four 13.2 machine-guns; the natural retaliation was the dropping of five bombs about 80 metres astern of us, which did no damage. Our Christmas pies!

On the 29th of December the *Scirè* arrived at La Spezia. Admiral Bacci, now chief of the North Tyrrhenean Sector, was waiting for us, on the pier; he brought us greetings and congratulations from Admiral Riccardi, Under Secretary of State for the Navy.

I was glad of this tribute to my gallant crew, who had worked so hard, with such efficiency and courage, in bringing our submarine back to harbour after 27 days of operational service, 22 of them at sea, and had covered without mishap 3500 miles, thus contributing to a great victory for Italy.

How had it fared with the operators, whom we had left in the open sea, outside Alexandria harbour, astride their fragile torpedoes, plunged beneath the waves in the darkness of night, surrounded by enemies in ambush? The three crews had left the submarine in company and commenced approach along the pre-arranged routes.

The sea was very calm, the night dark. Lights in the harbour permitted the pilots to determine their position, which they found to be precisely as planned. They went ahead so coolly that at one point, as de la Penne relates in his report, "as we were ahead of schedule, we opened our ration tins and had a meal. We were then 500 metres from the Ras el Tin Lighthouse."

At last they reached the net defences at the harbour's entrance.

"We saw some people at the end of the pier and heard them talking; one of them was walking about with a lighted oil-lamp.

We also saw a large motorboat cruising in silence off the pier and dropping depth-charges. These charges were rather a nuisance to us."

While the six heads, only just above water, were looking, with all the concentrated attention of which they were capable, for a gap in the net, three British destroyers suddenly appeared at the entrance to the harbour, waiting to go in: guide lights were switched on to show them the way and the net gates were thrown wide open. Without a second's hesitation our three assault craft slipped into the harbour with the British destroyers: they were in! They had lost sight of one another during this manœuvre, but they were now close to their targets. The latter had been distributed as follows: de la Penne was to take the battleship *Valiant*, Marceglia the battleship *Queen Elizabeth* and Martellotta was to look for the aircraft-carrier; if she were not in harbour, he was to attack a loaded tanker in the hope that the oil or petrol which would issue from it would spread over the water and thus furnish excellent fuel for the floating incendiary bombs the operators were to scatter before abandoning their 'pigs'.

We will now take up the stories of the individual crews.

DE LA PENNE—BIANCHI. Inside the harbour, after passing the interned French warships, the presence of which was well known, de la Penne sighted, at the presumed anchorage, the huge dark mass of the target assigned to him, the 32,000 ton battleship *Valiant*. As he approached her, he encountered the anti-torpedo net barrier: he got through it *surfaced* "in order to lose as little time as possible, for I found that my physical condition, owing to the cold, would be unlikely to let me hold out much longer". (His diver's suit had been leaking ever since he had left the submarine.) He had no difficulty with negotiation of the net: he was now 30 metres from the *Valiant*; it was 19

147

minutes past two. He touched the hull, giving it a slight bump; in performing the evolution necessary to get beneath the hull, his 'pig' seemed to take on extra weight and went to the bottom in 17 metres of water; de la Penne dived after it and discovered to his amazement that there was no sign of his second pilot. He rose to the surface to look for him, but could not see him; everything was quiet aboard the battleship; no alarm had been given. De la Penne left Bianchi to his fate, returned to the bottom and tried to start the engine of his craft to get it underneath the hull, as it had meanwhile moved some distance away. But the engine would not start; a rapid check-over soon showed what the trouble was: a steel wire had got entangled in the propeller.

What was to be done? All alone, with his craft immobilized on the sea-bed a few metres from the target, de la Penne resolved to try the only possible expedient: this was to drag the 'pig' by main force, finding his direction from the compass, beneath the battleship. Speed was essential, for he feared that at any moment the British might pick up his second pilot, who had probably fainted and would be floating about close by . . . ; the alarm would be given, depth-charges would be dropped, his operation and those of his companions would be doomed to certain failure, for they would be at work only a few hundred metres away. With all his strength, panting and sweating, he dragged at the craft; his goggles became obscured and the mud he was stirring up prevented his reading the compass, his breath began to come in great gasps and it became difficult to breathe at all through the mask, but he stuck to it and made progress; he could hear, close above him, the noises made aboard the ship, especially the sound of an alternating pump, which he used to find his direction. After 40 minutes of superhuman effort, making a few inches at every pull, he at last bumped his head against the hull. He made a cursory survey of the position: he seemed to be at about the middle of the ship, an excellent spot for causing maximum damage. He was now almost exhausted; but he used the last vestiges of his strength to set the time fuses; in accordance with the orders he had received he regulated them so as to cause the explosion at five o'clock precisely (Italian time, corresponding with six o'clock local time). He did not release his incendiary bombs, for when they rose to the surface they would reveal the presence and the position of the threat now established under the hull with the fuses in action. He left his craft on the sea-bed under the vessel and swam to the surface. The moment he got his head above water he removed his mask and sank it; the fresh, pure air revived him; he began to swim slowly away from the ship. But someone called out to him, a searchlight picked him out, a burst of machine-gun fire brought him to a halt. He swam back towards the vessel and climbed out of the water on to the mooring-buoy at the bows of the *Valiant*. He found there his second pilot Bianchi, who, after fainting, had risen to the surface like a balloon and on regaining consciousness had hidden himself on the buoy so as not risk causing an alarm which would have disturbed the work of his leader. "Aboard they were making facetious remarks, believing that our operation had failed; they were talking contemptuously about Italians. I called Bianchi's attention to the pro-bability that in a few hours they would have changed their minds about the Italians." It was then about 3.30. At last a motorboat turned up and the two 'shipwrecked' men were picked up by it and taken aboard the battleship. A British officer asked who they were, where they had come from and expressed ironical sympathy with their lack of success. The two operators, who were now prisoners of war, made clear who they were, by handing over their military identity cards. They refused to answer any other questions. They were taken in the motorboat, separated from each other, to a hut ashore, near the Ras el Tin Light-house. Bianchi was the first to be cross-examined: on leaving the hut he made a sign to de la Penne indicating that he had said nothing. It was then the latter's turn: naturally, he held his tongue; the Britisher, who had a revolver in his hand, seemed to be an excitable sort of fellow, "I'll soon find a way to make you talk," he said, in excellent Italian. The men were taken back aboard the *Valiant*: it was then four o'clock.

They were received by the commanding officer, Captain Morgan, who asked them where the charge was located. On their refusing to answer, the two men, accompanied by the officer of the watch and escorted by an armed picket, were placed in one of the holds forward, between the two gun-turrets, not very far from the point at which the charge would explode.

We will now let de la Penne take up the tale.

"Our escort were rather white about the gills and behaved very nicely to us; they gave me rum to drink and offered me cigarettes; they also tried to make us talk. Bianchi sat down and went to sleep. I perceived from the ribbons on the sailors' caps that we were aboard the battleship *Valiant*. When there were about 10 minutes left before the explosion, I asked if I could speak to the commanding officer. I was taken aft, into his presence. I told him that in a few minutes his ship would blow up, that there was nothing he could do about it and that, if he wished, he could still get his crew into a place of safety. He again asked me where I had placed the charge and as I did not reply had me escorted back to the hold. As we went along I heard the loudspeakers giving orders to abandon ship, as the vessel had been attacked by Italians, and saw people running aft. When I was again in the hold I said to Bianchi, as I came down the ladder, that things had turned out badly and that it was all up with us, but that we could be content, since we had succeeded, in spite of everything, in bringing the operation to a successful conclusion. Bianchi, however, did not answer me. I looked for him and could not find him. I supposed that the British, believing that I had confessed, had removed him. A few minutes passed (they were infernal ones for me: would the explosion take place?) and then it came. The vessel reared, with extreme violence. All the lights went out and the hold became filled with smoke. I was surrounded by shackles which had been hanging from the ceiling and had now fallen. I was unhurt, except for pain in a knee, which had been grazed by one of the shackles in its fall. The vessel was listing to port. I opened one of the port-holes very near sea level, hoping to be able to get through it and escape. This proved to be impossible, as the port-hole was too small, and I gave up the idea: but I left the port open, hoping that through it more water would enter. I waited for a few moments. The hold was now illuminated by the light which entered through the port. I concluded that it would be rash to stay there any longer, noticing that the vessel was now lying on the bottom and continuing slowly to list to port. I climbed up the ladder and, finding the hatchway open, began to walk aft; there was no one about. But there were still many of the crew at the stern. They got up as I passed them; I went on till I reached the Captain. At that moment he was engaged in giving orders for salvaging his ship. I asked him what he had done with my diver. He did not reply and the officer of the watch told me to be silent. The ship had now listed through 4–5 degrees and come to a stand-still. I saw from a clock that it was a quarter past six. I went further aft, where a number of officers were standing, and began to watch the battleship *Queen Elizabeth*, which lay about 500 metres astern of us.

The crew of that battleship were standing in her bows. A few seconds passed and then the *Queen Elizabeth*, too, blew up. She rose a few inches out of the water and fragments of iron and other objects flew out of her funnel, mixed with oil which even reached the deck of the *Valiant*, splashing everyone of us standing on her stern. An officer came up and asked me to tell him on my word of honour if there were any other charges under the ship. I made no reply and was then again taken back to the hold. After about a quarter of an hour I was escorted up to the officers' mess, where at last I could sit down, and where I found Bianchi. Shortly afterwards I was put aboard a motor-boat, which took me back to Ras el Tin.

I noticed that the anchor, which had been hanging at the bows, was now underwater. During transit an officer asked me whether we had got in through the gaps in the mole. At Ras el Tin we were locked in two cells and kept there until towards evening. I asked whether I could be given a little sunlight, as I was again very cold. A soldier came, felt my pulse and told me that I was perfectly all right.

Towards evening we were put into a small lorry and transported therein to a prisoner of war camp in Alexandria. I found some Italians in the camp who had heard the explosions that morning. We lay down on the ground, without having had any food, and, though we were soaked through, we slept till the following morning. I was taken to the infirmary for treatment of my knee injury and some Italian orderlies gave me an excellent dish of macaroni. The next morning I was removed to Cairo." (From the report handed in by Lieutenant Luigi de la Penne on his return from prison.)

In 1944, after de la Penne and Bianchi had come back to Italy from prison, they were awarded the gold medal for gallantry in war. And he who pinned the medal on the chest of de la Penne was none other than Admiral Morgan, formerly commanding officer of the *Valiant* and at that time chief of the allied naval mission in Italy.

MARCEGLIA—SCHERGAT. Approach commenced in company with de la Penne on the pre-arranged course. About midnight they saw the guide lights at the entrance to the harbour switched on; it was clear that units were either going in or coming out. Violent shocks were felt against the casing of the 'pig', as though it had crashed against some metallic obstacle, accompanied by strong contraction of the leg muscles of the pilots: these were the effects of depth-charges dropped by the enemy at the entrance to the harbour to prevent 'unwelcome visits'. As they slipped into the entrance channel they noticed, much to their surprise and satisfaction, that the net gates had been opened. Shortly afterwards, towards one o'clock, they had to take rapid evasive action to avoid being run down by three destroyers which were just coming in. Marceglia resumed the pre-arranged course: "in no time at all I found myself face to face with the whole massive bulk of my target." He came upon the anti-torpedo net, got through it and, now that the way was clear, submerged beneath the hull, in line with the funnel. With the aid of his second pilot, Marceglia precisely carried out the manœuvre: he clamped a loop-line connecting the two bilge keels and attached the warhead of his torpedo to the central point of the line, so that it hung about a metre and a half below the hull; then he set the fuse in motion. It was then 3.15 a.m. (Italian time).

"I tried to analyse my sensations at that moment. I found that I did not feel particularly thrilled, but only rather tired and just starting to get cold. We got astride our craft again: my diver made me urgent signs to surface, as he was just about all in. I pumped in air to surface; the craft only detached itself from the bottom with difficulty, then at last it started to rise, at first slowly, later more rapidly. So as not to burst out of the water too suddenly, I had to exhaust; the air bubbles attracted the attention of the watch aft. He switched on a searchlight and we surfaced right into its rays. We ducked down on the craft to make the target as small as possible and prevent our goggles from reflecting the light. Shortly afterwards the searchlight was switched off; we started on our return, which took us past the bows of the ship; a man was walking up and down the fo'c'sle deck, I could see his cigarette glowing; everything was quiet aboard. We got out of the obstructed zone and, at last, took off our masks; it was very cold; I couldn't prevent my teeth chattering. We stopped again and began distributing our incendiaries after setting the fuses." (From a report by Engineer Captain Antonio Marceglia.)

They then set off for the spot on which they were to land: it was the area which, according to our maps and intelligence reports, was the least strictly guarded and furnished the most convenient access to the city.

While still some distance from land they set going the fuse of the craft's self-destructor and sank her; they swam ashore, removed their breathing sets and rubber suits, cut everything to pieces and buried the strips under the rocks. Then they waded ashore: it was 4.30 a.m.; they had been in the water exactly eight hours.

Marceglia and Schergat succeeded in leaving the harbour area unobserved. Posing as French sailors, they entered the city of Alexandria; after wandering about for some time, they made their way to the station to take the train for Rosetta and try to rejoin the submarine which would be lying about 10 miles out to sea at certain pre-arranged times, a night or two later. But at this point their troubles began: the sterling with which they were supplied did not circulate in Egypt; they wasted a lot of time trying to get it changed and were not able to leave until the evening. At Rosetta they spent the night in a squalid little inn, hiding from frequent visits by the police; next day, in the evening, they made for the seashore, but were stopped by the Egyptian police, recognized as Italians and turned over to the British naval authorities.

Their attempt to evade capture was thus frustrated.

Marceglia's operation may be characterized as a 'perfect' one, meaning by this phrase that it was performed without a hitch at every stage and nothing unforeseen happened. In a letter he wrote me some years later he observed: "As you can see, Sir, our performance had nothing heroic about it; its success was due solely to the preparations made, the specially favourable conditions under which it took place and above all the determination to succeed at all costs."

Preparations, determination and luck were rewarded with the gold medal for gallantry in war, which both Marceglia and Schergat obtained on their release from prison.

MARTELLOTTA—MARINO. Martellotta writes in his report:

"Aboard the submarine *Scirè* at 1630 on the 18th December 1941, I received from Lieutenant-Commander Borghese the following operational orders: 'Attack to be made on a large loaded tanker and six incendiaries to be distributed in its immediate neighbourhood.'

The presence which had been notified of 12 loaded tankers in harbour at Alexandria, with a total tonnage of 120,000, was sufficient indication of the importance of the order received: the fire which might be started would be capable of reaching such proportions as to bring about the entire destruction of the harbour itself, with all the units present and all the shore installations.

Nevertheless, I felt obliged to reply: 'Sir, I shall obey your orders; but I should like you to know that my diver and I would rather have attacked a warship.'

The Captain smiled at this remark of mine and, to please me, since he was aware that there was a possibility of an aircraft-carrier having returned to the harbour, he modified the original operational orders to read: 'Search to be made for the aircraft-carrier at its two normal anchorages and attack to be made on it if found; otherwise, all other targets consisting of active war units to be ignored and a large loaded tanker to be attacked with distribution of the six incendiaries in its immediate neighbourhood.' "

Martellotta had a certain amount of trouble in opening the door of the cylinder and asked Spaccarelli to help him (this was the difficulty which involved Spaccarelli in the adventure related above); he finally joined the other two crews and continued approach in their company as far as the entrance net gate.

"I felt shocks from depth-charges and violent pressure against my legs, as though they were being crushed against the craft by some heavy object. I put on my mask and, so as to avoid injury from the frequent shocks being inflicted at vulnerable parts of my body, I ducked in such a way as to lie low in the water, but with heart, lungs and head above the surface. I told Marino, my diver, to put on his mask also and to take up a similar position, but facing aft, since I was unable myself to keep an eye open in that direction, engaged as I was in looking ahead and having only the limited area of visibility which the mask allowed.

We arrived in these positions at the entrance to the harbour . . . We did not find obstructions, as we had expected, at the pier-heads: the channel was clear.

We went ahead very slowly. Suddenly, my diver, Marino, thumped me on the shoulder and said: 'Hard a-starboard.' I instantly swerved in the direction indicated, putting on speed, but the craft struck the buoys of the fixed interior barrier, being driven against them by the waves from the bow of a ship which had caught me up as it entered the harbour. It was a destroyer, showing no lights and going at about 10 knots; I distinctly heard chains clashing at her bows and saw members of the crew on deck getting ready to moor. It was then 0030 hours on the 19th December. I got going again and, taking advantage of the waves made by a second destroyer as it entered the harbour, I slipped in with it, still surfaced and passing within about 20 metres of the guardship."

Martellotta, therefore, was now inside the harbour; he started looking for the aircraft-carrier at its two habitual anchorages; he could not find her (as a matter of fact she was not in harbour that night). But he did sight a large warship; believing her to be a battleship, he initiated attack; he had already got under her hull when he discovered that she was, on the contrary, a cruiser and with great reluctance, in obedience to orders received, abandoned the attack; just as he was clearing her after-davits he was caught in the rays of a pocket-torch aboard her: some seconds of utter immobility ensued, during which he felt as if even his heart had stopped beating; then the torch went out. He made for the zone of the tankers. Martellotta was now beginning to notice signs of strain: his head ached and he had to vomit; he could no longer keep the mouthpiece of the mask between his lips; he took it off and went ahead surfaced. There were the tankers. "I sighted a large one, heavily loaded, which I guessed to be about 16,000 tons." Not being able to submerge, he decided to carry out the attack from the surface: while Martellotta kept the 'pig' under the stern of the tanker, the second pilot, Marino, fastened the charge beneath the hull. By 2.55 the fuse had been set going. While this operation was proceeding, a smaller tanker had come alongside the one under attack.

"When Marino rose to the surface and saw her, he said: 'Let's hope she stays here another three hours and then she'll have her hash settled too.' Next, we started off again, for distribution of the incendiaries: we moored them, after setting their fuses, about 100 metres from the tanker and 20 metres apart."

The operation having been carried out in detail so far, the final stage began: this would be the attempt to escape so as not to fall into the hands of the enemy. They got ashore at the agreed place without incident, destroyed, by way of preventive action, their breathing sets and divers' suits and sank the 'pig' after setting the self-destructor fuse. Then they went ashore.

"I set off with Marino to get clear of the harbour zone and enter the city: we were stopped at a control point and arrested by some Egyptian customs officials and police, who summoned a second lieutenant and six privates of the British Marines. We were taken to an office occupied by two lieutenants of the Egyptian police, who started cross-examining us; while I was answering the questions put to me in as evasive and vague a manner as I could, a British naval commander arrived and requested the senior of the two Egyptian officers to hand us over to the British. The Egyptian refused to do so in the absence of any authority from his Government, pointing out that, as he had found us to be Italians from the documents we carried and Egypt was not at war with Italy, he would have to get special instructions.

The British Commander, after obtaining the necessary authorization from his Admiral, made a personal application to the Egyptian Government for the instructions required and succeeded in getting us handed over.

My waterproof watch was on the table with the other articles taken possession of and I never took my eyes off it. Shortly after 5.54 a.m. a violent explosion was heard, which shook the whole building. A few minutes later, as we were getting into a car to follow the British officer, a second explosion was heard, further away, and after the car had started a third. At the Ras el Tin naval headquarters we were briefly interrogated, courteously enough, and then despatched to the concentration camp for prisoners of war at Cairo." (From the report of Gunner Captain Vincenzo Martellotta.)

Martellotta and Marino, on their release from captivity, were also awarded the gold medal for gallantry in war.

·   ·   ·   ·   ·

The Italian War Bulletin N. 585 of the 8th of January, 1942, gives the following account of the success of the operation:

"On the night of the 18th December assault craft of the Italian Royal Navy entered the harbour of Alexandria and attacked two British battleships anchored there. It has only just been confirmed that a battleship of the *Valiant* class was seriously damaged and put into dock for repairs, and is still there."

The following Bulletin, N. 586 of the 9th of January, rounds off the information as follows:

"In the operation conducted by assault craft of the Italian Royal Navy in the harbour of Alexandria and reported in yesterday's Bulletin we now have definite further intelligence that, in addition to the *Valiant*, a second battleship of the *Barham* class was also damaged."

Such was the modest announcement of a naval victory unparalleled throughout the war for precision of execution and importance of strategic results. At the cost of six men captured, there had been sunk, in addition to a large tanker, two 32,000 ton battleships, the last of those at the disposal of the British in the Mediterranean. Crippled by the charges applied to their hulls by the daring members of the Tenth Light Flotilla, the vessels were at a later date, after much expenditure of energy and materials, refloated, patched up for the time being and then transferred to quiet and distant yards for refit: but they made no further contribution to the war and immediately after the cessation of hostilities they were removed for demolition.

The losses of the *Valiant* and the *Queen Elizabeth*, following those of the *Ark Royal* and the *Barham* in the Mediterranean and almost contemporaneous with the destruction of the *Repulse* and the extremely recent *Prince of Wales* in Indonesia at the hands of Japanese aviators, brought about a most critical situation for the British Navy, which was only retrieved after a long lapse of time and then only by means of American assistance.

The strategic position in the Mediterranean was now reversed: for the first (and last) time in the course of the war the Italian Navy achieved crushing superiority and dominated the Mediterranean; it

157

could therefore resume, with practical immunity, supplies to the armies overseas and carry out transport of the German *Afrika Corps* to Libya, thus causing the defeat, a few months later, of the British Army, which was driven out of Cyrenaica.

Even more could have been done: Italy's naval superiority at that time was such as to permit her armed forces to undertake a direct attack against the pivot of the war in the Mediterranean (and perhaps not only in that theatre of war), namely, Malta. An invasion force transported by a convoy protected by the entire Italian Fleet, when our battleships would be opposed by *no* such British vessels, would have eliminated that obstacle in the heart of the Mediterranean, which had done us so much harm already and was to do us even more later on. Such an operation would have disposed of the difficulties which the Italian Navy had to encounter, for months afterwards, in supplying our African army.

In view of the disproportion between naval forces, the operation would certainly have succeeded, though it might have been accompanied by serious losses. When the thorn in the flank of Italy's line of communication across the Mediterranean had thus been eliminated, the occupation of Egypt would only have been a question of time, bringing with it incalculable consequences for the outcome of the war.

The responsibility for losing this opportunity rests, in my opinion, on the Italian General Staff and, still more, upon the German High Command which, by refusing to supply the necessary fuel for our warships and aircraft, "again displayed its underestimation of sea power in the general conduct of the war and in particular of the importance of the Mediterranean in the general picture of the entire conflict". (From the report of Admiral Weichold, a German liaison officer attached to the Italian Supreme Naval Command, submitted to the Anglo-Americans after the war.)

The great victory at Alexandria was therefore only partially exploited: the British were given time to draw naval and air reinforcements to the Mediterranean to such an extent that a few months later the situation was again reversed, to our disadvantage; it continued to deteriorate until the final collapse, of which the withdrawal from North Africa in May 1943 was the obvious proof.

But how great the danger which threatened the enemy was, and how near we were, after the blow delivered at Alexandria, to achieving decisive victory, was indicated, more clearly than by anyone else, by the man who, being in charge of the conduct of the war on the other side, realized it most fully: Winston Churchill. In a speech before a secret session of the House of Commons on the 23rd of April, 1942, after announcing the loss of the *Ark Royal*, the *Barham*, the *Repulse* and the *Prince of Wales*, he continued as follows:

"A further sinister stroke was to come. On the early morning of December 19 half a dozen Italians in unusual diving suits were captured floundering about in the harbour of Alexandria. Extreme precautions have been taken for some time past against the varieties of human torpedo or one-man submarine entering our harbours. Not only are nets and other obstructions used but underwater charges are exploded at frequent irregular intervals in the fairway. None the less these men had penetrated the harbour. Four hours later explosions occurred in the bottoms of the *Valiant* and the *Queen Elizabeth*, produced by limpet bombs fixed with extraordinary courage and ingenuity, the effect of which was to blow large holes in the bottoms of both ships and to flood several compartments, thus putting them both out of action for many months. One ship will soon be ready again, the other is still in the floating dock at Alexandria, a constant target for enemy air attack. Thus we no longer had any battle squadron in the Mediterranean. *Barham* had gone and now *Valiant* and *Queen Elizabeth* were completely out of action. Both these ships floated on an even keel, they looked all right from the air. The enemy were for some time unaware of the success of their attack,[1] and it is only now that I feel it possible to make this disclosure to the House even in the strictness of a Secret Session. The Italian fleet still contains four or five battleships, several times repaired, of the new *Littorio* or of the modernized class. The sea defence of the Nile valley had to be confided to our submarine and destroyer flotillas, with a few cruisers, and of course to shore based Air forces. For this reason it was necessary to transfer a part of our shore based torpedo-carrying aircraft from the south and east coasts of England, where they were soon to be needed, to the north African shore . . ."

The decoration, that of the Military Order of Savoy, which was

[1] This assertion is disproved by the Italian war Bulletins quoted above. (Author's note.)

conferred upon me, on the King's own initiative, after the Alexandria operations, was accompanied by the following citation:

"Commanding officer of a submarine detailed to the Tenth Light Flotilla for special assault craft operations, he had already successfully carried out three daring and difficult undertakings; he studied and prepared, with great technical competence and shrewdness, the plan of a fourth operation, for forcing a further enemy base. He took his submarine close in to the heavily fortified harbour, facing with cool determination the risks incurred from the defence measures and vigilance of the enemy, in order to put the assault craft in the best possible position for forcing the enemy base. He then launched the assault craft in an action which achieved a brilliant success, leading as it did to the infliction of serious damage upon two enemy battleships."

LIEUTENANT-COMMANDER GIOBBE.

Hoisting the colours on H.M.S. *Queen Elizabeth*, flagship of the Mediterranean Fleet. Admiral Sir Andrew Cunningham (now Viscount Cunningham) can be see in the centre, right, saluting as the colours are hoisted. March 1942.

CHAPTER XII

SPRING 1942: TORPEDO ASSAULT BOATS AT THE SIEGE OF MALTA; THE *AMBRA* AT ALEXANDRIA

I leave the Scirè—*The crew's decision to remain—Zelich in command—2nd April, 1942: the Duke of Aosta decorates us —Lieutenant Ungarelli's exemplary spirit of camaraderie at sea—Preparations for a raid on Malta: Admiral Tur's task force—Reconnaissance by a swimmer—The heroic death of Borg Pisani—Alexandria again: a bold plan—Arillo's operation with the submarine* Ambra—*'Alexandria was more easily forced by the Tenth than photographed by our aircraft.'*

AFTER the mission to Alexandria in December 1941 the Ministry again ordered me to relinquish the command of the *Scirè* and devote all my energies to the Tenth, as chief of the underwater Department, a task I had already been fulfilling for some time. The Flotilla continued to develop: it comprised the study, construction and employment of new weapons, a great increase in personnel, the planning of operations of greater importance at distances which became steadily greater; then there was the extension of its activity to new fields; this complex mass of tasks was a full-time job for the few officers who had the necessary competence and experience in this highly specialized branch. Such were the considerations advanced to me by the Ministry against my humble request to remain with the *Scirè*; I was well aware, indeed, how well founded the Ministry's reasons were.

"On the other hand," I was told, "You have carried out five operations in command of the *Scirè*: four to Gibraltar and one to Alexandria, and all were brought to a successful conclusion. You have shown how the submarine may be adapted to this particular service and transformed it by technical improvements into an arm strikingly more efficient than its original structure envisaged; you have also given the crew the high degree of training required. Finally, you have found and used the routes and types of

L   161 navigation which enabled you to take the *Scirè* repeatedly, with due order and precision, to zones in the immediate neighbourhood of those enemy harbours which were most assiduously watched and defended, despite the growing intensification of the defensive measures taken. It is time that other officers replaced you at this work and that you devoted all your energies and the results of your experience to the Flotilla."

In obeying this order I asked the Ministry to allow the entire crew of the *Scirè* to leave the submarine and take up appointments elsewhere: it was very distasteful to me to have to abandon the crew which had shared the risks of the previous operations with me and to which I was bound by ties of brotherly affection, and to leave it to run the gauntlet of further equally perilous operations, while I remained in safety ashore. The Ministry granted my request: and on a day which I shall never forget I told the crew of the *Scirè* the news. I had to take up a shore appointment, I said, at the orders of my superiors and there was nothing to be done about it; I should take leave of them with the deepest reluctance. Those of the crew who desired to take up other work, which would certainly be less risky, could ask to be transferred accordingly. They had all done more than their duty and the Navy recognized that and therefore gave them this chance. But once more the crew of the *Scirè* was to display a shining example of the spirit of self-sacrifice and utter devotion to duty. All of them, barring a few exceptions, wanted to remain on board. "We are very sorry indeed, sir, that you are going to leave us and we thank you for having thought of giving us the chance to transfer. But the choice between any sort of safe employment and our attachment to the grand ship on which we serve is one we have no hesitation about: we want to stay with the *Scirè*." Such was the verdict of Tajer, sturdiest of Engineer Captains, who had only been a few months married, of Benini and of Olcese, the two Sub-Lieutenants who had given me such valuable co-operation in navigating the ship, and who were always capable, unassuming and cool under any circumstances; it was the verdict, too, of Ravera, the chief mechanic, Rapetti, the chief electrician, Farina, the chief torpedo-gunner, Lodati, the wireless sergeant, Barbieri, the boatswain, and Canali, the assistant torpedo-gunner, all splendid petty officers in whom I had always had the greatest confidence and who showed, on this occasion, that they fully deserved it; such was the verdict, too, of almost all the seamen. The deliberate and conscious resolve of the crew to stick by the ship, exposed as she was to dangers which increased with every operation, and also only too well aware of the probable end of a struggle in which fortune had been defied and forced to yield the victory much too often already, was a magnificent instance of collective courage: in other words of that quality by which we estimate the worth of peoples and nations.

I can still see my men drawn up on Veleria pier in La Spezia dockyard on the 2nd of April, 1942, on the occasion of the award of decorations for gallantry. Three crews were present; that of the *Scirè* being in the centre and the two German crews of Gugenberger and von Tiesenhausen, who sank, respectively, the aircraft-carrier *Ark Royal* and the battleship *Barham*, on each side. The decorations were pinned upon our tunics in the King's name by the Duke of Aosta. The three victorious submarines were moored side by side, the *Scirè* in the middle, with their flags flying, and seemed themselves, too, to participate in the ceremony in virtue of that inexpressible but powerfully felt bond linking a crew to its ship.

The function was characterized by military simplicity; the public were not admitted. The citations were read: each seaman received his decorations. Those belonging to the *Scirè* got four, one for each of the operations performed. It had been my wish, as expressed to and approved by the Ministry, that the entire crew should be decorated; for the effort to bring an operation to its conclusion had been a collective one and its reward should therefore also be collective.

I have a vivid recollection of my seamen, happy in the dignified pride with which they wore the medals (by tradition kept on all through that day and then replaced, for practical reasons, by the ribbons), maintaining a calm and unassuming attitude when they received them from the royal prince, such as they had always maintained during the performance of the most arduous tasks aboard throughout the operations, even at moments of the greatest tension.

The command of the *Scirè* was transferred to Lieutenant-Commander Bruno Zelich, one of my own batch, a brave officer with a great deal of experience in the submarine service and of high professional capacity; he had been chosen, for these reasons, from among the few submarine commanders who had applied for that post.

After the new commanding officer had been introduced, I took leave, with much cordiality, of the seamen. My old crew presented me with a photograph of the *Scirè*, with their names inscribed round the frame, and gave me a rousing send-off. I then paid a last visit to the submarine which had served us so well and so often and at last, with a tight feeling round my heart, tore myself away.

I was never to see the *Scirè* again, nor any of those whom I had left aboard her.

As part of the activities of our armed forces directed to the siege of the island of Malta a detachment of motor-torpedo-boats, under the command of Sub-Lieutenant Ongarillo Ungarelli, had been transferred to Augusta at the beginning of 1942. Its task was to lie in wait at night outside the entrances to La Valletta harbour and thus to furnish, in proximity to the island, an addition to the many other obstacles which the supply vessels had to deal with. There were dozens of hours of such patrolling, a few hundred metres from the enemy coast, on any night when the state of the weather permitted it; the pilots were daring enough, while they waited for their targets, to make a regular habit of mooring their craft to the buoys indicating access to the safety channels leading to the harbour. On a number of occasions British patrols were encountered and boldly challenged, but no big enemy units ever came within range. On one of these missions Ungarelli gave a gallant proof of *camaraderie* at sea: one of his torpedo assault boats having been set on fire by enemy aircraft and its pilot wounded, Ungarelli instantly came alongside her in his own craft, paying no attention to the risks he ran from the imminent explosion of the petrol tanks and torpedo charges aboard; he succeeded in rescuing P.O./mechanic Minelli, the wounded man, and in making good his escape an instant before the burning boat blew up in a cloud of fire and smoke. For this deed Ungarelli was awarded the silver medal for gallantry.

In the spring of 1942 the operations undertaken by the detachment of the Tenth transferred to Augusta became very numerous and assumed novel forms. Preparations were, in fact, in progress at that time for a forcible occupation of the island of Malta, the defences of which had already been softened up by regular heavy air-raids and the garrison brought to the verge of exhaustion owing to the blockade established by our air and sea forces, which had practically brought supplies to a standstill. A special force under the command of Admiral Tur was in training for the object in question. It consisted, in addition to landing craft suitably adapted for the purpose, of marine groups for attacking the island by sea, or parachutists who were to descend upon it from the sky, and of some Army and Militia divisions for the completion of the occupation initiated by the raiding marines.

Between Admiral Tur's task force and the Tenth a fraternal bond of collaboration came into existence; Captain Buttazzoni's swimming parachutists belonging to that arm and our own Gamma Group swimmers formed liaison elements between the two organizations.

A parallelism of method and purpose was thus constituted which was later to bear excellent fruit in a number of actions carried out in common.

It was actually at the request of the Special Force Command that the Tenth was summoned to a new undertaking, the identification of the plan of fixed and mobile defences existing at Malta. The idea was to approach the island by the various means in which we were specially trained, in order to discover the nature of the fixed defences in operation and test the vigilance of the enemy and the resistance he might put up to approaching forces.

This task was performed with great courage by some of our best surface pilots, Ungarelli, Lieutenant Giuseppe Cosulich, Midshipman Fracassini and a number of others. They proceeded on several occasions, in their tiny motorboats, right round the island, sometimes coming in to within a few dozen metres of the coast, taking note of its most prominent features and picking up useful data for every aspect of the prepared invasion.

Two operations carried out within the framework of these activities especially deserve to be recorded.

On the 18th of May an action took place involving the torpedo-boat *Abba* and a detachment of light craft commanded by Lieutenant Freschi, in support of the torpedo assault craft 218 (Lieutenant Cosulich, P.O./mechanic Aldo Pia) and 214 (Sub-Lieutenant Ungarelli and P.O./mechanic Arnaldo De Angeli).

Cosulich took one of the swimmers of the Tenth to the Bay of Marsa Scala, on the north-east coast of Malta; the volunteer's task was to carry out reconnaissance by swimming to within the shortest possible distance from the coast and noting the existence of any obstacles, barbed wire obstructions, nests of machine-guns or sentry-posts, etc., and then return to the motorboat to describe what he had seen. Assault swimmer Giuseppe Guglielmo of our Gamma Group was chosen to carry out this work. The operation proceeded in normal fashion. Cosulich duly took his motorboat into Marsa Scala bay; Guglielmo plunged into the sea and started his reconnaissance, exploring the inlet metre by metre, while he lay on an air-cushion propelling himself with his arms. This was one of the methods in regular use by our swimmers. After some time, in order to get a more accurate idea of certain aspects of the coast, he made straight for it and, tucking the deflated cushion under his arm, took a short reconnoitring stroll ashore, making a mental note of anything that interested him. On his return into the sea with his mission accomplished he failed to find any sign of the motorboat, though Cosulich, who had agreed to wait until 3.15 a.m., had remained on the watch for him until 4.10, when dawn had already begun to break. Guglielmo was therefore obliged to take refuge ashore, in broad daylight, and was there eventually captured by the British. Cosulich, however, returned without mishap to his base and, though Guglielmo was missing, was able to furnish useful intelligence regarding what he had seen.

The same night Ungarelli left Sicily, taking with him on his craft Carmelo Borg Pisani, a Maltese student patriotically devoted to Italy, who had volunteered to fill in important gaps in our knowledge of Malta's defences. He was to go ashore on the island and supply us by radio transmitter with the information needed for the invasion operations. Ungarelli's undertaking succeeded perfectly. He coasted along the east of the island and took up a position south-west of it, where, owing to the steep cliffs, he considered that it would be less carefully watched. At the pre-arranged spot, 150 metres from the coast, Borg Pisani, with his transmitter and the scanty equipment necessary, left the motorboat and reached the island without mishap in a rubber canoe. Ungarelli returned to his base. We learned eventually that Borg Pisani was very soon captured by the British and, after five months of strict interrogation, was tried and condemned to death. He was hanged on the 28th of November. He left a farewell message written with a charred stick on the door of his cell, in Italian: "God does not love slaves and cowards." He was posthumously awarded the gold medal for gallantry in war.

While the Augusta detachment continued its assiduous siege of Malta, performing frequent operations which, though they did not achieve any striking success, nevertheless demanded constant displays of courage and skilled seamanship from the pilots, the Tenth Light Flotilla was engaging in intense activity elsewhere.

At that time the Inspectorate-General of Light Craft was instituted. Its task was to discipline and co-ordinate activities by all the light craft flotillas, torpedo-boats and patrol vessels; the Tenth Flotilla was included under its jurisdiction. The Duke of Aosta, the Inspector-General, had followed the development of the new types of craft right from the start with admiration, sympathy and personal services; he became our protector in high quarters, to our very great advantage, especially where morale, so overwhelmingly important in the delicate business of dealing with volunteers, was concerned.

The conditions of the two battleships hit at Alexandria were meanwhile the object of a great deal of our attention, based upon reports by air reconnaissance. A photograph taken on the same day, the 19th of December, a few hours after the charges had exploded, was examined by myself personally on my return from the operation, and gave us a clear idea of the results achieved: one of the vessels was shown resting on the bottom, with a list, her stern at water level; the other, also visibly lying on the bottom, was entirely surrounded by floating platforms, rafts, tankers and a submarine; she was evidently unloading to lighten herself. Further photographs showed the *Queen Elizabeth* in course of being raised and, later, her introduction into the large floating repair dock at Alexandria.

In April we learned that after a hasty refit the *Queen Elizabeth* would shortly leave the dock on her way to a distant shipyard to undergo more thorough repairs; we considered the time opportune to launch an attack with a view to frustrating this project.

Our plan was conceived as follows: a submarine was to take the same route as the *Scirè* and approach Alexandria carrying three piloted torpedoes. After entering the harbour (we understood that, following the experiences in December, our enterprise would be a good deal more difficult on account of the new defensive measures the British must have, without doubt, put in hand since then) two of the piloted torpedoes would reach the large repair dock in which the *Queen Elizabeth* lay, apply the charges and blow it up; as a result of the explosion the 32,000 tons of the battleship and the 40,000 of the dock would become such an inextricable chaos of twisted steel, guns, armour plating and framework as to put out of action definitely not only the

167

Queen Elizabeth, already condemned owing to her keel being broken by the charge of Marceglia, but also the dock itself.

For ships, repair docks are the equivalent of beds for men. After hours of intense activity a bed is the place to stretch out and recuperate, to get rid of all the poison and waste matter accumulated in the system as a result of the energy expended; when an organism ceases to function appropriately, the first thing to do is to go to bed so as to allow treatment in the best possible conditions. So it is with ships: after some months of service any ship needs careening in dock, where the part of the hull normally submerged can be exposed to sunlight, cleaned and cleared of the deposits of marine flora and fauna, and then covered with anti-parasitic paint. Further cleaning is undertaken to water inlets, shafts and propellers, and inspections are made of armour-plating, all essential to the preservation in good condition, the safe operation and the serviceability of the vessel. If, therefore, the substructure or part under water of a hull is damaged by a torpedo, by stranding, by collision or by contact with mines, etc., as easily happens in war, the ship must be promptly put in dock; in some cases a readily available dock may prove the salvation of a unit which would otherwise be lost owing to the entry of water at the leak.

In the Eastern Mediterranean the British Navy only disposed of a single dock in which battleships could be careened: this was the floating dock at Alexandria. The nearest other dock of the type was at Durban in South Africa, that at Singapore being now useless, as it was occupied by the Japanese. The destruction of the dock at Alexandria would therefore have meant an extremely serious, irreparable loss.

The third pilot was to use the opportunity to attempt to wipe out a vessel and among the few ships of any importance still at Alexandria the *Medway*, the parent ship of the submarines stationed there, was the one chosen. It was in fact desired to carry our offensive into the sector of the enemy naval forces most troublesome at the time and these, since the elimination of the battleships, no longer consisted of the surface units, which now kept very quiet, but of the submarines.

The operation was slated to take place with the favourable moon in May; it was logical to suppose that vigilance at the British base, which had been so abruptly roused at dawn on the 19th of December, would have had the time, during four months of tranquillity, to relax again.

The usual methodical and carefully worked out preparations were applied to men and materials. With the approval of the Board of naval construction at La Spezia arsenal a series of tests were undertaken to find the most vulnerable point of a floating dock and to determine the quantity of explosive required to ensure its destruction.

Operational orders and detailed instruction were almost exact repetitions of those which had given such good results, when applied by the *Scirè*, in the previous action against Alexandria.

Forza, the commanding officer of the Tenth Flotilla, wanted to take part also and requested to be allowed to direct the mission from the submarine. The Supreme Naval Command, however, took another, more reasonable decision: he was sent to Athens to co-ordinate the various services necessary, such as air reconnaissance, the collection of intelligence and weather reports, and wireless liaison.

As soon as the works of adaptation and a long period of training had been completed, the submarine *Ambra*, under the command of Lieutenant Arillo, left La Spezia on her first special mission on the 29th of April, 1942, with three 'human torpedoes' lodged in her cylinders. At Leros she took the operators, who had arrived by air, aboard. They were Surgeon Sub-Lieutenant Giorgio Spaccarelli with P.O./diver Armando Memoli; Midshipman Giovanni Magello with P.O./diver Giuseppe Morbelli; and Engineer Sub-Lieutenant Luigi Feltrinelli with P.O./diver Luciano Favale. The reserves were Commissariat Captain Egil Chersi, P.O./diver Rodolfo Beuk and P.O./ diver Ario Lazzari. The medical officer of the expedition was Surgeon Sub-Lieutenant Elvio Moscatelli.

On the 12th of May the *Ambra* left Leros heading for Alexandria. On the evening of the 14th, she was just off that harbour. The current had carried her a little off her course to the west, relatively to the spot agreed upon for dropping the operators, which was the same as had been used by the *Scirè*. (*See* map facing p. 140.)

Since he was very near the entrance to the harbour, Arillo felt that it would be opportune to take a good look around before dropping the operators.

"1925 hours. We are resting on the bottom in 10.5 metres of water. At this depth the hydrophones are not very reliable. In view, also, of the activities of searchlights and star-shells which we observed last night I decided to send out Captain Chersi on a surface patrol, dropping him from the forward hatch, with the submarine submerged. I instructed him to indicate the best time for us to surface, bearing in mind that the craft would have to start whatever the circumstances.

2005 hours. Chersi is out with Lazzari and Beuk.

2025 hours. All clear signal from Chersi.

2032 hours. Surfaced. A number of searchlights sweeping the sea systematically. At the moment of surfacing they were directed west (to starboard) and were slowly revolving eastwards. The Ras el Tin lighthouse was in action. A number of lights visible on the coast, which was clearly discernible. I at once checked my position and found out that, as I had foreseen, the *Ambra* was inside the line of 'lobster-pots'."

A few seconds later a big star-shell burst over the entrance to the harbour and made the submarine clearly visible.

"2037 hours. Release operation ended. Although I was almost certain that the presence of the submarine had now been discovered, I ordered the operators to carry on with the mission to its conclusion. They were extremely cool, cheerful and in high spirits.

2038 hours. Submerged.

2055 hours. Heard through the hydrophones the three human torpedoes on their way.

2105 hours. Started return after difficult job getting clear of the sandbank on which the submarine was stuck." (From the report of Lieutenant Mario Arillo.)

On the 24th of May Arillo, who completed his task with great ability and resolution, brought the *Ambra* back to La Spezia.

In his report he summarized the main points of the action which developed.

"1. The current had caused the submarine to drift off from the ordered launching point in a westerly direction.

2. For the first time dropping the operators from a hatch was tried out with satisfactory results. This method presents the very great advantage of permitting the dropping to be made with the submarine never surfacing.

3. An observer was sent out, also for the first time, from the bottom, to reconnoitre the surface.

4. Vigilance in the harbour appeared to have been much increased. Searchlights and star-shells, aircraft and cruising patrol vessels must have made the enemy feel remarkably safe."

The targets had been assigned as follows: Magello and Spaccarelli were to go for the floating dock; Feltrinelli was to attack the submarine parent ship *Medway*. They were all also to strew two incendiary bombs each in the hope, once more, of setting fire to the harbour. The three crews began approach on the pre-arranged course, but were immediately bewildered by the glare due to numerous searchlights, about 20 altogether, which were slowly sweeping over the sea, almost uninterruptedly, in the very zones through which the pilots had to pass. They were, therefore, often obliged to submerge for long periods to avoid the risk of being spotted. This led both to a reduction of speed and to inability to reconnoitre the coast. For these reasons the pilots finally thought they could never make up for the delay on schedule, in view of the considerable distance still to be covered during the few hours of darkness which remained available, and came to the conclusion that they would never be able to bring the operation to a successful end. Accordingly, after some hours of floundering about in unidentified waters, over depths which did not correspond to those they expected, the three leaders each decided separately to abandon the undertaking and try to keep out of sight, so that, if they were discovered or captured by the enemy, their companions, who, they each hoped, might meanwhile succeed in penetrating the harbour, would not be prejudiced.

Magello and Morbelli, therefore, after having spent the whole night looking for the entrance, without even having been able to spot the harbour area, sank their craft at dawn and tried to hide in the wreck of a half-submerged steamer; they were surprised there by an Egyptian fishing-boat and immediately afterwards captured by a squad of British police; Spaccarelli and Memoli found themselves, just before daybreak, near an unknown beach. Here they sank their craft and landed; they soon fell into the hands of Egyptian police, who forthwith handed them over to the British; and finally Feltrinelli and Favale, finding themselves behind schedule on account of engine trouble as well as for the other reasons, destroyed their craft and went ashore just before three o'clock. They managed to elude the sentries and control posts and proceeded into the city. In the course of a number of adventures in which they were helped by a few intrepid and patriotic Italians resident in Egypt, they were able to retain their freedom in Alexandria for about a month; but on the 29th of June they were caught in the network of British police investigation, which was tirelessly searching for them: thus for them, too, began a hard life as prisoners of war.

The causes of the complete failure of this mission may be summarized as follows:

1. The operation had been planned without any time margin for unforeseen events; the conjunction of many favourable circumstances would have been required for success and not all of these actually occurred.

2. The operators were dropped a mile or two to the west of the pre-arranged point; they were unaware of this fact and followed their prescribed course; consequently they arrived at points similarly transposed in the same direction.

3. The shift in the submarine's position had been caused by a current (flowing in the opposite direction to that normally found) which naturally also influenced the approach course of the human torpedoes, increasing their drift west. For these last two reasons the pilots did not get to the harbour entrance or even its adjacent piers.

4. The sharp look-out kept by the enemy, the continual dropping of depth-charges, the effects of which, though reduced by the considerable distance, were none the less a source of trouble, the presence of numerous patrolboats and especially the uninterrupted employment of many powerful searchlights aimed at sea level, which made the zone to be crossed as bright as by day, forced the pilots to dodge about and submerge at frequent intervals, with consequent loss of time which could not be made up in view of the hours of darkness available, the distance to be covered and the speed of their craft.

5. The dazzling effect of the searchlights, moreover, impeded reconnaissance of the coast by the pilots and, for this reason, they were unable to correct the navigational errors resulting from the shift in the release point.

On the subject of the co-operation given by the Italian and German Air Forces and regarding the difficulties encountered in obtaining photographs of the harbour just before the operation, Commander Forza writes:

"The lack of air reconnaissance, though it was not of any importance so far as the targets themselves were concerned (both the floating dock and the submarine parent ship were permanently in the harbour) is nevertheless a matter that should receive serious consideration. It will be necessary in future to provide the German and Italian Air Forces (preferably the latter) with aircraft suitable for executing photographic reconnaissance with the necessary margin of security, thus eliminating the present state of affairs, in which Alexandria is more easily forced by the Tenth than photographed by our aircraft." (From the report of Commander Ernesto Forza.)

In the obstinate and relentless secret war between ourselves and the British around *their* fortified posts and in the waters of *their* harbours, the enemy, after the heavy punishment they had taken in December 1941, had scored a point. But the Tenth Light Flotilla had not lost the game; the able and courageous conduct of Arillo and the superb daring, even with fortune against it, of those making the assault, were giving the British fair warning: they were still exposed to the menace. New levies of bold Italian seamen, competing in generous rivalry with their seniors, continued to attack steadily and inexhaustibly, like the waves of the sea

CHAPTER XIII

THE TENTH FLOTILLA, AT THE SIEGE OF SEVASTOPOL IN THE BLACK SEA

The siege of Sevastopol—Submarines, light craft and assault motorboats in the Black Sea—The Moccagatta Column—Lenzi in command—Transfer from La Spezia to the Crimea— Todaro at his post—The assault boats in ambush and attack —Massarini hits a 13,000 ton vessel—Romano, the Russians at his heels, in sight of the Turkish coast—Four pilots against 40 Russians—Feint landing—Occupation of Balaclava— Cugia takes 13 prisoners—The action at Fort Gorki: another 80 prisoners—Massarini and Cugia torpedoed on the beach— To the Caspian—Brilliant return of the Column from Mariupol to La Spezia.

IN the course of their rapid occupation of the Crimea the German troops had encountered obstinate resistance from the various defence works of the strongly fortified seaport of Sevastopol; although the gallant defenders of the besieged fortress were completely surrounded on the landward side and under heavy bombardment from the air, they were able to withstand the formidable pressure of the German attack owing to the supplies and reinforcements which reached them by sea.

In March 1942 the Germans requested the assistance of the Italian Navy for the purpose of blockading the sea approaches to Sevastopol, interrupting the traffic bringing supplies to the besieged city and thus ensuring elimination of the last pockets of resistance on the route to the Caspian Sea, so that they could attain the ultimate objective of the campaign, the Caucasus.

The Italian Navy, in compliance with the suggestion of their German allies, detached a light Flotilla to the Black Sea under the command of Captain Mimbelli, together with some 'CB' pocket submarines. These units performed the tasks assigned to them with conspicuous success (one of the light craft sank a Russian cruiser and the CBs sank two submarines). The Tenth Flotilla was also ordered to give as much assistance as possible to the accomplishment of the purpose in view.

We decided to send a group of torpedo-carrying and explosive motorboats to the Black Sea, with instructions to provide a continuous service of offensive patrol in the neighbourhood of the port of Sevastopol and on the only possible supply routes.

The extremely special nature of our assault craft, necessitating personnel and materials of a particular type, both for maintenance and employment, as well as the experience gained by previous groups detached from the Tenth to operational destinations at outlying points, gave us the idea of sending the expedition as a motorized column. The vehicles would carry not only the craft but also the personnel, materials and equipment required for their use, thus ensuring the group complete independence; the column would, moreover, be able, owing to its mobility, to follow changes in the land-front. As soon as the column arrived at the most advanced point of the German lines, the craft would be launched and could then contribute, from the sea, to the demolition of the centres of resistance still in being on the coast. It was really the idea, though reduced to a minute scale, of the amphibious combat group, which later had such a tremendous and decisive influence on the course of the war, especially in the case of the American armed forces in the Pacific.

Todaro, head of the surface Department, was entrusted with the formation of the column and set to work with his usual energy, ability and enthusiasm. He summoned to his assistance, with a view to appointing him to the command of the column on its formation, his former second-in-command in the submarine service, Lieutenant-Commander Aldo Lenzi. The latter was a brave officer, always cool and in a good temper, just as tireless at his work and in action, as he loved elegance and comfort in his hours of ease, and of a gay and optimistic disposition. He welcomed his new post, which was a novelty for him as it was for seamen in general, with the keenest zest and at once began operations.

In April, executive orders were received. On the 6th of May the Duke of Aosta, the inspecting admiral, was present at the imposing spectacle of the review of the 'Moccagatta Column of the Tenth Light Flotilla' as it paraded in full war kit and ready to set out. It was made up as follows:

5 MTSM torpedo-carrying motorboats ⎫
5 MTM explosive boats ⎬ lorry-borne;
1 command 'bus, also containing bunks for all pilots; ⎭

1 motorized wireless unit, serving also as office for the column and
   spare part store;
1 Commanding Officer's car;
1 orderly's motor-cycle;
3 tractors;
5 lorries with
5 special trailers for transporting the 5 MTSMs;
2 trailers for transporting torpedoes;
1 motorized workshop, equipped for repairing vehicles, motorboats
   and torpedoes;
1 petrol-tank lorry holding 12,000 litres;
3 tanker-trailers;
1 ammunition trailer;
1 truck equipped with crane for lifting the motorboats.

The armament of the column consisted, apart from personal equipment, of 2 anti-aircraft 20 mm. machine-guns, on tow. Supplies of
petrol, ammunition, machines, spare parts and reserve victuals were
sufficient to enable the column to function independently for several
months.

The personnel section included Lieutenant-Commander Lenzi,
officer-in-charge and pilot; Lieutenants Romano and Massarini and
Sub-Lieutenants Cugia and Peliti, pilots; 14 petty officers, 8 of whom
(Pascolo, Zane, Grillo, Montanari, Ferrarini, Lavoratori, Barberi and
Berti) were pilots; and 29 assistant petty officers and other ranks,
making 48 men in all.

The astonishing rapidity with which the column was got ready,
despite enormous difficulties in the supply of materials owing to war-
time restrictions, was due, apart from the technical and organizing
ability and the determination and energy of Todaro and his collaborators, to the active participation of the Inspectorate-General of
Light Craft; a telephone call from the headquarters of the Duke of
Aosta often solved a problem and enabled situations and difficulties
arising as a result of red tape, which would normally have taken
months to eliminate, to be disposed of in an instant.

On the 6th of May the column, which was to reach the Crimea by
rail, left La Spezia. It proceeded by way of Verona, the Brenner,
Vienna, Cracow, Rostov, Leopoli and Tarnopol, reaching the former
Russian frontier on the 15th. It then went on through Dnepropetrovsk

Map of the Base in the Crimea

The submarine *Scirè*

and reached Simferopol, the end of the railway journey, on the 19th. Here the column left the train for its natural mode of progress, the road. On the 21st, 40 vehicles strong, it arrived at Yalta; "during its passage the column was presented with gifts of flowers by children and peasants." (This quotation and those that follow are taken from the diary of the Moccagatta Column, kept by the commanding officer, Lenzi.)

Finally, on the 22nd of May, the column reached its last destination, Foros, a pretty little town on the pleasant southern coast of the Crimea, not far from Balaclava and to the south of Sevastopol. Here the expedition camped in a glade of nut-trees. The first job to be undertaken was the construction of a small gauge railway and a wooden slipway to get the craft to the coast and to launch them. The work was promptly executed, thanks to the active assistance of a company of German sappers.

There were frequent raids by Russian aircraft which daily bombed and machine-gunned the expedition. Our own two 20 mm. guns were brought into action, these being the only anti-aircraft weapons in the zone. There were a few trifling disputes with the local German Commands, which Lenzi eventually settled in our favour by his good sense and comradely spirit, accompanied as they were by an unshakable dignity and self-respect, qualities which secured him the esteem and deference of our allies.

On the 29th, Todaro arrived in Foros, for he always liked to visit his departments on active service. On the 31st, the group, which had already received the most important local Italian and German authorities (Mimbelli, who was stationed at Yalta with the light craft; Admiral Freiberg, commanding the German Fleet in the Black Sea), was inspected by General von Manstein, in command of all the Axis armed forces in the Crimea

The situation was as follows: the Crimea was wholly in the hands of the Germans, with the exception of the two strongholds of Sevastopol and Balaclava, under siege, their obstinate resistance being exclusively maintained by sea. The task of our craft was to keep watch in front of the harbours and along the access routes, so as to break the flow of supplies and thus enfeeble the defence in order to facilitate the final assault of the German troops. The first operation, carried out by Todaro on the 4th of June, began a series of continual actions, which went on night after night, whenever the state of the sea permitted. To describe them all in detail would be impossible, as well as monotonous,

M

for few of them presented features of special interest: but the activities of the 48 men of the Moccagatta Column during that period, with two or three of their crews in ambush every night in front of the enemy's harbours, and the perpetual daily toil of repairing the craft after damage due to the sea or to frequent encounters with the enemy, under ceaseless machine-gunning and bombing from the air, constituted a silent, effective and admirably unselfish contribution to the fighting, greatly to the credit of all who took part in it. I shall confine myself to recording the more striking of the episodes that occurred as the result of the determination and fighting spirit of our gallant pilots, who were as aggressive and obstinate in their behaviour as so many mastiffs. (*See* map facing p. 176.)

On the 6th of June the five torpedo-carrying motorboats went to sea in support of German assault craft acting against a Russian convoy; on the 10th, Massarini fired a torpedo at the Russian light cruiser *Tashkent* three miles south of Cape Khersones; on the 11th, Todaro delivered a torpedo attack against a Russian torpedo-boat; on the 13th, the assault boat manned by Massarini and Grillo made a daring attack, at extremely close quarters, upon a large motorship of 13,000 tons, escorted by a torpedo-boat and two light craft; the vessel was struck by torpedo and ran ashore, where it was destroyed by aircraft. It was full of ammunition destined for Sevastopol and represented the enemy's last attempt to reinforce the besieged stronghold. On the 18th Romano, while in ambush with his boat at Balaclava, was surprised by two Russian light craft, which started chasing him: to escape them he was obliged to get further and further out to sea, with his pursuers at close quarters, till he sighted the Turkish coast; only when the Russians inexplicably ceased to follow him could he return to base; the same night

> "Two Russian boats were sighted south of Cape Chikiney and engaged by the Lenzi-Montanari and Todaro-Pascolo crews with automatic rifles. The Russian vessels were armed with heavy machine-guns and automatic rifles. The range was kept at 200 metres and the encounter lasted about 20 minutes. Our craft were repeatedly hit and Sergeant Pascolo lost his left arm. At 5.45 a.m. our two assault craft returned to moorings."

On the 29th of June the five torpedo-carrying craft were again at sea, in company with the German Stormboats, with the object of making a diversionary landing on the coast between Cape Feolent and Balaclava, the intention being to tie down the Russian defence and distract it from the main landing, which was to take place in another direction. So as to draw the enemy's attention more effectively, our crews shouted, fired shots, dodged about and made as much noise as possible; in the end, by way of a final display of fireworks, an explosive boat was run ashore in the bay of St. George, piloted by P.O. Barberi (brother of the Barberi who had been on the Suda operation). The violent explosion that ensued added to the confusion which it was desired to create. On the 1st of July, while the Rumanians were taking Balaclava, most courageously, at the point of the bayonet, our five assault craft entered the harbour, preventing any attempt at defence or flight by sea.

"At Balaclava we were received by the Rumanian Colonel Dimitrescu and two companies of infantry. We were regaled with champagne and onions."

On the 4th of July Todaro left Foros to see to the needs of his department and returned to Italy; the activities of the column remained as indefatigable as ever.

"On the 6th July, at 1720 hours, the German local Command notified us of the presence of a boat full of Russians near Foros. An assault craft manned by Cugia and Ferrarini went in search of the enemy. The Russians at first looked like offering resistance, but a few machine-gun bursts some metres from their bows made them think better of it and they surrendered. Thirteen prisoners were accordingly captured. They said they had been at sea for 11 days, but this cannot have been the exact truth. All of them had a few days' growth of beard; they had only sugar aboard and no water. The condition of their boat, roughly patched up as she was, would have prohibited so long a period at sea, for there had been a gale blowing off the coast during the last few days. There was some bloodstained clothing aboard, yet no one was wounded. Later on, I cross-examined one of them, who was an electrical engineer: he told me he could say no more than he had said already; after the war, if we ever met, he would tell me all about it. We gave them something to eat and drink. Some refused to believe that they had been captured by Italian Fascists, for if that were so, said they, their captors would have immediately massacred them. I told them that this was one of the usual yarns of their 'commissars'; but that they could see the truth for themselves. They could not get over their astonishment and some muttered, in Russian, 'Quite decent fellows, these Fascists'."

Meanwhile Sevastopol, with its supplies by sea cut off, was at last stormed by the Germans.

"7th July. Went with Cugia and Massarini by car to Sevastopol. The place was in utter ruins. A cruiser and a destroyer had sunk in the harbour; all docks and workshops had been shattered. Corpses were floating in the water and lying in the streets under clouds of flies. In a courtyard some wounded Russian civilians were crouching on the steps or stretched on the ground, silently waiting for death. No one uttered a cry or a groan; some of the living were still lying among the dead bodies which had not yet been removed. Nothing but dust, heat, flies, dead and yet more dead. Passers-by were avoiding the neighbourhood of a dug-up mine as they walked, or stepping over corpses. And so it went on, first a mine and then a corpse. . . ."

"9th July. Action at Fort Gorki. We shan't forget it in a hurry. Colonel Weber, after the action, told me that not even during the previous war, at Verdun, had he seen so much destruction."

Fort Gorki, near Cape Feolent, was the last pocket of Russian resistance that held out after the fall of Sevastopol. It was built on a towering cliff, with a sheer drop to the sea, and consisted of a series of deep entrenchments and galleries hollowed out in the rock, some of them having an outlet to the sea. Mimbelli's light craft and Lenzi's assault boats received orders to take part in the final attack by blockading the sea exits from the fort. Four units went into action (Lenzi, Romano, Massarini and Cugia); a third member of the crew was taken aboard each of the craft; all were armed with tommy-guns and hand-grenades. At the climax of the action Lenzi left one man aboard each craft and took the rest ashore; the tiny detachment of eight bold seamen entered the galleries from the sea and advanced up them at the double, giving the impression of a much larger force by shouting, hurling

180

their grenades and firing bursts. They took the defenders in the rear, caught them by surprise and made a valiant contribution to the ultimate collapse of the obstinate resistance. A bag of 80 prisoners raked in by the pilots in those rocky caverns was the result of the participation of our men in the action.

"Everyone behaved wonderfully well, the crews turning themselves into infantrymen as if they were old hands at the job, and operations developed as if they had been the subject of prolonged preliminary planning and repeated rehearsals. The assault craft were the last to return to base, having been at sea for as long as 14 hours and 30 minutes."

With the fall of the last pockets of resistance, the object of our group's presence in the Crimea had ceased to exist. But, small as it was, the group had been extremely active and the German Command, which highly appreciated our men's sterling qualities and declared that there would be opportunities for employing their craft, asked for them to be retained for possible further use in support of the operations of the troops.

"15th July. This morning an officer of the German local Command sent us a message to the effect that firing was not permitted except before ten in the morning and with previous authorization. It may be observed that this order had been in force for some time but that no one, least of all the Germans, had taken any notice of it. I was also informed that fishing with explosives was prohibited. This was a practice largely indulged in by our German allies, the only difference between them and us being that, as they had no divers, they left pounds upon pounds of fish at the bottom which our divers, when we got to the spot, carried off under their noses. I sent back to say that I had ordered the Italian seamen to pay exactly the same attention to instructions from headquarters as the German troops did and that, consequently, they had nothing to worry about. This afternoon, as usual, there was a great deal of firing in the woods. I sent my interpreter to the German local Command to ask, in view of the fact that it was quite a bit later than 10 a.m., in which direction I should send my men to co-operate in repelling the Russian landing. The German Command tried to find a few excuses, and put the best face it could on the matter. Accordingly, for a week at least, I was to be left in peace and not pestered by their eternal *verboten*!"

"30th July. At a simple military ceremony Lenzi, Romano, Cugia, Barberi and Montanari were decorated by the Germans with the Iron Cross, for their services at sea."

On the 13th of August part of the Moccagatta Column left Foros, after a stay of two months and a half, and moved on its own lorries, further east, to Theodosia, to lie in wait for submarines, which often made their appearance in front of the harbour and the adjacent coast. Twenty-four hours later, on the night of the 14th, three craft were already at sea; the succession of night patrols began again.

"1st September. At 9.45 a.m., in the presence of all ranks, our flag was struck and the last fraction of the Column departed from Foros amid the sobbing and wailing of the ladies left behind."

The entire group was then collected at Yalta to await its new destination.

"21st September. A Russian submarine in the entrance channel to Yalta harbour, 1000 metres off shore, fired two torpedoes at a small convoy which was coming in; the torpedoes missed the target and exploded on the coast.

Massarini and Cugia, who were sunbathing on the beach a few dozen metres from the spot where the explosions took place, were half buried in showers of stones and earth, but only received light flesh-wounds. Five of our German allies were killed near them. I had a stiff job convincing the operators that they had been torpedoed and not, as they thought, bombed from the air. The discovery that they had been torpedoed in person on the beach in bathing-trunks did not go down very well with the two famous torpedo-experts!"

"23rd September. Preparations in hand for departure of the Column for Mariupol on the Sea of Azov, a stage on the planned route towards the Caspian Sea.

The last three days have been characterized, busy as we were, by continual disputes with the German naval authorities, who object to our taking with us the ten German sailors who have been attached to us for some time now. The matter was finally settled by the declaration on our side that I was going to take the ten seamen with me and that if the Germans liked they could come and get them, in which case I should stay where I was. So eventually the German sailors were left with us.

There was no question of arguing on our part: in view of our reduced numbers, those few German hands were as necessary to us as the air we breathed."

From the 24th to the 27th of September the column travelled by the route Yalta–Simferopol–Melitopol–Mariupol.

"During the run, our tractors and lorries every now and then, strange to say, bumped into geese and chickens, which were then picked up and cooked when we camped in the evening. On going more closely into the matter I discovered, much to my surprise, that the unfortunate creatures had had their fate sealed by a preliminary burst of machine-gun fire!"

At Mariupol the usual skirmishes took place with our German allies, who were reluctant to give our men decent quarters; there were some peculiar and inconclusive interviews with Vice-Admiral Kopf, "a gentleman somewhat stricken in years, a little slow in the uptake and hard of hearing into the bargain". In the end Lenzi issued an ultimatum containing a threat of the immediate return of the whole column to Italy; the result was the prompt assignment to it of one of the finest buildings in the whole city, whence one of the 'PAK' Commands was ejected.

Our expeditionary force had been weakened by a number of cases of sickness and the loss of P.O./pilot Berti, who had died of typhus in hospital; but it had also been reinforced by the arrival from Italy of the new pilots, Gunner Sub-Lieutenant Volonteri and Surgeon Sub-Lieutenant Ciravegna. It remained at Mariupol for some months, waiting for the German troops to get on to the Caspian. The column spent the time putting its equipment in order, for materials were showing the strain of several months' intense activity, and devoting itself to operations of a different description.

"25th October. By raiding the neighbouring maize-fields far and wide, in defiance of the numerous rural police, I have managed to secure an independent food-supply for the Column to last through the winter. It is rather weird to see assault craft seamen sitting in their quarters husking maize like a lot of country boys, but all's fair in war! Nocturnal hare-hunts are also organized and bags vary from 13 to 15 head a time. Maize and hare have become the staple nutriment of the Column. The whole business keeps our bellies full and, apart from that, keeps our 'night-spotting' senses on the alert."

But as the winter came on, the fortune of war turned in favour of the Russians; the Germans began to withdraw along the whole front, including that on which the Italian forces in Russia were destined to be rolled up.

The Moccagatta Column, now commanded by Romano (Lenzi had been called back to Italy in December to take up another Command), left Mariupol in January; it made its way by sea to Constanta (in Rumania); after crossing the whole of East Europe in the face of difficulties which can well be imagined, it re-entered La Spezia in March 1943, *with all its motorized transport, sea-going craft, equipment and reserves*, after 10 months away from its base.

Thus the Moccagatta Column, displaying great gallantry, achieved the objects for which it had been organized and despatched to the Black Sea; it contributed largely to the interruption of the supply traffic to the base of Sevastopol. In particular, the failure of the ammunition vessel to arrive at its destination after being torpedoed by Massarini convinced the Russians that it was useless to renew the attempt and had a decisive influence upon the ultimate capitulation of the besieged city. The expedition demonstrated besides the organizing ability of the Tenth's Command and revealed the possibility of employing our assault craft either in effective contribution to close blockade of a naval base or in support, as an outlying wing at sea, of land operations. The conduct of the men confirmed the belief that in any circumstances and anywhere the seamen of the Tenth could be relied on to maintain their honour, their loyalty and their courage.

CHAPTER XIV

SUMMER 1942: OPERATIONS *CEFALO,*
SOGLIOLA AND *COSTANZA*—ROUND TRIP
THROUGH EUROPE—END OF THE *SCIRÈ*

The Cefalo *goes fishing—Approach to Alexandria—The*
Giobbe Motorized Column at El Daba—Fine exploit by Car-
minati—Alba Fiorita—Berlin: the Officers' Club—The
Germans create a Tenth Light Flotilla and come to school in
Italy—Paris: Admiral Doenitz—Bordeaux: kangaroos—San
Sebastian, Madrid, Lisbon—Last mission of the Scirè *—Gold*
medal for her flag.

WHILE the little squadron of Ungarelli's assault craft, detached to
Augusta, continued to participate in the siege of Malta, the Tenth
Light Flotilla had been engaged in a new form of activity, directed to
the same object.

As already mentioned, some steam-trawlers had been assigned to the
surface department. The idea was to utilize them in the setting of a new
kind of trap for the enemy vessels sailing from Gibraltar in the direction of
the central Mediterranean, with the purpose of carrying supplies to Malta.

By taking advantage of the aspect of these trawlers, which was
very innocent, it was intended to keep them fairly close to the routes
followed by the enemy, which were already precisely known; on
receipt of information by radio from the Supreme Naval Command
that the enemy fleet had left Gibraltar, the trawlers would approach
the zone which it would probably cross that night and there launch
some torpedo-carrying motorboats which they had ready concealed
aboard. The motorboats, taking advantage of their small size and high
speed, would thus be able to attack in waters where their presence was
utterly unexpected, being only able to remain at sea for a brief period
and because the distance to which the trawlers had carried them from
Italian bases was so great.

The trawler thus assumed the new function of transporting the
assault craft to the vicinity of the enemy fleet by sea and acted as a
mobile launching base.

This plan, which was approved in higher quarters, was rapidly carried out: the *Cefalo*, one of the three trawlers we disposed of, was rigged out for the purpose; she took aboard two torpedo motorboats and again loaded up her original equipment of nets and fishing gear; at the same time arrangements were made with the Supreme Naval Command for the transmission of information if a convoy were sighted. The *Cefalo*, after adaptation to her new duties, resumed her former aspect of an ancient steam-trawler, rusty and dirty, leisurely and smoky, literally covered with nets, some hoisted on deck, others trailing in the water; under the heaps of ropes, floats and nets it would have been impossible to guess the presence of murderous weapons of war, ready to dash at high speed against the enemy. Such was the Tenth Light's version of the 'Q-ships' of the previous war.

With two crews, consisting of Lieutenant De Qual, Sub-Lieutenant Garutti and Sergeant Torriani, all three pilots, the *Cefalo* carried out her first operation between the 14th and the 30th of July, 1942. Out of the 16 days spent in lying in ambush, mostly off the coasts of Spain and the Balearic Isles, on only four was the sea calm enough to allow the boats to be launched, had a favourable opportunity been signalled by the Supreme Naval Command; this latter event, however, did not take place. A continual process went on of casting the nets (whenever a ship was sighted), for the better playing of the part assigned, and hauling them back aboard again as soon as the horizon was clear, so as to be ready for action. The operation led to no result, as did also a subsequent one, still under De Qual's command, between the 5th and 18th of August. But the cruise of this small Italian vessel, which ventured alone and undefended into waters entirely under the enemy's control, deserves to be mentioned, not only as an example of the many stratagems thought out for inflicting damage on the enemy in any way possible, but also as doing honour to the pilots who volunteered for these risky operations and to the whole crew of the trawler, consisting of seamen of the merchant navy on war service: these seamen, who ran the same risk as the regular sailors, acted in brotherly association with them in fulfilling the one duty of serving their country at sea.

At this time, preparations were being made for an operation to the Eastern Mediterranean, in which two other trawlers, seconded to the Tenth Light Flotilla, took part.

In June 1942, while the army in Africa was besieging Tobruk, it was decided, in view of the experience at Sevastopol, that the Tenth should make its contribution by ambushing the supply vessels which reached the besieged by sea; with this object plans were made for the establishment of a surface units base in North Africa, near the beleaguered stronghold. At the same time, the trawler *Costanza* (300 tons) was to carry out, in the Eastern Mediterranean, missions of the same kind as those of the *Cefalo* in the Western Mediterranean, by intercepting the Malta traffic coming from Alexandria.

But, owing to circumstances, these two programmes underwent modifications when they were carried out.

In consequence of the victorious advance of the combined Italian and German forces in Africa, which, owing to our naval supremacy since December 1941, had been reinforced on a generous scale, Tobruk had fallen and the front had been pushed as far as El Alamein, not far from Alexandria. Small British units frequently disturbed our line of communications along the Balbia coastal highway by gunfire from the sea.

The plan was to intercept these British units with surprise action by our torpedo-carrying motorboats, posting them on the routes which the British vessels would be obliged to take. On the other hand, experience in the Black Sea suggested our participation in the land operations by disturbing the enemy's front from the rear through encircling its outlying wing towards the sea.

Finally, as regards the occupation of Alexandria, which now seemed imminent, it was desired, for obvious reasons of military and political prestige, that we should precede our German ally by sea. It was considered only fair that the flag of the Italian Navy should be the first to be hoisted in token of victory over the waters of the harbour of Alexandria, which had already been raided by the Tenth Light Flotilla.

In July 1942 the *Costanza*, with three torpedo-carrying motorboats aboard, left Naples: she had, in addition to the crew, the following operators of the Tenth: Lieutenant Giuseppe Cosulich, in command of the fighting service of the vessel and himself a pilot; Sub-Lieutenant Piero Carminati, pilot; Sub-Lieutenant Elio Scardamaglia, pilot, and Captain Vincenzo Portesi, chief engineer. The ship reached Tobruk by following the coastal routes by way of Naples, Salerno, Vibo Valentia, Messina, Cotrone, Taranto, Otranto, Corfu, Prevesa, Patrasso, the Piraeus and Suda.

At the same time the trawler *Sogliola* also arrived at Tobruk, coming from La Spezia with four explosive boats aboard and the operators Sub-Lieutenants Edoardo Longobardi and Mameli Rattazzi.

That same evening the two units were dispersed, for security reasons, in a creek in the vicinity. But this measure did not save them from being bombed by aircraft, probably quite by chance, during the night, though luckily no casualties or damage resulted.

On the following night the units moved to Derna. Here, a few days later, our commanding officer, Forza, joined them by air from Italy, to take charge of the operation. After taking stock of the situation on the spot and assessing the strength of enemy air activity, he decided to abandon the original idea of transporting the craft to the neighbourhood of the front lines at the extremely slow speed of the trawlers and to move them by land instead, taking advantage of local resources. The undertaking was not an easy one, for neither the vehicles nor the materials required to transform a naval into a land expedition were very plentiful. But after about 15 days, an advance section of the column was ready to leave, carrying three torpedo craft and their auxiliary services. The formation was given the name of 'Lieutenant-Commander Giobbe's Motorized Column'.

It was decided to put the craft which had been got ready into action at once. After reconnaissance along the coast, the column halted, at the beginning of the second half of August, in the vicinity of El Daba (White Sands) which was about 50 kilometres from El Alamein and the only point near the lines where the coast formed a slight indentation visible from the sea. This first column included Forza, Cosulich, Rattazzi, Carminati and Portesi. The rest of the expedition, with Longobardi, joined this advanced group later on, but was then ordered to return to Derna, as no chance was seen of employing the explosive motorboats.

At El Daba the column encamped in tents. Slipways were constructed for launching and hoisting the craft, a field radio station was established and the assistance of 50 men from the San Marco battalion was enlisted for the heavy labour. The base was situated in the midst of the coastal defence posts and was connected with Marsa Matruh, Group Headquarters of the Italian North Africa Flotilla, by telephone.

On the night following arrival at El Daba, while the craft were still lorry-borne, enemy destroyers shelled the coast. Their objective was a petrol dump on the road behind the base. No counteraction could be attempted at the time, but steps were taken to enable effective retaliation in case of repetition of the enemy action.

On the night of the 28th–29th of August, when there was a full moon, the enemy again shelled the coast from four large destroyers of the *Jervis* class. So as not to lose a moment, Carminati and his assistant pilot, Sani, swam out to the only motorboat available, which was moored in the offing, and dashed at full speed towards the enemy vessels, the position of which was revealed by the flashes of their guns.

On reaching the formation, Carminati boldly attacked, firing his torpedo at a range of 150 metres, and severely damaged the leading unit. While disengaging, the crew were subjected to violent retaliation by all arms aboard the destroyers and were subsequently attacked with bombs and machine-gun fire at low level by one of the enemy aircraft escorting the naval formation. Fire broke out aboard the craft; the two men of the crew were flung into the sea by the bursting of a bomb which fell a few metres from the craft just as they had left their pilot-seats and were trying to put out the flames. They managed to swim ashore.

At dawn on the 29th the British destroyers were still in sight at 4000 metres off shore. Three of them attempted to take in tow the unit which had been brought to a standstill by Carminati's torpedo and had a heavy list. A message was immediately sent from our base to request the intervention of aircraft. As there was not a single long-range gun anywhere on the coast, German machine-guns and an anti-aircraft battery from the airfield at Fuca fired a few bursts without succeeding in hitting the targets, the range being too great. An hour after the request had been made for aircraft, a formation consisting of nine Stuka dive-bombers and two Messerschmitt fighters appeared above the enemy ships. The fighters, mistaking the situation, attacked our motorboat with machine-guns, as it was drifting about, with its engines still functioning and no one aboard it, a few hundred metres off shore. The frantic signals made by our men on the beach were of no avail.

A petty officer and some seamen, who had been sent out just before, in a boat, to try and salvage the craft, barely escaped with their lives from the assaults of the aircraft, which shortly afterwards blew up their objective. The Stukas dive-bombed the destroyers without success. The enemy vessels, after retaliating violently with anti-aircraft fire against the German air attack, finally managed to take their distressed unit in tow and withdrew in the direction of Alexandria.

Some time later, when the formation was already out of sight, another group of Stukas flew over the base in pursuit of the enemy units; but not even in this second attack did they hit their objectives.

During the expedition's stay at El Daba, Cosulich and Rattazzi made sorties out to sea with the object of intercepting British naval formations making for the coast under our control and also in order to ambush naval traffic outside Alexandria harbour.

Cosulich sighted two units steaming at high speed and followed them for more than an hour before he could reach a favourable position for attack; but, as he was not able to develop his maximum speed on account of the heavy seas, he had to give up the chase.

Rattazzi succeeded in reaching the entrance to Alexandria harbour and returned late in the morning after an unprofitable period of ambush, due to the absence of enemy traffic.

Only a limited number of operations proved possible and they produced no positive results owing to accidental circumstances of one kind or another. The distance between their starting-point and Alexandria harbour was 140 miles there and back, equal to the range of our craft. In view of visibility conditions and the activities of enemy aircraft, the period available for ambush was not more than two hours. Finally the absence of enemy traffic outside Alexandria harbour at night and many difficulties connected with the lack of gear for raising and launching the craft, repairs, camouflage and maintenance at this improvised base, were all reasons for the negative result of the operations.

During this period enemy aircraft attacked almost every night, with star-shells and bombs, the zone in which the assault craft base had been established; the column was also once machine-gunned at night, at low levels, fortunately without any damage.

Towards the middle of September the Italo-German forces at El Alamein tried to break through the enemy lines for the final advance but were obliged to fall back to their starting-points almost at once: the concentration of opposing troops was formidable and British air activity grew daily more intense. The hope of obtaining a decisive victory in North Africa dwindled away, with fatal consequences for the outcome of the war. In view of these events it was decided to withdraw the column to positions further back. Towards the end of September the expedition reached Derna. It was there that the ceremony took place of the awards to Carminati and Sani for their gallant

action of the 29th of August. After this, while Forza returned to Italy
to resume his duties as commander of the Tenth, the column, with the
addition of the craft previously left at Derna, moved on to Alba
Fiorita, a pretty village built by our peasants in the neighbourhood
of Apollonia. This locality was chosen on account of the proximity of
a solidly built wooden pier particularly suitable for launching the craft.

The *Sogliola* and the *Costanza*, with their task completed, returned
to Italy.

The pioneer divers turned out by our school were meanwhile
being employed on an increasing scale. They were taken aboard all
warships of smaller tonnage which did not carry divers, in order that
they might render the useful services pertaining to this speciality: such
were inspection of hulls, cleaning of inlets, minor underwater repairs,
clearing of propellers from cables or other materials which had become
entangled in them. Pioneers were also taken aboard larger vessels in
order to carry out the inspection of hulls at night in case the enemy
might have given us the same type of treatment as we had given him.

Important operations were also carried out by our 'underwater'
men in a different and entirely novel sphere. At Tobruk, after we had
retaken that stronghold, a number of enemy vessels had been found
sunk or half submerged. Under direction by officers of the secret
intelligence service, they were minutely examined by our divers, who
were enabled, owing to the lightness and self-sufficiency of their equipment, to penetrate to places inaccessible to ordinary divers: in this way
secret papers and documents were salvaged which proved of great use
to our intelligence service. Particular mention is due to the investigations carried out on the wreck of the destroyer *Mohawk*, which had
been sunk by an Italian destroyer after a violent duel off the shoals of
Kerkenah in Tunisia. For despite the risks inherent in the nature of
submarine explorations and the ceaseless offensive by enemy aircraft
our divers were able to recover, almost intact, the secret papers of the
unit.

I have thought fit to record these activities, inconspicuous as they
were, as a tribute to the conscientious devotion with which our seamen
silently performed these duties.

After I had relinquished command of the *Scirè*, developments in the
activities of the underwater Department of the Tenth Light Flotilla,

which now took up all my time, obliged me to arrange a prolonged stay abroad. I had to go to Berlin for an exchange of information with our allies concerning naval sabotage; to Paris, where I had to obtain documentation from the German general submarine headquarters which might be of use in connection with our projected actions against North American and South African naval bases; I then had to visit the Italian Flotilla of Atlantic submarines at Bordeaux, to attend exercises and tests relating to the oceanic operations in question; and lastly I was also to go to San Sebastian, Madrid and Lisbon, to see to the organization of naval sabotage groups.

Such was my programme; it was interesting from a professional point of view, for the object was to lay the foundations of an extension of the activities of the Tenth to new sectors of great promise for the future; these were closer military collaboration with our German allies, the widening of the field of action of the assault craft by taking them beyond the Mediterranean, as far as the American bases on the Atlantic and the British in South Africa, the formation of small groups of naval saboteurs (swimmers) to be distributed, suitably disguised, in neutral ports, beginning with those in the Iberian peninsula, which were most frequented by enemy merchant ships.

But the programme was also interesting from a personal point of view: to 'make the round' of the capitals of Europe in the middle of a war, from Rome to Berlin, Paris, Madrid and Lisbon, was a piece of luck which does not often come one's way; I was being given the chance, not so much rare as unique, of obtaining what would be practically a bird's-eye view of the panorama of Europe at one of the most dramatic moments of its history of so many thousand years.

It was not the first time I had been in Germany during the war. I had been there on certain service missions in between the operations of the *Scirè*. The Germans had no training in or knowledge of the domain of naval assault craft (apart from ourselves, only the Japanese, so far as I am aware, had paid any attention before the war to the study of these new weapons, which were employed with success in the attack on Pearl Harbour on the 7th of December, 1940). Nor were these weapons particularly suited to the German military mind, since they demanded, in addition to skill in the water and seamanlike qualities, conspicuous gifts of personal initiative and individual enterprise. During the first months of the war the Germans did not seem interested in what we had accomplished in this field. Now, with the

192

Crew of the submarine *Scirè* on return from the Alexandria attack.
The author is in the centre.

The submarine *Scirè* between two German *U*-boats in La Spezia,
2nd April, 1942. Award of decorations to the crew of the *Scirè*—
she is to the left of the *U*-boat in the background.

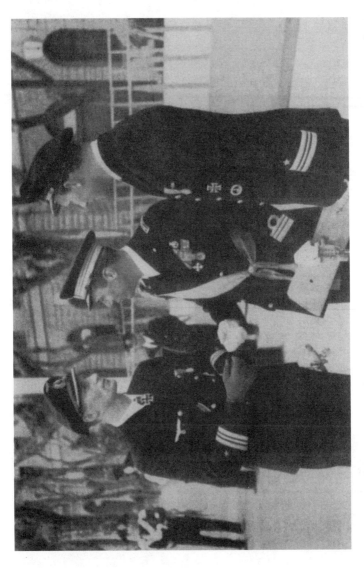

Left to right: VON TIESENHAUSEN (who sank the *Barham*), COMMANDER J. V. BORGHESE, and GUGENBERGER (who sank the *Ark Royal*) taken on 2nd April, 1942.

passage of time and the extinction of the hopes of a lightning victory, when the maritime character of the war had been accentuated in consequence of its extension over the whole world, they had rediscovered, after a delay which was to prove fatal, the old principle that sea power is the dominant and decisive factor in international conflict and their attention had been drawn to the successes achieved by the Italians in the Mediterranean with assault craft (weapons so particularly suitable for a navy inferior in strength to its adversary, which was the case with the German Navy even more than it was with our own). Accordingly, the German naval authorities had decided to develop this speciality and had, therefore, solicited closer contact with the Tenth. Up to that time, the directives we received had been: to show our allies something, but not everything; to reveal such secrets as had presumably already fallen into the hands of the enemy, but not those which we still retained intact; to say nothing of new technical inventions still in the phase of study and experiment. We had obeyed these orders, though the principle that inspired them was not at all clear. It seemed to us, in fact, that divergences, doubts or reservations arising among allies in war ought to find expression and solution in the political field; while in the military domain, where we were fighting for our lives side by side against the same adversary, the closest and most loyal collaboration was not only useful but essential. Such is, precisely, the whole point of military alliances: they are supposed to have the advantage of enabling the adversary to be struck at his weakest point with the entire weight of the *totality of the forces in association* and not by each in isolation, as nevertheless occurred, for reasons which I cannot stay to discuss, throughout the whole course of the war in the case of the Germans and the Italians.

It was however a principle of conduct with the Command of the Tenth to render our military collaboration with our allies active and effective, while always keeping closely to our terms of reference; for we were candid enough to believe that it was the duty of any soldier in time of war to use every means which could assist in obtaining victory for his own side.

In Berlin, which was the Berlin of the summer of '42, where, in spite of the perfect functioning of every cog in the immense machine of 'a nation at war', there could be felt in the air, a year after the commencement of hostilities with Russia, not perhaps, yet, any presentiment of defeat, but a certain disappointment that the expected rapid victory had not materialized, I had a series of interviews with highly placed officers charged with laying the foundations of a German 'Tenth Light'.

The spirit in which the task had been undertaken was typically German: on one side a group of scientists had been mobilized for the study of the weapons proposed, while, as to the question of personnel, the matter was discussed in terms of companies, battalions and even divisions of naval assault men! In Brandenburg I was taken to see their organization; a tremendous stretch of territory, including a lake for tests by water, had been requisitioned; all round it, scattered throughout the beautiful countryside, were houses and farms, in each one of which a group of technicians or of young people from the sabotage schools, who were completing their training, had been established. From everything I saw (and my opinion was confirmed by the way the Germans began this particular warfare) I drew the conclusion that they were barely initiated into the sphere of underwater surprise weapons: they had not yet produced anything that could compare with our human torpedo and 'explosive limpets', but were wasting time in somewhat crude and childish experiments which we had long since discarded.

They had, however, made very considerable progress in the field of sabotage on land. I remember visiting an enormous depot, which it was possible to enter as a German and leave, after a few hours' tour of various departments, completely metamorphosed into an Englishman, a Swiss, an Egyptian or a citizen of any other State whatever, not only furnished with a perfect set of forged personal documents, but also provided with suits, underclothing, cigarettes and periodicals, all of which bore the authentic trade-marks of any country desired. I was shown a great variety of inventions of every description, of the most innocent aspect, which were capable, at any moment required, of turning into instruments of destruction. In addition to the well-known thermos-flask (a careless traveller leaves it in the train or in his cabin on the steamer and it unexpectedly explodes, scattering incendiary material), I was struck by the following items among the traps of simpler construction, which are the most effective: pieces of coal, apparently similar to the rest, which are dropped into a ship's coal-bunker and start a fire there; and a fibre suit-case which arouses no suspicion even after the most minute investigation: here it was the material itself, of which the case was made, that exploded; a tiny time-fuse, which produced the explosion, was hidden in the lock, which was of absolutely normal appearance.

I came to various agreements with the German authorities, within the limits imposed by my Ministry; the most important was for the Germans to send some of their officers and seamen to attend the training courses of the Tenth and study our methods of schooling; after becoming expert, they were to assume the function of instructors at the schools which would meanwhile be set up in Germany.

In pursuance of these agreements, a number of German swimmer pupils, under the command of Lieutenant von Martiny, including some who, on account of their pre-war activities (such as pearl and sponge fishing), were already familiar with the use of the breathing gear, attended the training courses of our Gamma Group in charge of Lieutenant Wolk. It was also agreed to proceed to the exchange of materials: we passed on our breathing sets and divers' suits (rubber articles of first-rate manufacture from one of our great industrial concerns) and they handed over to us quantities of their plastic explosive, extremely formidable in effect and very suitable to our requirements, together with certain other materials which we found useful.

During my stay in Berlin I was invited to dine at the old-established and aristocratic Officers' Club. I was struck by the fact that the rooms were adorned with large portraits of the Kings and Queens of Prussia and of the last Emperors of Germany; it seemed, in that atmosphere, as though nothing had happened since 1918.

On that occasion a colonel in charge of a department of counter-espionage, an officer who had formerly belonged to the Austrian Army, now merged in the German, made me some prophetic observations (in a voice loud enough to be heard by everyone) on the outcome of the war. He said:

"We shall go on fighting to the end, for that is our duty and we can do nothing else: but the game was lost as soon as it started. In spite of the gruelling experiences of the first world war, the Germans have repeated the same fundamental error: they consider the function of strategy to be confined to continental and terrestrial limits, forgetting that Britain cannot be defeated except by sea. The restricted mentality which conceives modern warfare in terms of armies fighting to conquer border territories must succumb to that which studies the great problems of a three dimensional strategy, by air, by sea and on land, and takes the entire globe, considered as an unlimited field, for its province.

Perhaps, after we have paid a terrible price for this error, which will leave disastrous traces in Germany, we shall be able to show, in the third world war, that we have learnt the lessons we have been taught by history."

These words made an impression on me for they represented beliefs which I myself shared. The strategic principles which governed the conduct of the war by the German General Staff, mistaken and calamitous as they might be, could be justified by reference to the geographical position of Germany. But the Italian General Staff, which showed that it shared these ideas, had no such excuse. Although someone had proclaimed as long ago as 1932 that 'Italy is an island' and on another occasion that 'if the Mediterranean represents a road for Britain, for Italy it represents life itself', yet the strategic conceptions of our General Staff remained those of 1914. Our armed forces were organized and developed in inverse proportion to our needs: what was the use of building up an enormous, overgrown army without specialists? What was it for? To dig trenches? Where? The fleet was large, but still not large enough, and the Air Force was utterly inadequate. A glance at the map of the Mediterranean is enough to show that Italy needs a powerful Air Force to ensure control of the Mediterranean and North African skies; she also needs a powerful fleet to collaborate with the Air Force in keeping the sea routes, which are so vital to us, open; she only needs a small, highly mobile and well equipped army, consisting of specialized units, which can be rapidly transported overseas, this last facility being a decisive factor in any Mediterranean war.

The Alpine barrier, in a war restricted to the limits of the victorious campaigns of 1915–18, enabled the safety of our land frontiers to be guaranteed by small forces: such defence would be the natural business of our sturdy alpine troops.

'Italy is an island', but our General Staff, with an inadequate fleet and an absurd Air Force staring them in the face, continued to train dozens and dozens of divisions of infantry, all armed with the model 1891 rifle, all carrying entrenching tools, all in grey-green uniforms, with gaiters and mountaineering boots; the Staff was bogged down in notions derived from the wars of independence: 'The enemy is the German'. It was in vain that Crispi, the islander, gave us Eritrea; it was in vain that Giolitti, though a 'continental' Italian, made the fourth shore of the Mediterranean safe for Italy; it was in vain that Mussolini, by creating our African Empire, opened up the sea routes for his country; these problems did not ruffle the surface of the minds of our General Staff, with the result that in its training of the armed forces and in its conduct of the war, it fell utterly short of its duty and involved the country in military disaster.

Paris is so lovely a city that not even the trappings of war and military occupation can alter its inviting aspect.

I was taken to the German Submarine Headquarters, established in a mansion in the Bois de Boulogne, by Lieutenant-Commander Fausto Sestini, then serving as liaison officer of the Italian Navy at that Headquarters.

Admiral Doenitz, Commander-in-Chief of the German submarine arm since the beginning of the war, received me with great courtesy and was very hospitable. He was a tall man, with the pleasant face of a typical seaman, bright-eyed and quietly smiling; he had the genial manners of a born fighting man and expressed much sympathy with and esteem for the activities of the Tenth. In order to assist me in the researches which were the object of my mission, he gave me access to his secret archives with unhesitating affability and reliance on my good faith; he asked me to consider myself an officer of his staff during my stay in Paris.

The submarine war against the convoys bringing supplies from America to the enemy forces in Africa, Europe and Russia was then at its height: it was extremely interesting to study the organization in Paris which directed the movements of hundreds of individual submarines, thousands of miles away, in all the oceans of the world. So far as I could see, the Command functioned perfectly and its dependent branches rendered most effective service. Doenitz spread, wherever he went, recognition of his extremely agreeable and humane personality, together with that of his relentless application of Service standards; his department was greatly benefited by this state of affairs, as always happens where there is a calm atmosphere and 'chivvying by the boss' does not exist. He was a most energetic organizer and did not spare himself, so that he was able to make high demands on his

197

collaborators and subordinates. He ate and drank with the greatest moderation. As is well known, it was an excellent principle in the German armed forces that the same fare was prescribed for all who served, whatever rank they held; as a result of war-time restrictions on food such fare was reduced to what was strictly essential only. Although in Paris black market operations were practised on a vast scale and orders could be given in any restaurant for all sorts of delicacies not shown on the brief menu, yet in the German Submarine Headquarters mess, where Doenitz regularly took his midday and evening meals, the composition of the dishes was strictly that laid down in the rationing regulations. Here is the menu of a lunch I shared with Doenitz and his officers: cabbage soup (optional), two centimetres of cheese out of a tube and a few grammes of black bread; that was all. As a guest, the only one among all the officers present, I was allowed the privilege of taking *one* glass of wine per meal.

With effective collaboration from the German officers and the valuable aid of my friend Sestini, a regular expert in the German language and psychology, I was able in a few days to collect all the data I needed: it was a matter of summarizing, out of the hundreds of reports received from the submarines sent out by our allies, information concerning the harbours of North America, Brazil and South Africa, so as to determine which of the Atlantic bases, on account of their volume of traffic or as the regular stations of battleships, could most profitably be attacked by our assault craft; their hydrographic characteristics and defence systems had also to be ascertained.

As I looked through these reports I found some of great interest. I remember one from Lieutenant Prien on the forcing of the base at Scapa Flow, which resulted in the sinking of the battleship *Royal Oak*; this was an extremely bold undertaking, in which fortune favoured the risks taken by the courageous Prien, who, after other brilliant actions, went down with his ship.

I preserve the most cordial recollections of the hospitality of the German Submarine Headquarters and of the personality of Admiral Doenitz. My good wishes often go out to that honourable and gallant seaman in his prison at Spandau, where, after being sentenced to 10 years' imprisonment by the Nuremberg Tribunal, he is now atoning for misdeeds attributed to him by the victors, the chief of which, though not acknowledged by the hypocritical participators in that tragic judicial farce, was that of having fought on the side of the vanquished.

At Bordeaux I found an outpost of Italy, the base of our Atlantic submarines, commanded by Admiral Polacchini and including commanders made famous by frequent references to them in the war bulletins: such were Grossi, Fecia di Cossato, Salvatore Todaro (at that time with the Tenth), who all belonged to my own batch; also Gazzana, Prini, De Giacomo, Piomarta and many others.

This naval base, which had been created and was managed, with great ability, by Naval Engineer Major Fenu, was situated in the harbour at Bordeaux, on the Gironde, some dozens of miles from the sea, the personnel being accommodated in villas and châteaux in the environs of the city, among magnificent woods, in a delightful countryside. From Bordeaux our submarines operated on the Atlantic coasts of North and South America and of South Africa; some of them, acting as merchant vessels, made memorable voyages, travelling as far away as Japan, to which country they took German precision instruments and returned with cargoes of natural rubber.

I had arranged for a pocket submarine, the CA, an assault craft with which the Tenth had been experimenting for some time, to precede me to Bordeaux: she was of 12 tons, had a crew of two and was armed with two small torpedoes. I wanted to test the capacity of this craft for the service to which she was destined in our plans, that is to say, the forcing of the naval bases of North America.

The CA required, like all our assault craft, since it could not maintain itself at sea for long, a vessel which could bring it to within a short distance of the base to be attacked; it was by no means an easy problem to solve, in view of the size and weight of the submarine. The solution I had thought out and intended to test was to transport the CA on the deck of an ocean-going submarine, rather after the fashion of a baby kangaroo in its mother's pouch. The submarine *Leonardo da Vinci* was put at my disposal and soon adapted for the purpose by the hollowing out of a 'bed' in the deck, suitable for holding the midget submarine.

Directly the work was finished I assumed temporary command of the *Da Vinci* and started my tests in the maritime area between Bordeaux and La Palice. It was, without doubt, the first time that the strange spectacle was observed of a submarine proceeding with another smaller one perched on its back.

We had grave doubts as to the feasibility of launching the 'baby' without running into trouble, and under conditions which would allow her to proceed immediately on her mission towards the objective, leaving her transport to await her for a day or two on the high seas, at an agreed spot. The tricky manœuvre, however, succeeded perfectly: after surfaced and submerged navigation lasting some hours, I went down to a suitable depth; at the order, "Launch!" the CA, freed from the clamps which held it to the *Da Vinci*, detached itself at once and rose, dripping, to the surface, for all the world like a noisy and arrogant young duckling.

On being boarded by her crew, from a rubber dinghy, she was put in motion and went round and round us in several circles.

The test, therefore, had been successful and an important step forward had been taken on the road to realization of our plans for the future, which were certainly on the audacious side. I was encouraged by this happy result to attempt also the salvaging of the CA from the sea. I took the *Da Vinci* to a suitable depth and the CA manœuvred on the surface in such a way as to lie in line with her destination on deck: I then pumped in air very slowly and the *Da Vinci* thus rose quietly to the surface, catching the CA on the way up, so that by the time the submarine was afloat the baby kangaroo was snugly back again in its mother's pouch.

Our project had thus been found to be practicable: as further tests proved, it would be perfectly possible to carry the CA on the back of a submarine to the vicinity of an enemy base and also, if necessary, take it aboard again, after it had entered the harbour, fired its torpedoes against the target or put its naval saboteurs ashore, and then returned to the open sea.

The execution of the works of adaptation on the *Da Vinci* and those required on the CA to fit the craft for the needs of the important action it was to carry out could, I knew, be safely entrusted to the technical ability, the energy and the devotion of Major Fenu, his officers and the Italian workmen at the base of Bordeaux. The operation against New York had passed out of the planning stage into that of practical preparation.

I went from Bordeaux to San Sebastian by car; it was a splendid run along the excellent French roads, which the war had not affected, first over the Landes and then, from Biarritz to Irun and beyond, along the picturesque Atlantic coast. There was no trouble over entry into Spain and I got no particular thrill out of it, since I had a normal passport in my own name, with the single variant that under 'Profession' the description 'Naval Officer' had been replaced by the less conspicuous expression: 'Independent' (though in my opinion the phrases are by no means synonymous).

At San Sebastian, the summer capital of Spain, the fashionable bathing season was at its height. I met some Italian agents in the naval intelligence service who were in charge of the arrangements for the secret entry into Spain of our operators and their materials. I came to an understanding with them concerning the anticipated speeding up of our work. I was glad to be among Spaniards again, a most estimable people, whom I had got to know and appreciate during the civil war, when I commanded a submarine forming part of the Legion and served in the navy of General Franco.

Madrid was empty and hot. I met there our naval attaché, Captain Aristide Bona, whom I knew already, as he had been my commanding officer in the training-ship *Colombo* during her cruise under sail to North America in 1933. Here, too, I had conversations on the subject of the prosecution and acceleration of our operations against enemy merchant vessels in Spanish harbours.

And finally, in a *Junker* 52 belonging to the German civil air line, I reached Lisbon, the last stage of my journey and in some ways the most interesting. I already knew Lisbon, for I had spent some time there in 1923–25 when my father was Italian Ambassador to the Portuguese Government. Its natural situation, as it lies along the right bank of the Tagus, its architecture and the beauty of its surroundings, the gay and boisterous character of its inhabitants, all make the city extremely attractive and delightful.

The contrast of the war made this aspect of Lisbon even more striking: the city was the meeting-place of Europe and the rest of the world and was frequented by persons coming from the opposing fronts, who took advantage of the neutrality of the country which was their host to struggle, side by side, for commercial concessions or for prestige and to contend bitterly for the possession of a piece of information or a military secret. This cosmopolitan atmosphere and the impression received of isolation from the ancient continent, aflame with war, were accentuated by the fact that Lisbon was free from any of the consequences of the conflict that had now been burdening the rest of Europe for years; the shops were crammed with all kinds of good things, with British and German merchandise unobtainable in the countries of production, displayed side by side in the same window; there were no coupons, no black-out, no restrictions, no ban on dancing. It was a cheerful, smiling world, such as we had long since forgotten and which, perhaps, we should never see again.

I called on our naval attaché, Captain Cugia di Sant'Orsola, and on our Ambassador, Franzoni, who occupied the post held years before by my father. But these were formal visits; I set about the task entrusted to me almost alone. I had to take note of the general character of the enemy mercantile traffic frequenting the harbour; to identify its usual mooring positions, to study the chances of attacking the vessels and the facilities which existed for transporting our operators to the spot and keeping their whereabouts a secret. A blue blouse and canvas shoes enabled me to mingle with the porters and stevedores and to escape the observation, which was pretty sharp, of the staff guarding the approaches to the harbours; after I had found my way about a little, a derelict dredger and an ancient barge belonging to an Italian firm carrying out harbour works suggested a solution of the problem. . . .

I travelled from Lisbon to Madrid: I had interviews with our agents in the Algeciras and Gibraltar zones; I went on to Bordeaux, where I had a lucky meeting with an intimate friend, Carlo Fecia di Cossato, who had just come in with his submarine from a successful mission which had kept him three months at sea.

And then, after a brief stay in Paris, I returned to the headquarters of the Flotilla at La Spezia to put into practice the projects for which I had been laying the foundations.

At La Spezia I learned grievous news: the *Scirè*, while on her first operation after I had relinquished command, had been lost at sea with the whole of her crew!

In consequence of the threat to Alexandria which had developed with the rapid advance of the Italo-German troops to El Alamein, the British had provided for the dispersal of their ships from the harbour, of which they believed that they would soon be deprived. Some units had been sent to the Red Sea, others to the harbour at Haifa. It had been planned, during my absence, to deal with the latter vessels by means of an assault by swimmers provided with 'limpets', who were to be taken to the spot by the *Scirè*. As the port was only a secondary one, it was not anticipated that its forcing would present insuperable difficulties.

Lieutenant-Commander Max Candiani, head of the plans and operations department of the Flotilla, was sent to Rhodes on the 1st of August to direct the operation. A request for the necessary air co-operation was addressed to the Tenth Corps of the German Air Force (General Keisler) which had its headquarters at Candia (Crete).

Operational orders directed that on the evening of the 10th, one and a half miles from the entrance to Haifa harbour, the *Scirè* was to send out eight swimmers to attack targets inside the harbour; she would remain at her post, in case they got back, until three in the morning; then she was to set course for return to Leros. The swimmers were to have their targets assigned them by the commanding officer on the basis of the latest air reconnaissance reports which would be transmitted by radio in the following order of precedence:

(a) submarines; (b) cargo steamers; (c) destroyers and torpedo-boats; (d) cruisers; (e) support ships, troop transports, tankers and patrol vessels.

The *Scirè*, commanded by Zelich, reached Leros from La Spezia without mishap on the 2nd of August, with the material aboard required by the swimmers (divers' suits, breathing sets, explosive devices).

On the morning of the 6th the *Scirè* left Leros after taking aboard the following personnel of the assault swimmers group:

Observation swimmers: Commissariat Captain Egil Chersi, P.O./ diver Rodolfo Beuk.

Assault swimmers: Petty Officers Aurelio Morgan, Paolo Baronchelli, Eugenio Del Ben, Luca Ricciardi, Delfo Caprioli, Sauro Mengoni, Erminio Fioravanti, Guido Fontebuoni.

Surgeon to the expedition: Sub-Lieutenant Pietro Gnecco.

Photographic air reconnaissance of Haifa by the Tenth German Flight/Group proceeded normally, though some trouble was experienced, on the 7th and 9th; data as to the condition and whereabouts of the British ships in the harbour were passed on without delay to the *Scirè*. The headquarters of the Italian Aegean Air Force were also requested to assist in the operation:

"General Longo understands the nature of the request and assures me that he will do his best to comply with it, though the ceiling of the Italian aircraft does not permit photographic reconnaissance in this area, which is equipped with excellent radio direction-finders and strongly defended both with A.A. guns and by experienced fighters. The Germans use for this type of operation, and not without taking serious risks, special aircraft (J 86) with an operative ceiling of over 12,000 metres." (From Lieutenant-Commander Max Candiani's report.)

These remarks indicate that our Air Force, despite the unquestionable bravery of the pilots, was not in a condition, owing to the lack of serviceable machines, to photograph enemy bases; a tragic state of affairs!

According to the photographic air reconnaissance carried out by Germans on the 9th the following units were in harbour: 2 light cruisers, 3 destroyers, 8 steamers, 4 of which were large, and 4 large tankers, 5 patrolboats, 2 torpedo-boats and not a single submarine.

The weather forecast read calm sea with a spreading mist. Everything indicated a successful ending of the mission, should the *Scirè* have managed to accomplish the difficult task of reaching a point favourable for the dropping of the operators.

Extracts from Candiani's diary of the operation follow:

"13th August. From to-night onwards information regarding the operation carried out will be due from the *Scirè*.

14th August. Nothing yet heard from the *Scirè*; I deduce that the delay may be due to the desire of the submarine, in view of the presence of enemy units in the zone, not to incur the risk of radio messages being overheard.

1700 hours. Still no news. Sent message to *Scirè* requesting information.

2200 hours. No reply from submarine.

15th August. 0800 hours. Still no news. Requested Aegean Air Force to carry out special reconnaissance with three 1007 craft in the direction Rhodes–Haifa.

1500 hours. The three reconnaissance aircraft, which flew to within sight of Haifa, returned without information.

1800 hours. Requested Tenth German Group to carry out confirmation reconnaissance over Haifa, which I hope will enable me to get evidence as to the fate of the *Scirè*.

16th August. More unsuccessful attempts by the Tenth Group to carry out recognition over Haifa. The aircraft were attacked in every possible way and could not reach their objective.

Still no news of the *Scirè*.

17th August. 0500 hours. A 'J 86' has left Crete in a renewed attempt at reconnaissance.

0800 hours. Received message that aircraft had succeeded in photographing harbour from 9000 metres and will bring print to Rhodes.

2200 hours. Photograph obtained and examined. No vessel damaged and no trace of forcing of harbour. I infer that the *Scirè*, of which there is still no news whatever, never reached the stage of dropping the operators."

From information furnished by the British Admiralty we are aware today that the submarine *Scirè* was sunk off Haifa on the 10th of August by the torpedo-boat *Islay*. The 50 members of the crew and the 10 operators taken aboard for the mission disappeared into the sea with the unit. The bodies of two of the swimmers, of Captain Chersi and P.O. Del Ben, were washed ashore on Haifa beach four days later and buried in the city cemetery.

While the *Scirè*, with her usual audacity, was approaching to within the shortest possible distance from the harbour, repeating the prodigies of valour so often performed in the past, she became involved in the enemy's network of vigilance, either by being spotted from the air or through being discovered by hydrophonic means; in the swift and decisive duel that followed, and during which Zelich and all his men fought with extreme courage, the *Scirè* received her death-blow from depth-charges and ended her glorious life, with all her crew, at the bottom of the sea.

Her flag was decorated with the gold medal for gallantry in war, the citation being as follows:

"As a submarine operating in the Mediterranean she returned safely from a number of successful ambushing operations; was then appointed to act with assault divisions of the Navy in the heart of enemy waters and frequently participated in forcing the most heavily fortified bases of the Mediterranean. During repeated attempts to achieve the purpose in view, she encountered the gravest difficulties, provoked by the violence of enemy retaliation and by sea and current conditions. After overcoming, with the most utter disregard of danger, obstacles both artificial and natural, she succeeded in completing the task entrusted to her, surfacing at very short distances from the entrances to the very heavily fortified enemy naval bases selected and accordingly launching the special weapons, which caused the sinking of three large steamers at Gibraltar and, at Alexandria, serious damage to the two battleships *Queen Elizabeth* and *Valiant*, the total loss of these two vessels being only prevented by the shallow depths at which both units were anchored. Subsequently, in the course of a further particularly daring expedition, she was mercilessly attacked and disappeared in enemy waters, thus gloriously terminating her brilliant war-time career."

CHAPTER XV

SIEGE OF GIBRALTAR—THE VILLA CARMELA— TWO ATTACKS BY SWIMMERS—THE *OLTERRA*

*Gibraltar again—Signora Conchita needs sea air—The Villa
Carmela, most advanced base of the Italian Navy in enemy
waters—14th July: 12 swimmers versus a convoy:
four steamers hit—The derelict Olterra and a crazy idea of
Visintini's—A launching base at Algeciras for human torpedoes
—Our boys: 'merchant seamen' on the Olterra—15th
September: another steamer sunk by the swimmers—The
'Great Bear' flotilla—5th December: Force 'H' enters
Gibraltar—8th December: Visintini's last mission—A
mother: two sons fallen in action, two gold medals.*

GIBRALTAR, like Alexandria, was always one of our principal
objectives; as the headquarters of the British Fleet in the western
Mediterranean, a supply base for the Atlantic squadron and a most
important junction for enemy mercantile traffic, its harbour was the
marshalling yard for convoys from America and South Africa bound
for the Mediterranean and Britain. Huge convoys, of 30 or 40 steamers
at once, used to gather in Gibraltar roads, laden with food supplies for
the population of Britain and war material of every description, for
the most part of American origin; thence other convoys would leave
for the north, the south and the Mediterranean. It was, accordingly,
logical that the offensive activities of the Tenth should continue to be
concentrated on Gibraltar; another reason was that, owing to the
distance of this stronghold from Italy, our aircraft were unable to
interfere with enemy naval activity in that region; it became obvious
that, in practice, it was only our special seaborne craft which, on
account of the particular methods they used and the gallantry of their
commanders and pilots, were in a position to carry offensive action
by the armed forces of Italy as far as Gibraltar.

Study of the three operations conducted by the *Scirè* in Gibraltar
roads and consideration of the situation which had since arisen led to
the following conclusions:

1. The submarine had proved itself an ideal instrument for transport of the human torpedoes to within striking distance, but difficulties and risks grew, with each operation, in proportion to the development of measures of detection and defence taken by the enemy.

2. The submarine, owing to its very nature, could only execute a limited number of missions and could only take three craft with it on each; moreover, in view of the hours of darkness required to complete an operation, the months from late spring to autumn prohibited any such action, the nights being then too short.

3. The special geographical position of Gibraltar, in such close proximity to a neutral country, had enabled 22 out of the 24 operators sent out to return; the Birindelli-Paccagnini team was the only one that had fallen into the enemy's hands after the bold undertaking which had brought it, in October 1940, within a few metres of the *Barham*. It had been relatively easy for the Gibraltar operators to reach the Spanish coast, so might it not be equally easy for them to reach Gibraltar starting from the coast opposite?

4. Finally, a new element had cropped up in the situation: dozens of steamers laden with war supplies were to be found every day in the bay of Algeciras, a few hundred metres from the Spanish coast, beyond the reach of the protection of any harbour defence, and thus constituting an easy target.

Accordingly, we set out upon a fresh warpath; in addition to or instead of the transporting submarine we had to think out some other means of getting our operators to the coasts of Spain, a few hundred metres from the convoy vessels and a few miles from the entrance to the harbour. If we could find such a means the attacks could be kept up indefinitely, so as to give the enemy no rest; for, in addition to the actual damage which might be inflicted upon him, he would be obliged to resort to wide dispersal of his materials, energies and personnel in order to defend himself against a hidden menace, the source of which would be bound to remain a mystery to him. Naturally, in accordance with elementary rules of prudence and international convention, the whole business would have to be organized without the Spaniards knowing anything about it, so as to avoid, both for them and for ourselves, the risks which would be run if they were involved in our plot.

Some time ago a clever technician and a good Italian, Antonio Ramognino, had submitted to us the plan of a boat which might

The *Ambra* and her crew.

LIEUTENANT-COMMANDER MARIO ARILLO of the *Ambra*.

The Tenth in the Black Sea. Meeting between Commanding Officer TODARO and the German General VON MANSTEIN.

facilitate the approach of saboteurs to vessels destined for attack; some models were in course of construction and looked promising. I am not prepared to give a technical description of this craft, as it remains a secret and may still be used in the future. In the spring of 1942 Ramognino volunteered for active service, was appointed to the Navy and joined the Tenth Light. He was then sent by us to make investigations of the bay of Gibraltar, from Spain, in order to study on the spot the chances of establishing a coastal base from which his craft might go to sea. At his suggestion, and taking advantage of the fact that he had a Spanish wife, the charming *Signora* Conchita, we decided to rent a bungalow in the vicinity of Maiorga Point, on the north coast of Algeciras Bay near La Linea, and about 4000 metres from Gibraltar: it had a direct view of the maritime area where, at distances between 500 and 2000 metres from the beach, the merchant vessels of the British convoys were in the habit of anchoring (see map on p. 59). The Ramognino couple went to live in the bungalow, giving out that on account of Conchita's poor state of health she needed sea air and bathing. The couple, being on their honeymoon, were supposed to be only occupied with the house and their domestic affairs, but in fact they were getting the place ready for the double purpose which it was to serve. The first thing they did was to put in a window looking on to the bay and Gibraltar harbour, camouflaging it on the outside with a cage of ostentatiously twittering green parrakeets.

While we waited for Ramognino's boats to be completed, we thought of utilizing the Villa Carmela, the most advanced base of the Italian Navy in enemy waters, for the carrying out of an operation against the merchant vessels of the convoys anchored in front of it, the habits, mooring methods and defences of which we had already been studying. This would be a much easier task than the forcing of the harbour (for it would not be necessary to deal with obstructions) and also one which, owing to the short distance between the ships and the Spanish coast, would give the swimmers a chance; for the latter would not need any complex and heavy equipment which it would have been difficult to get into Spain, they would simply swim out with a few 'bugs' to fasten to the enemy hulls.

In July 1942 a batch of swimmers was issued with all the gear necessary for the operation—three 'bugs' per man. The detachment was commanded by Sub-Lieutenant Agostino Straulino, the well-

o

known champion racing yachtsman, and consisted of the following operators: Sub-Lieutenant Giorgio Baucer, Petty Officers Carlo Da Valle, Giovanni Lucchetti, Giuseppe Feroldi, Vago Giari, Bruno Di Lorenzo, Alfredo Schiavoni, Alessandro Bianchini, Evideo Boscolo, Rodolfo Lugano and Carlo Bucovaz, comprising 12 men in all.

They were smuggled into Spain and later, after the operation, were to be smuggled out of it. Six of them went to our submarine base at Bordeaux, whence they were taken into Spain in small groups by the naval agents placed at the disposal of the Tenth. Some were hidden in the false bottom of a lorry; others, less fortunate, went on foot, climbing the Pyrenees for hours and hours of wearisome footslogging. The other six, taken aboard an Italian cargo steamer as part of the crew, deserted, in accordance with their orders, at Barcelona, and were duly denounced for this crime by the skipper, who was not in the secret. Escorted by our agents, they were all swiftly transported to Madrid, where a forwarding station had been organized; finally they reached Cadiz by car and there went aboard our tanker, the *Fulgor*, in the guise of seamen who had arrived to replace the former crew. Thence, on the 11th and 12th, employing various improvised means for eluding the strict watch kept by the Spaniards at the three control points on the route, the operators made their way to Algeciras and went aboard an old Italian vessel, the *Olterra*, which had been interned and was lying at anchor in the harbour. It was from the *Olterra*, instructed by Visintini, who was one of those aboard, that they at last sighted the roadstead and the ships at anchor there which were their targets. At dawn on the 13th, one or two at a time, they were taken to the Villa Carmela; they were able to get a perfectly clear idea from the window of the best way to conduct the attack and the most suitable point for entering the water (out of sight of the Spanish sentries, who were numerous and vigilant on that part of the coast, and the many British spies that were about) as well as, finally, to choose their targets and study the details of their structure and anchorage.

On the night of the 13th–14th the action took place.

The operators, under cover of darkness, slipped silently out of the bungalow, dressed in their special suits and provided with explosive material previously despatched to the spot. They crossed a patch of garden and descended to the beach, protected from the notice of indiscreet eyes by a low wall and taking advantage of the dry bed of a watercourse. Finally they adjusted the fins to their feet and waded into the sea to begin the waterborne stage of their mission. A large convoy was in the roadstead; the leader of the group had already assigned his men their respective targets, and each had spent a long day studying his prospective victim. They began to swim, but by methods suitable for war, permitting speed without fatigue, no puffing and blowing or splashing, no gleams of phosphorescence, not a sound. They wore their seaweed-trailing head-nets, camouflage to deceive any possible watcher aboard the steamers.

The swimmers, bearing their tools of destruction, swam to the ships, eluding the sharp eyes aboard the British patrolboats, which darted about the roadstead in all directions at night. The operators became motionless and disappeared below the surface when the beam of a searchlight flashed over their heads, playing a shrewd and daring game which proved both their youthful zest and their grown men's cunning and discretion. A ripple too much, too impatient a stroke of the arm, might ruin everything. They plunged under the hulls, fastening the 'bugs' at the most vulnerable points; then they set out on their return swim, happy to have brought their tasks to a successful conclusion.

At 3.20 a.m. the first two operators swam ashore close to where one of our agents was waiting to pick them up.

"It is interesting to observe," he wrote in his report, "that, though I was standing in the lee of a bush less than 10 metres from the sea and was watching the water with the greatest attention, I never saw the two operators till they were already ashore and slipping across the sands towards our rendezvous. In my opinion it would be difficult to see them at a distance of more than 6–7 metres."

This circumstance was the result of their intensive and highly organized training at the hands of their instructor, Wolk.

Seven of the swimmers, however, were arrested, as they landed, by *carabineros*; through the prompt intervention of our consul at Algeciras, Bordigioni, they were set at liberty provisionally on condition that they held themselves at the disposal of the Spanish authorities. Two more managed to get ashore wholly unobserved and the twelfth landed, unseen, at La Linea bridge, reaching Algeciras on foot, where he reported to the Italian consulate; he had covered a distance, eluding all control-posts, of some 16 kilometres! The health of all except two remained unaffected: one was wounded in the foot by the propellers of a British patrolboat, the other received a violent shock after the explosion of a depth-charge and complained of pains at the backbone.

At the Villa Carmela they were attended and refreshed by the efficient and plucky *Signora* Conchita, who served them with cognac, coffee and liqueurs. After resuming their seamen's kit they were immediately afterwards taken by car to Cadiz, where they had a well-deserved rest on the *Fulgor* while awaiting repatriation, which took place, as had their arrival, in secret, one or two at a time, so that they left no trace of their movements behind them.

The results achieved, nevertheless, were not in proportion to the meticulous preparations that had been made or the valour displayed by the operators, owing to the imperfect functioning of some of the explosive devices.

Four steamers, however, were more or less seriously damaged to such an extent that they had to be hastily run ashore to prevent total loss.

They were the *Meta* of 1578 tons, the *Shuma* of 1494, the *Empire Snipe* of 2497 and the *Baron Douglas* of 3899, making a total tonnage of 9468.

On the unexpected occurrence of these explosions and settlings the other steamers in the roadstead were immediately transferred to the interior of the military harbour.

The British remained long in ignorance of the source of the attack. They only began to get an inkling of it when they picked up in the roadstead a rubber suit which had unexpectedly come to the surface. This precious and informative relic was immediately taken possession of and despatched by air to the Admiralty in London, where it was subjected to close examination.

The daring conduct of the 12 operators was recognized by the award of the silver medal for gallantry in war.

The behaviour of all the more or less confidentially employed persons who contributed to the success of this difficult and brilliant operation was excellent; officers of the Navy and of the Army and Italian civilians who composed our clandestine organization in Spain showed throughout the course of the mission, as they did in those which preceded and followed it, high levels of intelligence and patriotism; it is with great regret that for obvious reasons I am unable to give the names of all who deserve to be remembered. In the preparation and organization of the enterprise, Visintini played a predominant part; Ramognino's assistance, too, splendidly seconded by his wife's, was most useful.

On the 10th of June, 1940, on Italy's entry into the war, the steamer *Olterra*, belonging to a Genoese shipowner, happened to be in Gibraltar roads; in accordance with the orders received by radio the skipper took his vessel to the shallows of Spanish territorial waters and scuttled her to prevent this serviceable war booty from falling into the hands of the British. The ship remained there for 18 months, half under water, with a heavy list and exposed to the remorseless action of weather and waves; the few men of the crew retained aboard by the owner eked out a primitive and uncomfortable existence, their main function being to safeguard property rights in the vessel as prescribed by international law relating to wrecks at sea.

The existence of the *Olterra* was disclosed to the headquarters of the Tenth by Ramognino on his return from his mission of investigation in Spain; the idea, which was subsequently to take clearer shape, then immediately occurred to us of utilizing the wreck, with its very innocent appearance and its Italian flag, so near the stronghold of Gibraltar, for our offensive purposes.

The original idea soon passed into the stage of realization.

I tackled the shipowner without revealing to him the true reason for our sudden interest in his vessel, but merely referring vaguely to 'war needs of the Navy'. The owner proved to be accessible and a willing collaborator.

At our suggestion the owner instructed a Spanish salvage company to refloat the *Olterra*: he 'intended to refit his ship for handing over to a Spanish company which had made him a favourable offer for it'. The vessel was soon brought to the surface and was then towed into Algeciras harbour. Here, since the long retention of her engines and boilers under water had immobilized her, she was moored to the end of the outer pier. Ever since the 10th of June, 1940, a Spanish military guard had been posted there, the ship being regarded as interned owing to having been found in territorial waters on her country's declaration of war.

In this way we established a support point of our own, an Italian one in front of Gibraltar, on the other side of the roadstead, six miles from the stronghold; we now had to find the most effective way of using the opportunities thus afforded (see map on p. 59).

Absurd as the notion might appear and difficult as it might seem to put into practice, Visintini proposed that we should turn the *Olterra* into a fixed base for our assault craft: she would then replace, with tremendous advantages over her predecessor, the transporting submarine and take over the latter's functions as a launching station for human torpedoes. No objection was seen to the proposal, but first the *Olterra* would have to be adapted for the purpose.

We began by collecting a crew of our own to replace practically all the merchant seamen (the skipper, Amoretti, and the chief engineer, De Nigris, remained aboard and collaborated with us in first-rate and loyal style), both so as to keep our secret and because so great an increase of the crew of a vessel in that state would have aroused suspicion. Algeciras swarmed with British secret agents; and the *Olterra* was actually moored under the windows of the British consulate, its staff well swollen by naval intelligence service officers, after the fashion of British consulates in maritime cities all over the world.

Lieutenant Visintini, whom we have already met as the former bold invader of the harbour of Gibraltar, was appointed to command the *Olterra* group. He enjoyed our utmost confidence in view of his professional abilities and his personal traits of seriousness and deliberate audacity, but above all on account of the spirit of selfless devotion with which he discharged his duties. His brother Mario, a most gallant fighter pilot, had fallen shortly before in the last stages of the defence of Italian East Africa; he had gone up in a machine which by then was practically unserviceable, after having shot down no less than 17 enemy aircraft, to oppose, utterly alone now, the overwhelming odds of the British wing formations. The valour of the pilot had been betrayed by the inadequacy of his weapon, and he had gone to rejoin his father, who had been a strenuous patriot of Istria. . . . Now Visintini was addressing himself to a new enterprise, firmly determined to emulate his brother Mario who, he used to say, "Aids and directs me from Heaven".

Visintini chose the men of his group from among the technicians and seamen of the Tenth.

They were all sent to spend a few days on a steamer moored at Leghorn, to get some practice in the necessary 'deck technique'; they learnt from the merchant seamen aboard how to dress, eat, spit, smoke and use merchant-service slang; thus when they joined the *Olterra* they could not be suspected. They were given log books and forged cards and names, though using genuine passports, and were sent in groups of two or three at a time to join the *Olterra* at Algeciras: they were the new merchant crew relieving the old one and workmen detailed to carry out repairs to the steamer.

They included technicians appointed to set up a workshop in the *Olterra* for reconstruction of the human torpedoes to be sent from Italy piecemeal. The job was arduous and complicated, but in a few months, down in the hold, a complete workshop came into being, furnished with all the instruments and machinery necessary, including a Diesel group for charging the accumulators. A cistern was also rigged up for trimming and water-resistance testing of the torpedoes; it consisted of a flooded compartment of the hold. And one fine morning work started on the careening of the ship; the *Olterra*, with a heavy list and down astern, was seen to raise above water a large area of her port-side hull. An awning protected the seamen from the sun (and from indiscreet watchers) as they hammered and painted. No casual spectator could have supposed that an oxygen flame was cutting a huge hole in the ship's flank. By the evening the work was finished, the *Olterra* resumed her normal aspect and the hole had disappeared under water. In this way a direct connection had been made between the flooded compartment of the hold and the open sea, through which the 'pigs' could enter or leave the vessel wholly unobserved.

All this went on under the noses of the possibly bored Spanish sentries on deck and on the quay and in defiance of the undoubtedly attentive eyes of the British spies who infested the neighbourhood, well over a thousand kilometres from Italy and only 10 from Gibraltar.

Life aboard was apparently such as would be typical of any merchant ship undergoing refit or repairs. A few seamen, mostly dirty and dressed in ancient garments which had survived many a long voyage and were decorated with those characteristic patches, crudely stitched, irregularly shaped and multi-coloured, which seamen put on themselves during a voyage, with calloused fingers more used to the manipulation of ropes than to the niceties of needlework, were lounging on deck performing the usual tasks with weary gestures; they smoked pipes with chewed stems and bowls that emitted insufferable clouds of stinking tobacco smoke, sometimes proceeding from a cigarette-end; they had not shaved for months, there was practically no discipline and 'miking' was openly practised and tolrerated. During leave ashore the seamen frequented the taverns of the waterfront; they were always short of money and cursing the war, the owner, the skipper and the cook for getting them into this jam and leading them a dog's life of it. Sometimes, on payday, they would accept the company of some degraded and well-known local siren and return aboard late at night, rather drunk and discordantly hiccuping the lines of some old ballad that reminded them of the village at home. . . . Everyone in the locality knew them by this time and took no particular interest in them: they were just a typical crew spewed out by an old hulk that was mouldering slowly away in the miry waters of a neutral harbour. . . . The Spanish sentries aboard grew familiar with them; they called them by their Christian names, even by half Spanish, half Italian nicknames, the natural consequence of some conspicuous or ludicrous physical or mental characteristic; not such bad sorts, those poor devils of Italians. . . .

But lo and behold, one of these same Italians goes below (probably to sleep, the lazy hound); he drops down the ladder, passes along a corridor, knocks three times at an invisible door—it opens, there is another ladder. He descends it into the lowest depths of the ship, impenetrable to those who do not know the secret. Now for the surprise! A dozen men are at work, calmly, alertly and competently, among machines, dynamos, tools and electrical equipment all in perfect order and ready for action. " 'Morning, Captain!" In the cordial atmosphere of a military discipline imposed and acknowledged as a necessity and not as a pointless nuisance, orders are given and the lazy seaman who has just arrived assumes his true character: it is the chief electrician Rossi, come to see to his dynamo with the dexterous touch of an expert; or Carlini the carpenter; or Bonato the chief mechanic, come to connect the oxygen containers for charging the breathing sets. . . . The double life led aboard requires the most perfect control from everyone of every movement, every word. A single piece of carelessness would be enough to start suspicion. . . . But it's not going to happen: no one suspects anything and no one ever will, for months and months, not even when, over there in the roadstead, one steamer after another will blow up a few hundred metres from Gibraltar, under the noses of the dumbfounded British.

In the autumn of '42 Visintini was at La Spezia, at the headquarters of the Tenth. He submitted his report of what had been done: the

216

vessel was now ready to function as an assembly shop and launching base. From the close observation he had been carrying out (simply to lean over the rail of the *Olterra* was to get a direct view of Gibraltar right ahead) he had obtained data for the preparation of possible operations. The British had multiplied their preventive and defence systems, silent patrolboats cruised continually in the roadstead and in front of the harbour entrance, depth-charges were exploded every 10 minutes, hydrophones and other detection methods were in constant practice. But Visintini assured us that all this would not be enough to stop him: if the chance came, they would go all out for success. And if they failed . . . "Well, we should have done our best; and, for my own part, I should have joined my brother Mario . . ." (From Visintini's diary.)

Arrangements were made at La Spezia for the despatch of war materials to the *Olterra*; the great human torpedoes, seven metres long, weighing nearly two tons, were dismantled by sections; the warheads, the detonators, the fuses, the breathing sets, the divers' suits, were all packed in cases or crates constructed in such a way as to appear to the probing eye of the customs official or casual spectator nothing more than ordinary materials required for the refit of the *Olterra*: there were boiler tubes, pistons, engine cylinders and valves; there were oil-drums for the Diesel aboard (but there was another tin container inside the drum with the breathing sets in it). The containers were stamped with the Genoese shipowner's markings, since he was ostensibly forwarding material for the repair of his vessel. The torpedoes were followed by their pilots; Visintini and his second, the powerfully built, taciturn and devoted Sergeant Giovanni Magro, were accompanied by Gunner Sub-Lieutenant Vittorio Cella, a tall, fair, handsome young man, a Lombard of the Lombards, with Sergeant Salvatore Leone and Midshipman Girolamo Manisco, short, sturdy and quiet, all concentrated energy and determination, with P.O. Dino Varini.

The pilots, also disguised as seamen, joined the *Olterra*; they superintended the assembling of the craft to which their lives and, even more important, the success of the operation, would be entrusted; they studied, without appearing to do so, the movements of the enemy, the patrolboats cruising to and fro, the type of the obstructions erected, the times at which the harbour entrance gates were opened and the depth-charges dropped, the mooring-places of the vessels, the hours at which they arrived, the formation of the convoys and all the activities which went on in the enemy's stronghold over there, a few thousand metres from the *Olterra*. Elvio Moscatelli was the group's surgeon.

"It was his habit to put on an old suit and go out into the bay with the local Spanish fishermen; in this way, with a fishing-line in his hand, and selling fruit to the seamen of the Allied merchant ships, he used to watch what went on in the roadstead; he observed with special interest the British divers of the security service at their work of looking for explosive charges which he knew very well were not there. When, subsequently, he met Crabb (a British officer in charge of the underwater security service at Gibraltar during the war) in Italy, he did not wait to be introduced. Said Moscatelli: 'I know you well by sight; I have watched you and your men for hours and hours at a time!' "[1]

Visintini, a methodical and painstaking man who did not leave anything to chance, set up in one of the cabins of the ship, which had a port giving a view of Gibraltar, a regular observation post, from which officers who relieved one another at routine intervals kept a continuous watch, throughout all the 24 hours, on what went on in the enemy's camp; every part of it, every fresh occurrence and every movement was noted and included in the material studied for preparation of the mission. From the port, with the old ship's binoculars, one could see clearly everything that happened in Gibraltar, even the men walking about on the moles and the soldiers checking over the machine-guns aboard the vessels, or the sailors scrubbing the decks ... but no doubt, with better lenses, a more detailed study could have been made of the methods of opening and closing the net obstruction defending the north gate. The British consulate, right in front of the *Olterra*, boasted a pair of magnificent naval binoculars of colossal size, 64 magnification type, mounted on a tripod, for enabling those worthy fellows to keep in visual touch with their base. "That's just what we want!" Visintini casually observed on one occasion. Two days later the 64 magnification binoculars had reached their new destination: they remained directed at Gibraltar, but through the observation port of the *Olterra*; our operators stood at the lenses; it was legitimate war booty.

[1] Goldsworthy, *Sunday Express*, 25th of December, 1949 and later issues.

218

Fishing was the most popular of our men's recreations. A boat often left the *Olterra*, both by night and by day, with two seamen aboard; one rowed leisurely or lazily let the boat drift on the current under the lee of the convoy steamers, or as far as Gibraltar, as near as possible, while the other fished, line in hand. They were a couple of our men who wanted to clear up some doubtful point or ascertain some detail; the British patrolboats often passed very close to them, so that in the end their crews and periods of duty became well known to us. Thus the preparations went on, in the midst of the network of mobile and fixed defences and counter-espionage measures of the enemy; thus the men of the 'Great Bear Flotilla', as they called their group, under Visintini's directions, made ready to strike a decisive blow, as soon as a favourable opportunity arose, at the British Fleet.

Meanwhile, some time having elapsed since the previous operation, which had produced a certain amount of dismay at Gibraltar, owing to the mysterious apparition and vanishing of our swimmers, a similar action was undertaken.

On the night of the 15th of September three operators, Straulino, Di Lorenzo and Giari, in defiance of the intent watchfulness of the enemy, succeeded in attacking some steamers at the far end of the roadstead of Gibraltar and caused the sinking of the *Raven's Point* of 1787 tons.

The action proceeded by the same methods as that of the 15th of July, to wit:

(*a*) organization by our agents on Spanish territory;

(*b*) concentration of the operators at Algeciras aboard the *Olterra*;

(*c*) departure thence to take to the water at the Villa Carmela.

The number of operators was fixed at five. Two arrived in Barcelona in the guise of seamen aboard the *Mario Croce*; they deserted in the usual way, were picked up by one of our agents and taken straight to the *Olterra*. The other three were selected from among the seven operators who had participated in the action of the 14th–15th of July and who, after having been arrested by the *carabineros* on duty, were still holding themselves at the disposal of the local authorities; an equal number of seamen from the *Fulgor* took their places, undetected by the Spaniards. The material was smuggled into Spain by methods in which we had now acquired a good deal of practice. The concentration of the operators and their materials on the *Olterra* took place quite normally and without arousing any suspicion.

In the evening of the 14th the five swimmers, accompanied by one of our 'local experts', left the *Olterra* and arrived at the Villa Carmela, whence they set out to the spot at which they were to enter the water. It was decided at the last moment to cut down the number to three, this being the total of the objectives then in the roadstead. At 2340 hours the first swimmer entered the water, followed at a short interval by the other two. Each carried three explosive devices. The two reserve operators waited with one of the agents, hiding in the shadows of a building some 20 metres from the beach.

After seven hours, at 6.20 a.m. on the 15th, Straulino came ashore at the spot he had started from. He had not been able to carry out his task on account of the extremely close watch kept by the enemy around the target: three patrolboats attended the steamers, never going more than 50 metres away from them, and a rowing-boat, in each case, circled their quarters, while searchlights were switched on all the time. Straulino had twice attempted to reach the vessel assigned to him, but after his second attack, as a result of frequent submersions to evade detection by the patrolboats (on one occasion he fancied he might have been seen, for a number of small charges were dropped, fortunately without injuring him) and of an attempt to approach underwater, the oxygen in his breathing gear had given out, thus precluding all possibility of submersion for the purpose of applying the 'bugs'; he was therefore obliged to desist from the attack.

As it was now broad daylight Straulino and the operators who had remained ashore, after waiting in vain for their two companions, returned to the *Olterra*.

Thence they could perceive that one of the objectives, actually the steamer *Raven's Point* of 1787 tons, had begun to list and was rapidly sinking astern. Shortly afterwards her bows also went down. So the attack had accomplished some results after all!

Di Lorenzo, though he had had his breathing set cut through by the propellers of a patrolboat, had reached and attacked his own target, while Giari, not having been able, on account of the current, to get near the steamer assigned to him, had fastened his 'bugs' on a neighbouring vessel, which afterwards turned out to be the same as Di Lorenzo had attacked. Giari had swum back ashore and re-entered the Villa Carmela, unobserved, while Di Lorenzo, as he landed, had been surprised by a Spanish sentry and was now held captive by the *carabineros*.

The action had developed under particularly unfavourable conditions, i.e.:

(1) the great distance of the objectives from the spot at which the water had been entered. The British, in fact, after the July operation, no longer left any steamer, unless it had an explosive cargo, in the open roadstead, but collected them in the interior of the harbour or at the east end of the bay, in front of the military harbour;

(2) all night long there had not been a breath of wind and the sea had been extremely smooth, thus greatly increasing the risk of detection;

(3) current had been running at a higher speed than had been anticipated;

(4) there had been mobile watch kept in the roadstead during the night by five patrolboats, which moved continually round the steamers and dropped small depth-charges from time to time, and searchlight activity had been constant.

For this operation Straulino and Di Lorenzo were awarded the bronze medal, while Giari received a silver one.

Aboard the *Olterra* Visintini and his companions of the 'Great Bear Flotilla' were preparing, materially and mentally, for the great enterprise. The atmosphere in which they lived is evident from the contents of certain sheets of paper, hastily jotted down by Visintini, in pencil, in those days and addressed to the young wife, to whom they were handed over after his death, who jealously preserves them in memory of her unforgettable Licio:

"*23rd November* '42. . . . When I think of you, your image alone is enough to keep alive in me, most intensely, the spirit of a warrior *vir*. I know that I shall fight, with deliberate, cool and unqualified determination, because I want to feel the chains that weigh us down come loose, fall and rattle as they break. When I die, my beloved, it will be in the blaze of the freedom for which we are fighting.

24th November '42. . . . I can feel hatred rising again in me for those who failed to teach us to look hard into the the blue-grey, cold eyes of our enemies, the tyrants from the North. The duty

221

which I and my companions have to carry out is of *enormous* importance. Shall I be worthy of my trust?

27th November '42. Since I have been here I have ceased to belong to you, for my work occupies my thoughts completely. The stakes are enormous, but the prospects are excellent. Shall we succeed in carrying out my devilish plans? So far we have done wonderfully well; it is the clearest proof that Papa and Mario are guiding me, from the Beyond, in the path of a miraculous destiny. I tremble in the presence of such far-seeing beneficence and call upon all my energies and all my resources so that I may continue to deserve it. I know I am wearing myself out but that is of no importance. My sweet Maria and you, my poor, dear mother, with your prayers to Heaven and your invocations for God's mercy, do not despair if I seem so far away from you. We are once again involved in conflict, this time a decisive struggle, and it is for you to stand beside me, ever near, leaving my movements free and protecting my back from the cunning onslaughts of the enemy. Watch over me, my wife and my mother, while we six men prepare for the coming mortal combat.

30th November '42. A whole week has now passed since our last leave-taking . . . it seems an infinity to me, above all because no one can say whether our next meeting will be in a few hours, a day or a month. It even seems, so great is the uncertainty, that we may never meet again. . . . The thought, when it strikes me, clutches at my heart like a hand of cold steel. . . .

5th December '42. After four months of uncertainty, struggle and incessant work, my great plan is ripe. To-morrow evening 3 craft and 6 men will be ready to leave. . . . The enemy is an experienced veteran but we do not fear him, for our hearts are exalted and utterly resolved to conquer at all costs. For many evenings now we have been able to calculate, hour by hour and minute by minute, the various forms of deadly peril that await us and are designed to prevent us reaching our objectives. But bursting bombs and darting patrol-boats only strengthen our will to defy the enemy offensive and scorn it. The stakes are enormous, the game is a complicated and subtle one, but nothing can stop us now save death. Such a death will reward our ardour by conferring on our souls the eternal peace that follows a life conscientiously devoted to the service of our country.

On the eve of an event of such magnitude you will understand how completely matter is dominated by spirit and to what extent the latter tends to live its own life. . . . When I think that the adventure may turn out badly, my sorrow for you two who must live is lessened when I cannot help smiling to think that, by reason of the power of the laws of nature, one day, my beloved, you will have a baby boy who will be able to live through, in innocent gaiety, the careless springtide of youth."

An imposing naval squadron entered Gibraltar a few hours later: it consisted of the battleship *Nelson*, the battle-cruiser *Renown*, the aircraft-carriers *Furious* and *Formidable* and numerous smaller escort units.

"*6th December* '42. Last night, when I told you we were on the eve of an important event, I told the truth without realizing it, for, in view of the arrival of the British squadron, I have decided to take action to-morrow night. From this base, which we have set up 2000 miles from Italy, from this splendid island of the Italian spirit, we shall launch our liberating offensive. We shall set out and fight in the name of the immortal civilization of Rome and the sons who have proved worthy of her and who struggle and suffer bereavement in their families and in their homes.

And if God wills to protect us, our success, alone, will be an eloquent reply to the facile and barbarous triumphs of the haughty British power.

We, the pigmies, are resolved to strike you boldly to the heart, in the fleet which is your greatest pride. And we expect that this gesture of ours will cause the world to realize, once and for all, what stuff we Italians are made of.

Just that, and nothing more."

On the 7th of December Visintini again writes in his diary:

"The craft are ready and the charges are fused. The three torpedoes stand in line: they look like three tiny, but powerful, ships of war. We are going to sea and, whatever happens, we are determined to sell our skins at a very high price.

The objectives are: the *Nelson*, myself; the *Formidable*, Manisco;

the *Furious*, Cella. I believe I have made provision for every eventuality. At any rate, my conscience is perfectly clear because I know I have dedicated my whole being to the success of this operation. Before we leave I shall pray to God that He may crown our labours with the award of victory and that He may protect with His gracious favour Italy and my bereaved family!"

The same evening, the three crews, Visintini and Magro, Manisco and Varini, Cella and Leone, left the *Olterra* by the underwater outlet and made for Gibraltar, at hourly intervals. All three, after a short time, were obliged to return aboard, after discovering a fault in the assembly of the steering-gear; the trouble was soon adjusted and they took to the water again.

The defences surrounding the harbour in which vessels of such importance were now collected showed much activity; in addition to the usual patrolboats, cleaving the waters of the roadstead in every direction, and the searchlights incessantly sweeping the sea, depthcharges were being dropped at a steady interval of *three minutes* (*see* map on p. 59).

Visintini, who had been the first to start, was inspired with incomparable resolution. In spite of the explosions in the sea, with their violent repercussions, he traversed the roadstead and reached the obstructions which barred access to the harbour. This was the most serious of the obstacles: a way had to be opened through it, while depth-charges burst all around. With indomitable courage Visintini continued his operations: "Nothing can stop us now save death."

The zone of the explosions lay between him and his objective: *he entered it.*

There was a burst nearer at hand, then another, and yet another . . . the mission of Visintini and Magro had ended. Our comrade Licio had rejoined his father and his brother Mario; the faithful Magro accompanied him on that last journey.

Manisco, too, reached the stronghold; under the Detached Mole he was seen by a sentry, picked up by a searchlight and fired on by artillery and machine-guns: he tried to make off, so as to draw the enemy's retaliation on to himself and thus distract it from his companions; finally, after 20 minutes' submersion, pursued by depthcharges dropped from a patrolboat, stunned and harried by the bursts, he could only abandon the operation; he sank his craft and, rising to the

Foros base (in Foros Bay in the Crimea): maintenance work on a torpedo. TODARO in centre.

The Villa Carmela: observer point between the two windows.

British convoy seen from Villa Carmela beach.

surface, climbed, with his second, on to an American steamer anchored close by. They had scarcely got aboard before the crew, many of whom were Italo-Americans, surrounded the two pilots, aiding them and praising their exploit; everyone wanted to shake hands with them. The pilots stripped off their divers' suits, which they did not want to see fall into the hands of the British: the Americans themselves hastened to throw the garments into the sea.

Cella and Leone, surprised, while they still remained far from their objective, by the now general alarm of the stronghold, succeeded, despite pursuit by numerous patrolboats, in evading capture by a series of prolonged submersions. When at last Cella, at the ultimate stage of human endurance, decided to give up the undertaking, he surfaced and made for the *Olterra*; he then realized, with grief and stupefaction, that his second, Leone, had disappeared.

At dawn, out of the six brave men who had set out the evening before, only Cella returned to the *Olterra*: Visintini, Magro and Leone had perished in their daring attempt, Manisco and Varini were prisoners of war.

The following official British announcement was made:

"At 2.15 a.m on the 8th December, three Italian assault craft, carrying two men each, tried to penetrate the harbour at Gibraltar. One was seen by a sentry, caught by a searchlight, fired on and sunk by artillery and depth-charges. The crew was picked up by a merchant vessel moored near the Detached Mole and, though the two men were circumspect in what they said, it is believed that they were brought from Italy by the submarine *Ambra*. A second pair of men *entered the harbour* but perished as a result of depth-charge attack, while it seems that the third pair were killed before they could reach the harbour."

Some days later the bodies of Visintini and Magro came to the surface of the waters of Gibraltar harbour. They were buried at sea and accorded military honours. A wreath was presented. It was thrown by Lieutenants Crabb and Bailey of the underwater security service of Gibraltar. Their task had been, that night, to investigate the hulls of the ships after the attack, though they knew that at any moment they might be killed or mutilated by the explosion of a warhead with a radius of half a mile.

"It was a generous gesture, which was little understood by other personnel on the Rock."[1]

Today the mother of Visintini, who has given her two sons to her country, one as an aviator and the other as a seaman, bears, with melancholy pride, their memorial, pinned to her breast in the shape of two gold medals. Licio's widow, Maria, was unable to retain the consolation of her little Valeria, born a few months later, for the child failed to survive.

[1] Goldsworthy, *Sunday Express*, 25th of December, 1949.

CHAPTER XVI

THE *AMBRA* AT ALGIERS. THE TUNISIA CAMPAIGN

Mission of the Ambra *against convoys at Algiers—Attacks by human torpedoes and swimmers—Enemy losses—Our British competitors in the game attack Palermo—The* Cefalo *as a mobile base for assault craft—Pantelleria and Bizerta—Attempt to force Bona harbour: death of Todaro—The 'Giobbe Column' reaches Bizerta—The retreat from Tunisia.*

ON the 11th of November, 1942, the Anglo-Americans landed in French North Africa; the Tenth was ordered to participate, so far as possible, in opposing the flow of supplies to the powerful new army which our own forces, at once concentrated in Tunisia, had to confront.

Air reconnaissance showed that the harbour at Algiers and the roadstead outside were crammed with steamers unloading: it was decided to carry out a combined operation there, composed of human torpedoes for penetrating the harbour and assault swimmers for simultaneous attacks upon the shipping in the roadstead.

The submarine *Ambra* was appointed to act as transport, commanded as before by Lieutenant-Commander Arillo.

Operational orders stipulated that the submarine, after entering the roadstead, should despatch the operators while the vessel remained submerged; then she was to await their return, after the attacks had been executed, until 2 a.m., with a view to trying to pick them up; she was then to start her return voyage. The operators were to give precedence to targets outside the harbour itself.

A group of young volunteers on their first war-time assignment was selected to carry out the action.

As the general conflict went on and on and the activities of the Tenth continued to extend, the problem of providing personnel grew more and more difficult. A torpedo pilot needed at least a year's training before he could be operationally employed; there were few who, during their apprenticeship, were found to possess the physical and moral qualities required to carry through an operation; the examination for final selection was accordingly a stiff one and a very large number of candidates were rejected. Each mission meant that six operators were 'used up', i.e. as a rule, captured; it was necessary to hold at least as many in reserve, so as not to lose chances which might occur at any moment. Work went on at high pressure on the Serchio; though the pilots in training during the war (not before it, as should have been the case) were never exceedingly numerous, there were always enough of them to meet the operational requirements which continued to crop up from time to time.

In the case of the present undertaking, the targets being steamers and not warships, double warheads were adopted for the first time; in other words, the normal warhead containing 300 kg. of explosive, the quantity required to blow up a battleship, was replaced on the torpedoes by a charge of equal penetrating form as a whole, but divided into two sections, since 150 kg. of explosive were more than enough to sink a steamer, thus doubling the offensive capacity of the craft.

The adaptation of weapons to operational requirements as imposed by circumstances was one of the typical features of the Tenth's system of work. The normally applicable principle, *Find a use for the weapons available*, was replaced in our case by another, *In a given tactical situation, find the weapon and the modes of using it which will ensure control*. It was a profitable and interesting procedure, necessitating the use of an organ which High Commands, possibly owing to the habit of military discipline, often keep in a state of semi-coma, namely, the brain.

On the 4th of December the *Ambra* left La Spezia with the following operators aboard:

TORPEDO CREWS: Lieutenant Giorgio Badessi (group leader) with P.O./diver Carlo Pesel; Engineer Lieutenant Guido Arena with P.O./diver Ferdinando Cocchi; Midshipman Giorgio Reggioli with P.O./diver Colombo Pamolli. *Reserves*: Lieutenant Augusto Jacobacci with P.O. Battaglia.

ASSAULT SWIMMERS: Gunner Sub-Lieutenant Agostino Morello, group leader; P.O. Oreste Botti, Grenadier Sergeant Luigi Rolfini, Bersaglieri Sergeant Alberto Evangelisti, Sergeant Gaspare Ghiglione, P.O./diver Giuseppe Feroldi, P.O./gunner Evideo Boscolo, Stoker Rodolfo Lugano, Seaman Pioneer Giovanni Lucchetti and Private Luciano Luciani; 10 men in all.

Transport by submarine proceeded without a hitch. On the 8th of December heavy seas were a considerable handicap to the swimmers, particularly those who came from the Army, these, though excellent in a swimming pool, not having yet quite found their 'sea-legs'. But, if the physical condition had to suffer, the morale remained at a high level. All through the day, on the 11th, the *Ambra*, making for Algiers, proceeded submerged, taking every precaution to avoid being sighted by the enemy and slipping along the sea-bed so as to pass beneath the explosive barriers which, it was understood from intelligence received, protected the entrance of the bay. In the evening the submarine entered the roadstead and came to rest on the bottom. At a depth of 18 metres Lieutenant Jacobacci, provided, of course, with his breathing gear, emerged from the hatch.

He rose to the surface and began scouting operations: he took note of the situation and transmitted his information to the commander of the submarine, with whom he was connected by telephone. As Jacobacci found that the harbour was still some way off, the *Ambra* went further into the area of the roadstead, still slipping along the bottom, while the scout, on the surface, superintended and directed navigation.

He warned the submarine that a sunken destroyer lay about 400 metres ahead of her; finally, at 2145 hours, he telephoned the information that the submarine was now in the midst of a group of six steamers: the three nearest were of considerable size. The *Ambra* stopped: it now lay at about 2000 metres from the south entrance to the harbour. At 2230 hours the swimmers, who had lost a certain amount of time putting on their special equipment, began to emerge from the hatch; at 2300 hours they had all left; it was now the turn of the torpedo crews. At 2320 hours all the assault personnel had been despatched. The scout on the surface, who had been showing the operators, as fast as they came up, the positions of their targets, finished his duties and dived back aboard. During the period of waiting to pick up the operators a number of explosions of depth-charges, some of great violence, were heard aboard the submarine. At 2.30 a.m. Jacobacci carried out a further scouting investigation on the surface and returned to say that he had heard the voices of some of the swimmers who were looking for him but had not been able to make contact with them; the voices had also been heard by a neighbouring steamer, which had fired a few machine-gun bursts in their direction.

The time set for the return of the operators had already been exceeded by an hour: the *Ambra* could not wait any longer, especially as the incessant series of depth-charge explosions gave Arillo the clear impression that the base must have been alarmed. At 3 a.m. the *Ambra* started navigation to clear the roadstead. At this stage she came into violent collision, accompanied by ominous creaking and crashing noises, with a sunken wreck, and only disentangled herself with some difficulty. On the 15th of December she re-entered La Spezia with her arduous mission successfully completed.

Badessi, group leader of the piloted torpedoes, on coming to the surface, perceived that, owing to the delay in the despatch of the operators, the harbour could not be reached in time; he therefore assigned targets in the roadstead to each of his companions (giving two to each crew, the warheads being double). He himself reached his target, but his craft was not functioning properly, having been damaged, perhaps, by the heavy weather the submarine had encountered, and after five failures to attack he was at last compelled to desist. He then tried to return aboard; but not being able to find the scout, turned shorewards, taking in tow two swimmers he met on the way; after destroying his craft and making his way to the beach, he was almost at once captured, with his second pilot Pesel, by a French sentry-post.

Arena emerged from the submarine in very bad physical shape: he had a splitting headache and felt sick and weak. He was determined, nevertheless, to carry out his task and, relying on the loyal support of his companion Cocchi, he made straight for the targets assigned him by Badessi.

"After a few minutes, while navigating on the surface, I found I had run against a human body, which I pulled in for a few seconds, thinking it might be that of one of our swimmers in trouble. But I discovered at once that the body was clothed in the ordinary way, not in rubber, and so I let go of it: the corpse must have been that of a victim of one of our bombing raids on Algiers, which we had heard of by radio communiqué a few days before, while on the voyage." (Extract from Lieutenant Arena's report, made out on his return from prison.)

Towards one o'clock Arena heard, as Badessi, too, had, "the report of a single gun, followed by the sounding of two warnings by siren,

230

within a few minutes of each other, and two explosions, accompanied by the noise of motorboat engines. These events caused me to assume that we had been detected and that the alarm had been given." He continued on his way nevertheless. He reached the nearest steamer of the two assigned him, attacked it and, with the efficient aid of his second, Cocchi, fastened both his charges under the hull. On the way back he could not find the submarine and made for the shore, which he reached at 4 a.m., towing the swimmers Luciani and Ghiglione, whom he met on his way, still carrying the 'bugs'. By 6 a.m. all four had been captured by Scottish troops encamped in the vicinity.

Reggioli and Pamolli stated: "The sky was overcast, visibility not good and phosphorescence considerable." In compliance with Badessi's orders to attack ships in the roadstead, Reggioli traversed the sector assigned to him, on the look-out for the more important steamers. He identified a tanker of 9–10,000 tons and decided to attack her. The vessel had no bilge-keel ledges (a very rare case) and the attack was therefore concentrated on the propeller shafts. Immediately afterwards, with his second charge, Reggioli attacked a motorship of about 10,000 tons, this time at the centre of the keel. During clearance navigation he was caught in the beam of a minor searchlight and had two or three bursts of machine-gun fire aimed at him, luckily without effect.

He, too, failed to find the submarine and made for the shore, arriving there at 4.30 a.m.

"The explosions began at 5 and continued until 7 o'clock. From the place where we were we could see nothing owing to the darkness and a light sea-mist. The same day, from aboard the auxiliary cruiser *Maidstone*, to which we had been taken, we noticed, near the entrance to the harbour, a certain amount of wreckage at the point where we had attacked the first ship and, while we were on the road from Algiers to Camp 203, we saw the motorship which we had attacked (No. 59, flying the flag of the United States) stranded on the beach with her stern carried away.

At 7 o'clock we were on our way to the interior and at 7.30 we were handed over to a squadron of French spahis." (Extract from the report of Midshipman Reggioli, handed in on his return from prison.)

The swimmers' adventures may be summarized as follows: the

231

group leader, Morello, on surfacing, collected his men and, being within sight of the vessels to be attacked, distributed the targets:

"Before leaving on the operation I had received orders from Commanding Officer Borghese to send at least two operators against each ship of more than 10,000 tons. I therefore instructed Ghiglione and Luciani to attack the first vessel lying at the extreme left of the semi-circle formed by the steamers; Rolfini and Evangelisti were to attack the second, Lugano and Lucchetti the third and Boscolo and Feroldi the fourth. But as I noticed that the target which I myself, with Botti, had to attack was of considerable size, I ordered Feroldi to come with me.

I instructed Botti to attack this vessel on the starboard side, and told Feroldi to take her astern, while I went to port. I left them and approached the vessel; on my way I heard voices aboard her and saw someone leaning over the rail smoking. Suddenly, a small searchlight aboard was switched on and began to probe the water, catching me in its beam; as I had my camouflage net on, I turned the back of my head to the reflector and remained on the surface, being sure that the people aboard would never guess that what seemed a clump of seaweed was the head of an operator. It was about half-past twelve when I fastened my charges." (Extract from the report of Sub-Lieutenant Morello, handed in on his return from prison.)

Morello then swam off to look for the scout; he could not find him and made for the coast, where he arrived at 4 a.m.

Botti and Feroldi carried out their attack, under the ship already mined by Morello, without a hitch, in accordance with their orders.

Lucchetti was almost at once detected in the water, captured and taken aboard the very vessel which Morello attacked, actually at about the same time as the attack was being carried out. Such was probably the reason for the alarm given at the base, as heard by several of the operators. Rolfini and Evangelisti attacked their assigned target. Boscolo attacked this same vessel, it having proved impossible for him, owing to the current, to reach his own target; Ghiglione, Luciani and Lugano became exhausted and did not complete their tasks, being taken in tow by the torpedoes piloted by Badessi and Arena with their charges still on them.

The British Admiralty admitted the following losses:

"At 1230 hours on the 12th December several assault craft attacked merchant ships in the bay of Algiers and attached mines or explosive devices to the hulls of certain vessels. The steamers *Ocean Vanquisher* of 7174 tons and *Berta* of 1493 tons were sunk, the *Empire Centaur* of 7041 tons and the *Armattan* of 4587 tons were damaged; 16 Italians were captured."

During the operation as a whole, Reggioli and Arena sank one vessel each: another was damaged by Reggioli's second charge; a third, attacked by Morello, Feroldi and Botti, was presumed to have been sunk and, lastly, the ship attacked by Evangelisti, Rolfini and Boscolo was sunk or damaged.

Though the mission had been a success, its results were less than might have been expected from the employment of so many as 16 operators. Yet, even according to the British announcement, another 20,295 tons of enemy shipping had been put out of action.

The commanding officer, Arillo, was awarded, for this outstanding operation conducted with the *Ambra*, of which he had formerly been in charge during the Alexandria operation, the gold medal for gallantry in war; the successful operators were decorated, on their return from prison, with the silver medal.

In the official list of losses undergone during the war, published by the British Admiralty, there figure, among the other names mentioned, the following:

2nd January 1943. Palermo. *Chariots* XV, XVI, XIX, XXII, XXIII, of 1.2 tons.

8th January 1943. La Maddalena. *Chariots* X and XVIII, of 1.2 tons.

19th January 1943. Tripoli. *Chariots* XII, XIII, of 1.2 tons.

These 'chariots' were simply piloted torpedoes, which, with Britannic precision, were listed with their exact tonnage.

We never found out what happened during the British operation against La Maddalena. There are strong grounds for supposing that the two British piloted torpedoes, with their crews, disappeared at sea, for some unknown reason, before they ever got near the harbour they were making for.

The other attempt, the one against Tripoli, had the purpose to blow up the steamers which the Italians intended to scuttle at the entrance to the harbour in order to block the way for Allied maritime traffic directed to Tripoli with supplies and reinforcements for the 8th Army due to occupy the town.

The two chariots were carried to a point off Tripoli by the submarine *Thunderbolt* (ex *Thetis*). But both teams were unsuccessful: the one, composed of Sub-Lieutenant Stevens and the second man Buxton, who managed to penetrate the harbour, was immediately captured; the other, made up of Lieutenant Larkin and P.O./cook Barey, landed on the beach to the west of the harbour. They were taken prisoner right away by the Germans, but were able to escape after three days and join the British who had meanwhile arrived.

The members of both crews had forged papers describing them as Germans in order to mislead the Italians.

On the 3rd of January, 1943, in accordance with a telegraphic order received from the Ministry, I travelled to Palermo to hold an enquiry in connection with the sudden attack on that harbour, the night before, by assault craft. Out of the craft taking part in the action, two had been lost at sea before arrival at the harbour: one lost its officer, Lieutenant Cook, who was drowned, and was sunk by the second man, Seaman Worthy, who then swam to land; the remaining two managed to reach the harbour and penetrate the net barrier. The crew, consisting of Lieutenant Greenland and Seaman Ferrier, fastened their warhead to the hull, under construction and still only a shell, of the light cruiser *Ulpio Traiano*, 3300 tons; the extremely violent explosion smashed the light metallic structure, which remained, for its greater part, out of water, due to the shallow depth. The other crew (Sub-Lieutenant Dove and Seaman Freel) attached their charge to the propeller shaft of the merchant motorship *Viminale*, and caused the vessel such slight damage that a few days later she was able to leave the harbour for refit elsewhere. The British assailants had also attached to the hulls of some light units a number of rudimentary little charges rigged up in a primitive sort of way, which did not explode, owing to defects in their construction, and were promptly brought to the surface by our divers.

This attack, called 'Operation Principle', was the first the British made with human torpedoes: the Italian assault weapons had found imitators.

The five British operators who had survived were all captured in open country a few hours after they had landed; the two craft, which had no self-destructors, were picked up intact and closely examined. They were imitations of our first 'pigs', without any special innovations or improvements. Their divers' equipment (which was all found in the water) showed very serious technical shortcomings: in particular, the suit, which, unlike ours, covered the head completely, was very defective and probably the chief reason for the high mortality incurred by the British in such operations, even before they reached their objectives.

The cross-examination of the prisoners, to which I devoted some time, was rather interesting in some ways.

Though they were, naturally, somewhat reticent, and none of them were prepared to reveal the secrets entrusted to them, I nevertheless obtained some useful information in the course of these long conversations.

It appeared that the British, after our first unsuccessful attempts on Gibraltar, had picked up fragments of one of our piloted torpedoes (perhaps Birindelli's) and copied them. Training took place on board a vessel usually stationed in Scottish waters.

The prisoners were much astonished at the unexpected technical knowledge displayed by the examining officer and one of the British officers enquired, "But how comes it that you know so much about these craft and the way to use them?" When I told him I had been the commander of the submarine which had taken the Italian assailants to Gibraltar and Alexandria, the Britisher came smartly to attention and asked permission to be allowed to shake hands with me. He proceeded to inform me that the British pilots had pinned up in the main hall of their training school the reproduction of a page from an Italian illustrated paper bearing photographs of our pilots, for whom the greatest admiration was felt in the school. The Italians were considered the masters from whom the art could be learnt with a view to emulation. One of the prisoners, a diver with a frank, good-natured countenance, and evidently obsessed by a sportsman's enthusiasm for the submarine activity he had taken up, begged me, with the greatest persistence, for permission to join the Italian assault craft roster; he was obviously disconcerted by my amazed refusal. On the whole, the British were more carefully trained for the stage of concealment and camouflage after landing than for performance in the water; everything they wore had some hidden gadget in it: their buttons were tiny

235

compasses; files lurked in the turn-ups of their trousers for sawing through the bars of any prison in which they might find themselves; in the linings of their jackets they had silk maps sewn, showing the way to Switzerland; they were provided with Italian money and cigarettes and even the matches issued by our State monopoly; finally, a microscopic compass was found concealed inside one of their Italian cigarettes.

Considering the results achieved, the attempts of the British assault craft to attack our ships illustrated the sporting, competitive spirit of which the British have given many proofs in the past and which used to be so pleasing a trait in their character.

In pursuance of the activities directed to interception of enemy naval traffic to Malta and particularly in order to catch a very fast minelaying cruiser, the *Welshman*, which had succeeded, all by itself, in eluding every ambush on the route from Gibraltar to Malta, whither it carried essential replacement materials, we set up an assault craft base at Pantelleria. On the 21st of October, 1942, the *Cefalo* left La Spezia with three torpedo-carrying motorboats. After unloading them at Pantelleria, she became their support base.

The assault craft stationed there carried out ambush operations on the basis of information received from the Supreme Naval Command, off Tunisia. The group, under the command of Todaro, just back from the Black Sea, was composed of the pilots De Qual, Ungarelli, Garutti, Scardamaglia and Miniati, the Midshipmen pilots Malotti, Fracassini and Patané, and the P.O./pilots Tonissi, Barabino, Torriani, Virgilio, Patrizi, Papurello and Guercio. The enterprise was reinforced by other assault craft which reached Sicily by land, going on to Pantelleria under their own power or in motorized barges.

After the Allied landings in French North Africa (11th of November) and the consequent creation of a new front in Tunisia, the *Cefalo*, with new craft taken on at Trapani, went on to Bizerta, escorting a number of assault boats that were crossing from Sicily to Tunis by sea. At Bizerta a new base was established as one of the branches of the Tunisia Naval Command (Admiral Biancheri). Life there was made an inferno by continual air-raids (the entire anti-aircraft defence of Bizerta consisted of the solitary machine-gun of the *Cefalo*, for the numerous local batteries were manned by Frenchmen who either did not fire at all or else deliberately fired too late).

There was much lying in wait along the coast occupied by the enemy, particularly off Tabarca. Enemy vessels were never sighted, but there were frequent engagements with Allied motor gunboats, against which, owing to the difference of armament and the shallow draught of the enemy vessels, forming an insufficient underwater target for torpedoes, our only chance of survival was to break off the engagement immediately. During this period the sea, which was almost always high, held the tireless aggressiveness of Todaro and his pilots in check.

An action was planned for the forcing of the harbour at Bona, which had become a busy centre for enemy shipping, by swimmers, brought to the spot by assault motorboats. As its distance from Bizerta was too great for a direct voyage by our craft, the islet of La Galite, off Tabarca and situated about half-way between Bizerta and Bona, was selected as the starting point.

On the 13th of December the *Cefalo* crossed to La Galite with the expedition. The same evening two torpedo-carrying motorboats set out, one manned by Todaro and Barabino and carrying, instead of its torpedo, the three swimmers who were to break through to Bona (Coceani, Giari and Mistroni); the other boat, commanded by Ungarelli, acted as escort. Approach was slowed up by a rather rough sea; on arrival off the entirely blacked-out coast they cruised along it trying to identify the harbour. An air-raid, which was to have been carried out concurrently with the naval operation to allow sight of the harbour, did not materialize. The increasing roughness of the sea, together with mist and squalls of rain, preventing coastal reconnaissance, obliged the expedition to return to its base.

On the morning of the 14th the two craft were back at La Galite, aboard the *Cefalo*. The crews had thrown themselves on to their bunks to rest. At 8.15 a.m. two enemy aircraft machine-gunned the *Cefalo*; a bullet passed through the cabin wall and struck Todaro in the head, killing him instantly.

Such was the death in action of Salvatore Todaro, head of the surface Division of the Tenth Light Flotilla.

This brave officer, who had.already won, during the war, the Military Cross of Merit, two bronze and three silver medals, was posthumously awarded the gold medal for gallantry with the following most splendid citation:

"An exceptional officer, of particularly high military and civil capacity. Very able, resolute, tenacious, aggressive and daring, he first commanded a submarine and later an assault section, facing on innumerable occasions weapons vastly more powerful and numerous than his own and showing the enemy how the seamen of Italy can fight and conquer. He was a convinced champion of the power of the spirit, who never allowed his indifferent health to exhaust him and was never defeated by material difficulties, personal considerations or physical weariness. He always kept his aggressive will intact, together with his faith and devotion to duty, understood in its highest and most comprehensive sense. Never content with his fame and successes, caring nothing for himself but only for victory, he managed to obtain the command of enterprises which became more and more perilous, until at last, during one of these undertakings, he was machine-gunned by enemy aircraft and sacrificed his most valuable life to the growing greatness of our Country. Flawless as a man and as a warrior, he remains a magnificent example of cool, intelligent courage and utter self-dedication."

The *Cefalo*, riddled with machine-gun fire (the aircraft also released a couple of fragmentation bombs which destroyed Todaro's craft almost as soon as it had been made fast in its frame), began to sink, and shortly afterwards touched bottom. The crew managed to reach La Galite and tried to get into communication with the base at Bizerta through a local radio station with a French operator: but this attempt failed. In the end, using the *Cefalo's* apparatus, they got through. The same evening a torpedo-boat arrived from Bizerta with Commanding Officers Calosi and Buttazzoni, while Ungarelli went to inform Admiral Biancheri of what had happened.

On the islet of La Galite the men who loved him like a father and a brother gave the corpse of their revered commander military burial: a small, white, wooden cross was erected, facing the sea, to mark the spot of his last resting-place.

At the same time, actually on the 15th of December, there arrived at Bizerta, coming from Alba Fiorita, the column named after Commanding Officer Giobbe (it consisted of 4 torpedo-carrying motorboats and 6 E-boats, served by 5 lorries with 5 trailers, a tractor with a trailer, a smaller truck and two petrol-carriers). The column, in retreat before the British advance, had travelled, on its own, all along the Libyan coast highway, and had now reached its battle station on the new Tunisian front. On the death of Todaro, Lieutenant Cosulich assumed the command of our operational detachment in Tunisia.

Thanks to the labours of three assault swimmers (Coceani, Giari and Mistroni) the *Cefalo* was soon refloated and enabled to rejoin the base, while, under the command of Cosulich, the assault craft resumed their offensive from Bizerta.

A large number of ambuscading operations took place during the period January–April, designed to obstruct enemy shipping, which generally moved at night. During an air-raid by night, when a British aircraft fell into the sea, an assault boat manned by De Qual and Scardamaglia went in search of it; the gunner, one Macdonnel, was picked up and taken prisoner. Attempts to force the harbour at Bona were renewed; among others the assault swimmers Straulino, Coceani, Paciolla and Giari participated. In one of these operations, which took place on the 6th of April, the high seas that were running when the craft reached the entrance to the harbour prevented the despatch of the swimmers and considerably hindered the return of the three assault boats, piloted by Cosulich, Longobardi and Garutti, to the base.

With the fall of Tunisia (8th of May, 1943) our base also withdrew. On the evening of the 9th of May the craft of the Tenth Light were the last to leave Bizerta. Four motorboats, commanded respectively by Garutti, Tonissi, Barabino and Malotti, by bold seamanship, despite the unfavourable navigating conditions, reached Cagliari on the 10th of May; others were directed to Sicily; one craft, piloted by Sub-Lieutenant Patané, finished the last stage of the voyage under sail, with a jurymast, its fuel having run out.

The craft, thus repatriated from Tunisia in spite of so many difficulties, joined Ungarelli's squadron, stationed at Augusta.

The latter group, meanwhile, had not been inactive; they continued, incessantly, to lie in wait off Malta. In December 1942 an attack had been mounted by six swimmers transported by three motorboats (Commander Forza in charge) against vessels at La Valletta, but the enterprise was not carried to a conclusion owing to delays in approach navigation. A similar mission, repeated in April 1943 (two motorboats, one manned by Forza, Ungarelli and Wolk, the other by Fracassini, De Angelis and Ferrarini, carrying six swimmers), was broken off owing to adverse sea conditions.

239

CHAPTER XVII

THE FRONT SHRINKS—THE ACTIVITY OF THE TENTH EXPANDS. (MAY–SEPTEMBER 1943)

I take command of the Flotilla—Increased tasks—Attack on Gibraltar from the Olterra—The threat of invasion: Sardinia or Sicily?—On 10th July the question is answered—The Sicily assault boat flotilla defends that island—Lying in wait for enemy submarines at La Spezia: Mataluno's exploit— Gold medal for the Tenth's flag—Naval saboteurs in Spanish harbours—Adventures of Ferraro in Turkey—The Ambra at Syracuse—The 25th July—The 'Great Bear' flotilla again in action—Journey to Calabria—Two new operations planned: attacks on New York and Freetown and the forcing of Gibraltar by daylight—The 8th September.

ON the 1st of May, 1943, Commander Forza relinquished the command of the Tenth to go to sea and I was appointed to succeed him.

Our Flotilla had become a large unit with a highly specialized organization and function; all the *offensive* activities of the Navy were concentrated in it (with the exception of the submarine, light craft and torpedo services), since the squadrons of the Fleet had to perform defensive duties connected with their preservation against the ever-growing superiority, by air and sea, of our adversaries.

The fortunes of war were now frankly against us on all fronts and in all sectors. Now that the penetrating power of the German war potential had been shattered against the immensity of Russia and the deadly climate of that country, the main weight of American industrial production and armaments by air and sea had to be concentrated against Italy. Italy had lost Abyssinia, North Africa had been abandoned, superiority in the Mediterranean skies and seas had passed decisively to the enemy; we were practically a besieged country, surrounded on all sides by adversaries who were hurling destruction and ruin upon our cities from the air. The Italian Fleet, which had been operating, at the commencement of the war, from a base at Taranto, had been steadily withdrawing, before the pressure of the air offensive, to the

The Rock of Gibraltar and British convoy, as seen from the Villa Carmela. Signora CONCHITA RAMOGRINO in foreground.

Villa Carmela beach after the attack by assault swimmers. Note stockade and Spanish mounted sentry.

The Italian *original* (the 'pig') of the British 'chariot'.

north, and was now partly at La Spezia and partly at Genoa: this was a 'preservative' distribution perforce, since there were no other possibilities, the lack of petrol and the absence of aircraft which might have protected our skies preventing the use of ships in the operational sector of the war.

The Tenth, therefore, had to bear the burden of developing such offensive activity as, in the naval sphere, might be suggested by circumstances; it could only take the form of operations that, on account of their ambuscading character and their employment of extremely light units, costing absurdly little and entailing equally little wastage, owed their destructive power predominantly, not to their strength, but to the ingenuity, the resources of initiative and audacity, the determination and the reckless pugnacity of the men who carried them out.

Thus, while our armed forces of every type, on all fronts, were forced to the defensive and were steadily being ground down by the smashing blows delivered by an external enemy and the insidious intrigues of those who plotted against their own country from within, the Tenth Light Flotilla kept up its fighting potential with inexhaustible and increasing vigour, multiplying its operational activities and extending them to wider and more distant sectors; it resolutely sought out the enemy and boldly attacked him wherever he could be reached; it planned new operations even more audacious and death-dealing than the many others it had already accomplished.

During the period May–September 1943 the attacks delivered by the volunteers of the Tenth followed one another incessantly, from one end to the other of the Mediterranean.

Aboard the *Olterra*, after the glorious but unlucky enterprise of the Visintini group in December 1942, the internal organization had survived its gruelling test: none of those concerned on the other side had suspected anything out of the ordinary when Visintini, Magro, Leone, Manisco and Varini vanished from the ship, never to return.

Activity was resumed without a day's delay.

The 'Great Bear' Flotilla was reconstituted. Under the command of Lieutenant-Commander Ernesto Notari, leader of the group, the following came aboard the *Olterra*: Notari's second, P.O./diver Ario Lazzari, Lieutenant Camillo Tadini with P.O./diver Salvatore Mattera and Gunner Lieutenant Vittorio Cella, sole survivor of the mission of the 8th of December, 1942, with P.O./diver Eusebio Montalenti. Notari, an

Q

old underwater sea-dog, had been my pupil when, as long ago as 1933, I was in charge, aboard the salvage vessel *Titano*, of a course for divers at normal and exceptional depths; he had gone down to 150 metres in his steel diving-kit, beating what was then the world's record; he had been for some time a volunteer at the school on the Serchio estuary as a group leader and member of the piloted torpedoes course. He possessed an exceptionally robust 'diver-type' physique and was a serious sort of man, who spoke little; though he had passed the ideal age for the work in view, he belonged to the group of 'lads' who were in training to emulate the gallant veterans who had preceded them.

The despatch of men was followed by that of materials; more 'pigs' were forwarded to the *Olterra* by the clandestine methods previously employed: once more boiler tubes, engines, machine-parts, valves and various other fittings came aboard, invariably subjected to close examination by the Spanish customs officials, without any proof of the true nature of the goods leaking out. The workshop aboard resumed its labours: in a short time three torpedoes had been assembled and others, as reserves, were in preparation.

The experience gained on the operation of the 8th of December had persuaded us to abandon the attempt to force the harbour of Gibraltar by the same methods as before; the development of the British defence organization had rendered success by these means altogether too dubious.

It was decided, instead, to concentrate attack on the merchant shipping of the convoys which still continued to lie at anchor, in ever-growing numbers, in the roadstead; this target was easier to reach, since it was nearer and under less effective protection (though the enemy were at work on the construction of underwater net defences all round the area used as an anchorage by the vessels in question). The destruction of such targets, moreover, would be a more practical measure, since it would reduce, to the greatest extent possible, the flow of reinforcements to the troops fighting in Tunisia against the remnant of our African army and intending a direct assault, presumably, upon one of our larger islands, either Sardinia or Sicily.

On the night of the 8th of May, 1943, taking advantage of the favourable phase of the moon and of a storm that was raging in the bay of Gibraltar, making hydrophonic and visual detection more difficult for the enemy, Notari, Tadini and Cella, with their seconds, took to the sea, issuing, astride their craft, from the passage-way opened in the *Olterra's* side, a metre and a half below sea-level. The 'pigs' were also furnished on this occasion, as at Algiers, with double warheads, so that each crew was assigned two targets. The latter were selected by Notari from among those situated furthest from Algeciras, and therefore nearest to Gibraltar, for the reason that, though the difficulties, delay and dangers in reaching them might be thereby enhanced, there would thus be less likelihood of the British picking up any clue to the source of the attack, and suspicion would in this way be diverted from the *Olterra*. The pilots, in the course of this operation, met with great difficulties, both in avoiding the extremely alert vigilance of the enemy patrolboats covering the roadstead and owing to the violent currents provoked by the boisterous weather: they had to repeat the attack several times (Tadini, in particular, six times) and resort to various expedients in order to remain under the hulls of the steamers long enough to attach the explosive charges, while they struggled with the current's attempts to drag them from the spot; the result was that, as dawn approached, after a night of superhuman toil and incessant dangers faced with the greatest courage, each of the three crews succeeded in mining one steamer. Then, returning to the *Olterra* with their 'pigs' and entering the vessel through the secret passage, they resumed the appearance of ordinary seamen, strolling about the deck with an abstracted and nonchalant air, while each kept watch, out of the corner of his eye, on a doomed ship as it grew visible in the morning light, and eagerly awaited events. How often they glanced at the time during those few minutes! Then suddenly, with the usual punctuality characteristic of our fuses, one explosion after another took place and three heavily laden steamers blew up. They were the *Pat Harrison* (a Liberty ship of 7000 tons), the *Mahsud*, of 7500 tons, which were broken up and sank in shallow water, and the *Camerata* (4875 tons) which disappeared altogether.

Visintini had been justified: the organization to which he had contributed ideas and labour of such high value, the 'Great Bear' Flotilla of the *Olterra*, had scored its first success.

20,000 tons of enemy shipping had been added to the bag of the Tenth.

That night our agents had scattered along the north coast of the bay of Gibraltar items of divers' equipment which were picked up next morning by the Spaniards, as had been foreseen, and served to mislead the British.

"We never found any proof," writes Goldsworthy, "of the part played by the *Olterra* in this affair. From British Naval Headquarters on Gibraltar we could see, with the naked eye, the *Olterra's* superstructure above the exterior mole at Algeciras. The possibility that the *Olterra* might be associated in some way with the attacks by human torpedoes did not escape us, but there was never the least visible evidence to suggest the actual nature of her participation."

It was the result of technical skill in our organization, shrewd calculation, ceaseless self-control, unending false pretences and the valour of our men. For nearly a year Gibraltar was overshadowed by the menace of the Tenth from the *Olterra* and then, at last, the first sinkings were accomplished. The British, despite all their efforts, never succeeded in identifying the origin of these attacks; they were in the state of mind of a man in his own house, barricaded in his own room, who is struck, in the darkness of the night, by a series of blows, coming from he knows not where, which carry away at one moment his hand, at another his ear, tomorrow, perhaps, the tip of his nose, driving him crazy, less with pain than with rage at not being able to discover where his enemy is hiding and with dread lest the impalpable and mysterious aggressor may sooner or later strike into one of his vital organs (battleships).

On the evacuation of Tunisia (May 1943) the front became restricted to Italian territory at home, for the defence of which it was now a matter of urgency to provide. The Tenth was charged with the duty of distributing mobile defences along the coasts of Sicily and Sardinia; there was much uncertainty as to which of the two islands would be subjected to a wave of invasion.

Our surface units were dispersed in accordance with the new situation. So far as Sicily was concerned, steps were taken to reinforce Ungarelli's squadron, which had been stationed for some time at Augusta.

In Sardinia three operative bases were established; two groups of assault boats were stationed at Carloforte and Bosa Marina for the purpose of attacking any possible invasion fleet; Lenzi was appointed Commander-in-Chief, while De Qual and Massarini controlled the two separate bases. The *Sogliola*, on her return voyage from transport-

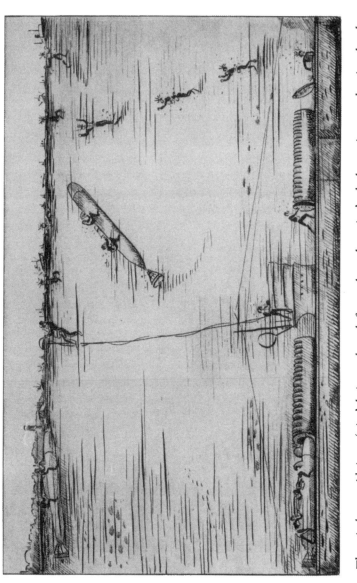

The *Ambra* at Algiers: 'pigs' being released from the submarine's deck—swimmers leaving hatch—and scout reporting back from the surface by telephone.

Aboard the *Olterra* at Algeciras; assembly of a human torpedo in the secret workshop.

ing the boats to Sardinia, was sunk by the gunfire of an enemy submarine; the *Pegaso* took her place.

The third base, which had special duties, was set up in the harbour at Cagliari; its preparation was a particularly laborious task. A group of swimmers, under the command of Sub-Lieutenant Faravelli, engaged, silently and unknown to the local civil and military authorities themselves, in the excavation of a sort of cavern in the massive masonry of the eastern mole of the harbour. It was made a storehouse for boxes of rations, equipment and explosives in such quantity as to permit of numerous offensive operations. The plan was conceived as follows: if the enemy landed at Cagliari, our group, taking advantage of the arrangements made, would 'go underground'. While the handful of swimmers, hidden in their secret place of concealment hollowed out in the mole, made sundry sudden attacks on the enemy shipping with 'bugs' and 'limpets', another group would take the most favourable opportunities (when the harbour was full of shipping, with important cargoes) to blow up petrol dumps ashore, causing oil to flow into the harbour and thus starting fires there. The preparation of this action in particular, which required a great deal of time and heavy work, was entrusted to Wolk, group leader of the swimmers, an officer possessing high organizing ability and of indisputable authority over his subordinates.

On the 10th of July all doubt as to the point of invasion was at an end: the enemy had gained a footing in Sicily.

The base at Cagliari was rapidly dismantled; but those under De Qual and Massarini remained in position, in case the enemy's next objective should turn out to be Sardinia.

In Sicily Ungarelli's flotilla, at the time of the enemy invasion, was in process of reconstruction so as to take in the units which had come in from Tunisia (Ungarelli himself arrived at Augusta on the 9th of July, from La Spezia, with a column of replacement materials and torpedoes, required for refit of the craft suffering from the effects of the gruelling activities in which they had participated). Augusta being invested from the landward side, it was rapidly evacuated and the craft had to fall back on Isola Bella, off Mazzaro, near Taormina.

From this base a number of ambuscading operations off Syracuse, Augusta and Catania were organized, as these harbours successively fell into the hands of the British, to lie in wait for their convoys. To reinforce resistance new craft and further pilots were directed to the spot from the Tenth's headquarters and Commanding Officer Lenzi came from Sardinia to take charge of the Tenth's group stationed in Sicily.

There were frequent encounters with enemy light craft. One morning two British cruisers and four destroyers appeared 2000 metres offshore and opened fire on the St. Agostino viaduct forming part of the main road from Taormina to Messina; the sudden and daring intervention of one of our boats (Lenzi and Barabino) was enough, by the threat it represented, to cause the withdrawal of the enemy ships under smoke-screens.

During the same period sabotage raids were also carried out, in collaboration with Buttazzoni's parachutists, behind the British lines. In particular, Ungarelli, Lenzi and Fracassini disembarked a group at Cape San Croce: after carrying out their orders the group made their way through the lines and returned to their bases. Other saboteurs, also transported by our craft, who had been caught in the rapid British advance, returned some days later direct to Calabria, negotiating the Straits of Messina in the rubber canoes with which they had been provided.

The fate of Sicily, however, could not, in the nature of things, depend only upon our tiny craft and their determined pilots: under the pressure of the enemy's advance the boats fell back on Messina. Here, too, there were frequent encounters, during the incessant night ambuscades, with light British units: an enemy motor-gunboat was seriously damaged by the explosion of a depth-charge dropped by one of our assault boats.

When Messina, too, was invested, the torpedo-carrying motorboat 262, nicknamed 'Fatty' on account of her swollen timbers, due to prolonged service at sea, manned by Lenzi and Barabino, was the last Italian naval unit to leave the harbour and abandon Sicily, making straight for the Calabrian coast, where, at once, with inexhaustible tenacity, a new assault craft base was organized to oppose the extension, now considered imminent, of the enemy's advance into continental Italy.

About 20 miles off shore, in a semi-circle round the gulf of La Spezia, as indeed was the case with all the main naval bases, a line of sailing boats was posted on scouting duty. They were equipped with acoustic detectors of a primitive type and patrolled slowly to and fro, their task being to give timely warning, to the stronghold where our battleships were anchored, of the appearance of enemy aircraft. This expedient was used, because we had no 'radar'.

For some time these boats, practically unarmed and manned by seamen under military orders, had been the object of attack by enemy submarines, which surfaced unexpectedly in the vicinity and now and again easily sank, with no risk to themselves, one of the boats by gunfire.

The headquarters of the North Tyrrhenian naval sector at La Spezia asked us to find some way of protecting the unfortunate boats which were performing such useful duties.

A trap was promptly set for the enemy submarines. Some of the guardships took a number of our torpedo-carrying boats in tow, the latter being camouflaged to resemble harmless skiffs. Their crews lay in wait, day and night, in the interiors of their craft, ready to make a dash for the submarine the moment she appeared. Long days of waiting followed, monotonous and enervating, and lengthened into weeks: the crews were relieved every 48 hours. At last patience was rewarded: Lieutenant Mataluno sighted from his craft a submarine which had just made a threatening appearance in the vicinity. Without a second's hesitation Mataluno cast off, started his engine, stripped away the camouflage awning and ran up his war ensign. Then he raced to the attack, launching his torpedo. The submarine saw him coming and instantly submerged. The alarm was given and craft of the anti-submarine group of La Spezia (Captain Zoli) dashed to the scene. A systematic chase began, the result of which, as so often in such cases, could not be ascertained.

Even though the action had no positive upshot, it was enough to put the enemy on his guard: the attacks on the motorboats of the exterior defence of La Spezia were not renewed and the latter were enabled to resume their modest but important functions in relative tranquillity.

On the 10th of June, 1943, the Italian Navy Day, the flag of the Tenth Light Flotilla was decorated with the gold medal, with the following citation:

"The Tenth Light Flotilla is the heir, in direct line, of the fame of those invaders of harbours who astonished the globe with their

247

deeds in the First World War and gave the Italian Navy a record
of achievement as yet unequalled. The Flotilla has proved that the
seed sown by the heroes of the past has borne good fruit. In
numerous undertakings of great daring, in contempt of all danger,
against difficulties of every kind, created as much by natural conditions as by the effectiveness of defensive installations at the
harbours, the gallant men of the assault divisions of the Navy,
trained and directed by the Tenth Light Flotilla, have contrived to
reach the enemy in the secure retreats of fortified harbours, sinking
two battleships, two cruisers, a destroyer and a large number of
steamers, totalling more than 100,000 tons.

The Tenth Light Flotilla, a select band of heroic spirits, is
faithful to its motto: *For our King and our Flag*."

Meanwhile, small groups of our swimmers were continually being
organized in certain neutral harbours frequented by enemy shipping.
Under various disguises which served to conceal their identities from
their hosts and from enemy spies, they acted at night, whenever a
favourable opportunity arose to attach the charges to the hulls of
steamers.

One such base was established aboard the Italian steamer *Gaeta*,
interned in the harbour at Huelva. The expedition, composed of three
persons under the command of a gallant petty officer, named Vianello,
embarked disguised as members of the crew; the group had much ill-
luck owing to the numerous spies employed by the British to watch
the harbour, the importance of which was due to the cargoes of
minerals, iron and copper, exported by the mines of Rio Tinto; some
charges were fastened to the steamers, but we could never find out
whether these attacks were successful. All that we knew for certain
was that every ship arriving at Gibraltar from Spanish ports was closely
examined by divers of the Security Service and that at least one vessel
out of those attacked at Huelva was cleared in time of the deadly loads
that, unknown to herself, she had brought with her.

Similar bases, camouflaged in accordance with the conditions
prevailing locally, were organized at Malaga, Barcelona, Lisbon and
Oporto. I do not propose to dwell upon their adventures, though some
would form an interesting chapter in the secret history of the war,
because the commencement of the activities of these groups coincided
with the unexpected events of September.

One of the most brilliant enterprises carried out during the war, Sub-Lieutenant Ferraro's secret mission, may however now be related in full.

It was apprehended from intelligence received that the Turkish ports of Alexandretta and Mersina were much frequented by enemy shipping; chromium, a metal essential for war production, was being loaded there. In collaboration with our Naval secret intelligence service an expedition was organized with the object of interfering with this traffic, thus carrying our offensive into a zone which had hitherto remained undisturbed.

In view of the hydrographic characteristics of the harbour at Alexandretta, an open roadstead where steamers are anchored at two or three thousand metres from the coast (and are there reached by lighters loaded with the mineral to be taken aboard), the type of weapon selected was the 'explosive limpet', carried by a swimmer.

One of the finest of our swimmers, Sub-Lieutenant Luigi Ferraro, was appointed to execute the operation. He was an athletic Italian from Tripoli, a former pupil of the Physical Culture Academy and later an officer in the coastal militia, who combined traits of determination and seriousness with exceptional physical and moral advantages. With the help of specialists he was disguised as a consular employee of the Ministry for Foreign Affairs and appointed to join the Italian Vice-consulate at Alexandretta. For this purpose it was necessary to arrange for him to cross the frontiers of Central Europe without arousing suspicion, especially among the extremely wary Turks, very reasonably anxious to maintain their neutrality; also to furnish him with documents justifying his presence in the office of the Vice-consul of Italy at Alexandretta who, in view of his official function, could not be compromised in the affair; the mission was therefore to take place under his protection but unknown to himself.

In order to obtain the necessary documents, a service passport, letters of credit for the consul, diplomatic immunity from customs examination and so on, it would have been necessary to apply officially to the Minister for Foreign Affairs; but there were many excellent reasons for going another way about it. In the first place, so as to preserve the military secret involved, which it was always risky to let out of our own restricted circle, and secondly, owing to a feeling of distrust, which was steadily on the increase, of the official bodies in Rome, where the atmosphere was one of masked defeatism which accorded ill with our plans. Lastly, the Ministry of Foreign Affairs, on which we had often previously relied for the solution of such problems, was becoming more and more reluctant to collaborate with us in this way, on the unexceptionable ground that the multiplication of bogus diplomats brought discredit on the institution, so that in the end even those who had a legitimate right to protection under diplomatic immunity would become involved in the distrust which the abuse of privilege would entail.

But there is always a way out: one of our petty officers was acquainted, on somewhat intimate terms, with a good-natured and quick-witted girl, a typist at the Ministry of Foreign Affairs; it did not prove difficult for him, in view of the highly patriotic reason for his request, to persuade her to work in with us. In this way we obtained the passport, some sheets of officially stamped notepaper and lastly the Ministry's rubber stamp itself (which was returned immediately after use).

On one of the first days of June 1943 the consular employee Luigi Ferraro, an elegant and nonchalant looking young man of handsome and promising appearance, reported to the Italian Vice-consul at Alexandretta, the Marquis Ignazio di Sanfelice, armed with every possible credential. He handed the consul, who was not expecting him, as his arrival had not been previously announced, a letter signed by the Minister for Foreign Affairs appointing him to the office staff to carry out special duties on behalf of the Ministry. The consul was formally requested to give him every possible assistance.

Ferraro had four suitcases with him, all rather heavy, and bearing diplomatic seals.

He soon established amicable relations with the clerk at the consulate, Giovanni Roccardi, really a lieutenant in the naval secret service.

It had in fact been Roccardi who, having been at Alexandretta for some time and hence well acquainted with the place and the people, had called the Ministry's attention to the possibility of acting against enemy traffic in the port; he was the originator of the idea of the mission and Ferraro's indispensable collaborator on the organizational and shore side of his activities.

Roccardi gave us the following description of the local conditions:

"Ferraro's arrival certainly made the operation possible from the technical point of view but by no means simplified the organizational problem, which was that of introducing into our small world, by its very nature extremely prone to gossip, a new subject of curiosity, without excessive shock. The atmosphere in which we had to work was that of a small frontier city, enlivened by the intrigues of six consulates, the American, the British, the French, the Greek, the German and the Italian. The population of 12,000, mostly Arabs, was not hostile, it was even potentially friendly to us, but it was kept in subjection by the suspicious attitude of the Turkish police and much influenced by enemy propaganda, which was disseminated by certain Greeks and Jews who were naturally very bitter against us and for the most part voluntary spies in the service of the British. The latter, accordingly, supported by interests connected with the construction of the harbour then in progress with the aid of British capital and engineers, and with the delivery of material under the Lend-Lease agreement, and with works included in the plans for the Alexandretta-Adana road, had all the authorities in the place practically in their pockets. American influence was at that time only in its infancy.

In addition to all this, the war-time restrictions in force in Turkey bore particularly hardly on the Hatay district, which was suspected of turcophobia and separatism; consequently, in that area examination of passports in trains, demands for credentials on all sorts of occasions, refusals to grant game and fishing licences to foreigners, etc., were especially severe.

However, I managed to get everything arranged satisfactorily and our work was carried through right under the noses of two agents of the British intelligence service, whose special duty it was to watch Italian citizens in general and presumably, in spite of our innocent aspects, ourselves in particular. My task was much facilitated by Ferraro's genial and expansive character which was certainly the last that might have been expected to be meditating dark projects concerned with dynamite." (From Lieutenant Roccardi's report.)

A few days after Ferraro's arrival he was introduced, under the wing of the expert Roccardi, into local consular and fashionable society; he was to be found on the beach every morning (and it was soon discovered by everybody that he could *not* swim) and every night at the café on the front, where he danced, drank and generally had a gay time of it, behaving exactly like any other young diplomat playing the usual diplomatic game. (*See* map opposite.)

He preferred sport to anything else; he was an adept at hand-ball and bowls. Every evening a large box was carried down to the beach from the Italian consul's bathing cabin and the games gear taken out of it in front of everyone; as soon as it began to get dark the games came to an end and the box was taken back to the cabin.

On the evening of the 30th of June, by which time the curiosity aroused by the newcomer to the small consular circle had died down, and the vigilance of the British agents had relaxed, for though they were extremely active they were not very intelligent, Ferraro and Roccardi lingered on the beach beyond the usual time; an exceptionally keen game of bowls had made them forget the lateness of the hour. As soon as they were alone, Ferraro darted like a squirrel into the consul's cabin, rummaged in the games box and shortly afterwards came out enveloped in a sheath of black rubber, fins on his feet, a mask on his face (the breathing gear) and two strange objects, oblong in shape and rather heavy, dangling from his waist, while his head was tied up with seaweed. It was an odd sort of beach get-up for a diplomat!

The black figure advanced circumspectly to the edge of the sea and entered the water; a moment later, soundlessly and without leaving visible trace of his progress, he had disappeared into the darkness of the night. He swam 2300 metres, until he reached a steamer. His first victim was the Greek vessel *Orion*, 7000 tons, with a cargo of chromium. Ferraro carried out the operation he had so often performed as a training exercise (he was one of our best swimmers and acted as instructor of the younger recruits); under the beams of the searchlights aboard and the alert eyes of the sentries he slipped very slowly along the side of the vessel (it was a tricky job, executed entirely with legs and fins, while the head remained motionless at the level of the water; he kept to the shadows cast by the lighters); on making contact with the steamer he switched on his breathing gear and dived, without a sound or a ripple. He moved, groping, along the hull, under the keel till he found the bilge-keel ledge, then detached those oblong 'objects' from his waist, fixed them to the ledge with the clamps, in the right position, so that nothing stuck out; at last they were properly adjusted; he released the safety-catches and came to the surface again; the whole job had only taken him a few minutes. In the

Alexandretta Harbour.

same cautious manner in which he had arrived he departed; by 4 a.m he was back in the consulate.

A week later the *Orion* finished taking in her cargo and weighed anchor, but she did not get far. While she was still in Syrian waters an explosion took place under her hull. She was so heavily laden that she sank in a few minutes. The survivors of the wreck were taken to hospital in Alexandretta; they said the ship had been torpedoed.

Intelligence was received from the neighbouring port of Mersina, on the 8th of July, that the steamer *Kaituna*, 10,000 tons, was lying at anchor there. She was a modern vessel, well equipped and well armed. Roccardi and Ferraro left for that city on the 9th, taking with them a small suitcase bearing diplomatic seals. That evening they went bathing. Next day they returned to Alexandretta, where their absence had not been noticed. The *Kaituna* did not leave until the 19th; only one of the two 'limpets' which had been attached exploded. To avoid sinking, she was obliged to run ashore on the coast of Cyprus; the British found the device, which had not exploded; but it was too late! Ferraro, by that time, had already mined two more ships and disappeared without leaving the slightest trace of his activities.

On the 30th of July Ferraro and Roccardi were again at Mersina:

"I took note of the position of the target and at 2200 hours put on practically the whole of my kit in the consulate and wrapped myself in a dressing-gown. Roccardi and I went down to the beach for our evening bathe. He helped me to carry the 'limpets' and to put on the rest of my gear. I went into action at 2245 hours.

After swimming about 500 metres I thought I could hear something. I stopped, listened and became aware, in the darkness, of the heavy breathing of some large animal very close to me. Then I saw, against the light, two big creatures leaping, puffing and blowing, a couple of metres away. More than once they came straight at me and I could feel under me the rush of water caused by the thrashing of their tails. I tried several times to frighten them off and strike them with my knife, but it was no use. They seemed, with astonishing devotion, to consider it their duty to accompany me practically the whole way. I reached my target, some 4000 metres from my starting point, at 2 a.m." (From Lieutenant Ferraro's report.)

After carrying out the attack with his usual coolness, Ferraro came ashore at 4 a.m. A few hours later he was in Alexandretta. But the *Sicilian Prince*, of 5000 tons, escaped her fate, for her departure was so long delayed that she was able to benefit by the inspection systematically carried out upon all British ships in Turkish waters after discovery of the unexploded 'limpet' under the *Kaituna*.

The Norwegian motorship *Fernplant*, 7000 tons, in the service of the British with a cargo of chromium, lying at Alexandretta, was not quite so fortunate. On the 2nd of August Ferraro attacked her in the same way as he had attacked the *Orion*. The motorship weighed anchor on the 4th; but a few hours later she was back in harbour.

"The apprehension and anxiety with which we awaited the sequel can be imagined. We resigned ourselves to expecting the explosion about midnight. The time came, and we stared, in suspense, at the target. But, to our incredulous amazement, the minutes passed and nothing happened. We came to the conclusion that it had only been a long time after weighing anchor that the vessel had attained sufficient speed to set the miniature propellers of the explosive devices in motion, so we discontinued observation. Next morning, as soon as it was light, I dashed to the window, sure that I should see the ship, stranded on her side, somewhere along the coast. Instead of that I saw her lying in perfectly good order at her anchorage. Something I had not dared to hope for had occurred: the vessel, at her departure, had not attained the necessary speed. It was a great relief when, at 1800 hours on the 5th, we saw her leave harbour. For some hours we went on keeping a look out, in case she came back a second time." (From the report of Lieutenant Ferraro.)

The *Fernplant* never returned to Alexandretta: a few hours later she reached her last destination at the bottom of the sea.

Three days later Ferraro, having used up all his charges, went down unexpectedly with a dose of malaria! He was at once repatriated; no trace of his past activity remained at Alexandretta.

In a single month Roccardi and Ferraro, working in perfect unison, had caused the sinkings of two ships with cargoes of chromium and damage to a third, with a total bag of 24,000 tons. Meanwhile, the British Intelligence Service pursued its enquiries.

. . . . .

As part of the defence of Sicily from the Allied invasion an attack was organized, shortly after disembarkation had taken place, against enemy shipping reported in the great harbour at Syracuse.

The submarine *Ambra*, now under the command of Lieutenant Ferrini, was appointed to conduct the operation. Arillo had been sent to Danzig to take over one of the German submarines under construction which had been handed over to us by Germany, richer as she was in material than in personnel.

In view of the distance which the operators would have to cover at Syracuse and of the few hours of darkness which would be available, and also bearing in mind our accurate knowledge of the obstructions in the harbour, the cylinders of the *Ambra* carried, instead of human torpedoes, three E-boats of the MTR type, capable of much longer periods at sea and much higher speed than piloted torpedoes. The operators selected were Lieutenant Garutti and P.O./pilots Tonissi, Guercio and Sguanci.

After 18 hours of submerged navigation along the coasts of Sicily, which were already occupied by the enemy, the submarine arrived, on the night of the 25th of July, at a point a few miles off Syracuse.

The submarine, on surfacing to check her position, was immediately detected by radar from the night-flyers on permanent guard duty in the zone. The dropping of a number of bombs showed that the hunt was up and the *Ambra* only succeeded in evading destruction by rapidly submerging to a deep level. But depth-charges inflicted serious damage upon her and the doors of the cylinders containing the E-boats were crushed by pressure and jammed in such a way as to prevent the craft being taken out; the submarine had to abandon the action.

It was only owing to the skill of the commanding officer and the gallantry of the crew that the *Ambra*, with wounded men aboard and grave structural injuries, with her atmosphere fouled by the gases released from the batteries demolished by the concussions of the depth-charges, was able to reach Naples.

On the 25th of July we received the following official information:

"His Majesty the King has accepted the resignation by His Excellency Benito Mussolini of his duties as Head of the Government, Prime Minister and Secretary of State, and has appointed as

Head of the Government, Prime Minister and Secretary of State, His Excellency, the Marshal of Italy, Pietro Badoglio."

The King, further, issued the following orders: "At this solemn crisis in the affairs of Italy everyone must stand firm at his post of duty, faith and battle." Meanwhile His Excellency, the Marshal of Italy, Pietro Badoglio, proclaimed: "The war goes on. Italy, reeling under the blows inflicted upon her invaded provinces and destroyed cities, remains faithful to her pledged word and jealously preserves her thousand-year-old traditions. . . ."

On the night of the 3rd–4th of August, 1943, the 'Great Bear' Flotilla, still under the command of Notari, and manned by the same crews as in the previous operation, carried out a further attack on the vessels of the convoys anchored in the roadstead at Gibraltar. The sea was very smooth, with the vivid phosphorescence of summer, and these factors constituted adverse natural phenomena against which, this time, we had to contend. Goldsworthy, at that time stationed at Gibraltar, gives the ensuing account of the progress of the operation; for once we will follow its course as seen from the other side.

". . . Three torpedoes were used.

Notari made a wide circuit close to the Spanish shore to keep out of the main glare of the searchlights.

Beneath the target, the 7000 ton U.S. Liberty ship *Harrison Gray Otis*, he encountered a new defence device, barbed wire hanging in the darkness.

He went deep to pass under it and reached the bottom of the ship.

His No. 2 was a Petty Officer, Giannoli, a last minute substitute, comparatively inexperienced on human torpedoes.

The plan, as usual, was to fasten the detachable warhead to a line between the bilge keel clamps; but Giannoli dropped the line and the warhead had to be clamped direct to the port bilge keel. While this was being completed the torpedo began to rise, threatening to break the surface.

Notari opened the diving valves too wide and suddenly the torpedo plunged down out of control. Lungs bursting, head splitting, Notari fumbled with the controls as the luminous depth gauge needle crept past its 34 metre (112 feet) limit—three times the normal training depth. As suddenly as it had gone down the torpedo began a wild rush to the surface. Notari expected to break his head against the bottom of the ship or rip his rubber suit to shreds on the barbed wire, but with a resounding splash he broke surface a yard from the ship's side.

Half conscious, unable to think or act, he lay over the controls, expecting shouts or rifle shots.

Nothing happened. Slowly Notari regained his wits.

Giannoli had vanished. The motor would only run at top speed, and at that speed diving was impossible. Notari took his only slender chance: a full speed retreat on the surface, for nearly four miles, expecting any moment that the fiery sparkle of his phosphorescent wake would bring a patrolboat in pursuit.

Then, to him, it seemed that a miracle happened. A school of porpoises, a familiar sight to Gibraltar yachtsmen, joined him and frolicked around him all the way to Algeciras, providing the perfect cover for his wake.

He made a wide circuit to avoid the Spanish sentry on the end of the Quay and reached the *Olterra*. (*See* map on p. 59.)

Meanwhile Giannoli, torn from his seat by the plunge of the torpedo, surfaced on the other side of the ship and thought Notari drowned.

He swam to the stern, stripped off his breathing gear and rubber suit, and for two hours shivered in his woollen combinations on the rudder of the ship.

When he judged the other crews would be back in the *Olterra*, and the time was approaching for the explosion of the warhead he had fixed himself, he swam along the side of the ship and shouted for help.

He was hauled on board, and his capture was flashed to naval headquarters.

A launch patrolling with the duty diver hurried to the *Harrison Gray Otis* to collect the prisoner and to search the ship.

Giannoli had been taken on to the launch and Petty Officer Bell, of the naval diving party, was putting his foot into the water when the 500 lb. charge exploded on the other side of the ship.

It blew a terrific hole in the engine room. A piece of metal passed right through the ship, out through the starboard plates,

SEA DEVILS

and killed the seaman guarding Giannoli in the wheelhouse of the launch.

Petty Officer Bell, who had escaped death by seconds, was searching the other ships within an hour.

Within minutes of the *Harrison Gray Otis* explosion, Midshipman Cella's warhead broke the 10,000 ton Norwegian tanker *Thorshovdi* in two and sent great masses of thick oil drifting across the bay.

The third charge heavily damaged the British 6000 ton *Stanridge*. All three ships sank in shallow water."[1]

Another 23,000 tons of enemy shipping had been added to the bag of the Tenth.

At the beginning of August Admiral de Courten, Minister of Marine under the new military Government of Badoglio, arrived at La Spezia on an official visit to the Tenth Light Flotilla.

He was accompanied, in addition to his personal suite, by Admiral Varoli Piazza, Chief of the General Staff of the Light Craft Inspectorate, a resolute, energetic and enthusiastic supporter of our war activities.

After the departments had been inspected, Admiral de Courten exhorted us, in a fighting speech, to maintain the struggle to the last.

"You represent the sighting spearhead of our Navy: you must continue on the road you have hitherto followed, intensify your offensive action and hold yourselves in readiness to exceed all previous efforts if the supreme hour of battle strikes. . . . As I embrace you all in the person of your commanding officer, I express the sentiment that unites us all in the struggle against the Anglo-American invaders, on whom we shall wage implacable war until we have thrown them back into the sea. . . ."

The enemy occupation of Sicily was completed in August. By then the assault craft flotilla, the last Italian units to leave Messina, had fallen back to Calabria. I wished to visit the zone of operations in order to establish a base for our craft there, which might serve to oppose possible attempts to invade the continent. I left La Spezia in a car, accompanied by Lieutenant Elio Scardamaglia, pilot, and my faithful

[1] Goldsworthy, *Sunday Express*, 25th of December, 1949, and subsequent issues.

orderly Pietro Cardia. From indomitable, martyred Naples onwards, our journey was a very sad one. We were the only party going south; along the Calabrian coast road we met the remnants of the Italian and German armed forces which had abandoned Sicily and were retreating northwards. What a contrast there was between them! While the German divisions, in perfect order, fully motorized, officers at the heads of the columns, moved up the peninsula in compact and disciplined bodies, with all their equipment and stores, the men in immaculate uniforms, washed and shaved, looking more like troops on parade than a routed army, there were to be seen, here and there among them, a few scattered groups of soldiers in grey-green rags, all on foot, most of them without boots, pale, unshaven, with neither officers nor orders, and with nowhere to go.

"Where are you off to?" I asked a sailor we met near Bagnara Calabra. "To Turin, where my girl friend lives." "Where do you come from?" "Palermo." "Who gave you leave?" He simply stared at me in bewilderment.

Thus, under my very eyes, the melancholy spectacle of an army in decay unrolled itself; I could well understand how it was that Sicily, which should have formed an insurmountable barrier to the invaders, had been lost in a little over a month.

The atmosphere of defeat and betrayal was everywhere apparent. One evening I found myself close to the headquarters of a coastal defence battalion, near Agropoli, and asked if I could stay the night there. While I was talking to the major in command (whose name I am sorry that I have forgotten, for it deserves to be duly recorded) he told me, at the top of his voice, in the village square, in front of his subordinates: "I can't wait until they sound the alarm for the enemy landing: I've already arranged for the battalion to surrender without firing a shot: at least this business will be over and I can go home." That was the way in which this gallant and loyal officer fulfilled his duty and carried out the task assigned to him!

In the field hospital at Polistena I found Lenzi. He had got a bomb splinter through one of his lungs at the very moment he was landing, with his assault boat, on the way back from Sicily, on the beach at Gioia Tauro. In view of the threat of an enemy invasion across the Straits I arranged for him to be taken north, to a place of safety, as soon as the state of his wound allowed him to be moved.

As I returned up the peninsula, for there was no possibility of the enemy setting foot in Calabria owing to the entire lack of suitable landing-places, my attention was drawn to the Gulf of Salerno, which seemed to me a favourable spot for a landing designed to take Calabria in the rear, that province, owing to the highly accidented character of its mountainous terrain, not lending itself easily to any plan of frontal attack. I decided, accordingly, that a flotilla of surface craft ought to be stationed there, actually at Amalfi, occupying a position between the gulfs of Salerno and Naples; from this post attacks by our assault craft could be launched against enemy convoys attempting to land. The base was immediately set up, under the command of Lieutenant Longobardi, pilot, and became a centre for the craft of our squadrons returning from Tunisia and Sicily, as well as for new forces drawn from the groups in training at La Spezia.

At the headquarters of the Flotilla, where nothing was known of the intrigues in progress in Rome, activity directed to inflicting maximum damage on the enemy was in full swing.

Two torpedo craft of 100 tons, destined for the Tenth and under construction in the yards at Monfalcone, were nearly ready for service; they were provided with the equipment required for transport of assault craft and were intended for operations planned against the harbours of the Eastern Mediterranean, which the transport ships based at La Spezia could not now reach, the Straits of Messina being under enemy control.

A base of the Tenth had been established at Venice, under the command of Lieutenant-Commander Baffigo, for fitting out and despatching the boats; men and materials were already on the spot and the preparation of a first mission was in hand.

Groups of our naval saboteurs, with their laborious apprenticeship behind them, were on the way to the neutral ports to which they had been appointed; some, who had already arrived, were organizing offensive action, taking every care not to give a hint of their true characters, against enemy shipping in sectors where it had hitherto remained undisturbed.

After a year of tests and experiments conducted on the Lake of Iseo by Sub-Lieutenant Massano, in some of which I had myself taken part, the midget assault submarine 'CA' had been adapted to her new functions and was ready for action. Simultaneously, at Bordeaux, where in the meantime command of the base of our Atlantic submarines had been assumed by Captain Enzo Grossi, the possibilities

I had formerly tested of using an ocean-going submarine for transporting the 'CA' to an enemy base had been realized. Two missions were in preparation with this craft, one being an attack on New York, taking the 'CA' up the Hudson into the very heart of the city; the psychological effect on the Americans, who had not yet undergone any war offensive on their own soil, would in our opinion far outweigh the material damage which might be inflicted (and ours was the only practicable plan, so far as I am aware, ever made to carry the war into the United States). The other operation provided for an attack against the important British stronghold of Freetown (Sierra Leone) where the British South Atlantic Squadron was stationed. The undoubted difficulties that such operations of very wide range involved were to a large extent neutralized by the factor of complete surprise; the appearance of assault craft of the Italian Navy, which had so far limited their efforts to the Mediterranean area, would certainly not be foreseen: defensive measures against so unexpected a type of attack were presumably not in being.

The action against New York was in an advanced stage of preparation and had been fixed to take place in December.

On the other hand, an entirely new operation was imminent against Gibraltar. Three submarines of about 1000 tons each, provided with four cylinders each for transporting the craft, had been assigned to the Tenth; they were the *Murena*, the *Sparide* and the *Grongo*. Of the three, which were all of the latest type, the *Murena* was ready for action. We also had ready the new piloted torpedo, the 'SSB', which had features strikingly superior to those of the previous types. So as to confound the opposing defences, the operational plan differed entirely from the methods we had hitherto employed. Our attacks had always been launched at night and on moonless nights into the bargain, in other words under protection of the most utter darkness.

Well! The *Murena* (commanded by Longanesi) was to release, from the Spanish side of the Straits of Gibraltar, at an advanced hour of the night, four explosive boats of the MTR type, which would silently proceed up the roadstead of Algeciras, hugging the neutral coast and arrive on the north side of the bay. Here they would take advantage of their microscopic dimensions to hide among the reeds at the mouths of the rivers. At 1100 hours, in broad daylight, they would burst from their hiding-places and, aiming at four steamers anchored in the roadstead, would boldly attack them. (*See* map p. 59.)

Experiénce had taught us that in consequence of the alarm given in the roadstead *the net barrier at the north gate of the fortress of Gibraltar would be raised* to allow scouts, torpedo-boats and salvage tugs to come to the aid of the vessels attacked. One of our piloted torpedoes of the new type would leave the *Olterra* at eight in the morning and cross the whole of the roadstead while submerged (six miles, three hours). It would then find itself at the entrance to the harbour at the very moment at which the barrier would be raised. It would, therefore, enter the harbour *at midday*, and, profiting by the disorder created by what was happening in the roadstead and the consequent distraction of vigilance in the interior of the harbour, would attack the largest warship present. The preparation of this daring exploit was far advanced. Sub-Lieutenant Scardamaglia, the pilot, leader of the group of MTRs, had already received his ticket for the aircraft which was to take him to Spain on the 9th of September, to reconnoitre the zone of operations on the spot, from the *Olterra*; while Lieutenant Jacobacci and P.O./diver Forni, who had been appointed to force the harbour, had been training for months, covering stretches in submersion with the piloted torpedo over distances equal to and longer than that proposed. The attack was to take place on the 2nd of October.

We were intent upon these preparations when, on the evening of the 8th of September, while I was at the Flotilla headquarters at La Spezia, I switched on the radio to hear the war news; like a bolt from the blue the announcement of the armistice already in force crashed down upon our projects, our activities and our hopes.

Such was the way in which I, the commander of the Tenth Light Flotilla, the fighting head of men on active service on all the European fronts, the possessor of important secrets and absolutely new weapons, responsible to the King and the nation for the due exercise of the war functions conferred upon me and for the lives of the men who had been entrusted to my care, learned from the hoarsely croaking radio (which I had casually switched on and might just as well have decided not to) that my Country, for which we were in arms and in conflict, had agreed to an armistice.

None of my numerous superiors, direct or indirect, had considered it necessary to give me prior warning, even with due reservations, of the fact.

I thought it queer.

THE END

APPENDIX

List of Hostile Vessels Sunk or Damaged by the Tenth Light Flotilla
up to the 8th September, 1943

1. Battleship *Queen Elizabeth*, 32,000 tons, Alexandria, December 1941.
2. Battleship *Valiant*, 32,000 tons, Alexandria, December 1941.
3. Cruiser *York*, 10,000 tons, Suda, March 1941.
4. Destroyer of the *Jervis* class,[1] 1690 tons, El Daba, August 1942.
5, 6, 7. Three merchant ships,[1] 32,000 tons,[2] Suda, March 1941.
8. Tanker,[1] 10,000 tons,[2] Alexandria, December 1941.
9. Naval tanker *Denby Dale*, 15,893 tons, Gibraltar, September 1941.
10. Motorship *Durham*, 10,900 tons, Gibraltar, September 1941.
11. Tanker *Fiona Shell*, 2444 tons, Gibraltar, September 1941.
12. Russian Motorship,[1] 13,000 tons,[2] Black Sea, June 1942.
13. Steamer *Meta*, 1578 tons, Gibraltar, July 1942.
14.   ,,   *Shuma*, 1494 tons, Gibraltar, July 1942.
15.   ,,   *Empire Snipe*, 2497 tons, Gibraltar, July 1942.
16.   ,,   *Baron Douglas*, 3899 tons, Gibraltar, July 1942.
17.   ,,   *Raven's Point*, 1887 tons, Gibraltar, July 1942.
18.   ,,   *Ocean Vanquisher*, 7174 tons, Algiers, December 1942.
19.   ,,   *Berta*, 1493 tons, Algiers, December 1942.
20.   ,,   *Empire Centaur*, 7041 tons, Algiers, December 1942.
21.   ,,   *Armattan*, 4567 tons, Algiers, December 1942.
22.   ,,   *N.59* (American), 7500 tons,[2] Algiers, December 1942.
23.   ,,   *Pat Harrison*, 7000 tons, Gibraltar, May 1943.
24.   ,,   *Mahsud*, 7500 tons, Gibraltar, May 1943.
25.   ,,   *Camerata*, 4875 tons, Gibraltar, May 1943.
26.   ,,   *Orion*, 7000 tons, Alexandretta, July 1943.
27.   ,,   *Kaituna*, 10,000 tons, Mersina, July 1943.
28. Motorship *Fernplant*, 7000 tons, Alexandretta, August 1943.
29. Steamer *Harrison Gray Otis*, 7000 tons, Gibraltar, August 1943.
30. Tanker *Thorshovdi*, 10,000 tons, Gibraltar, August 1943.
31. Steamer *Stanridge*, 6000 tons, Gibraltar, August 1943.

[1] Name not ascertained.
[2] Presumed tonnage.

Totals:

4 warships, aggregate tonnage	.. ..	75,690
27 merchant ships, aggregate tonnage	..	189,662
	Total tonnage	265,352

ABOUT THE EDITOR

PAOLO E. COLETTA has had two careers. He earned a doctorate from the University of Missouri at Columbia and taught there and at Stephens College before receiving a direct commission in the U.S. Naval Reserve. Following service aboard destroyers in the Pacific, he taught at South Dakota State College and the University of Louisville before starting a thirty-seven-year tour at the U.S. Naval Academy, from which he retired as a Distinguished Meritorious Professor in 1983. He also continued his service in the Naval Reserve, retiring at the grade of captain in 1973. Dr. Coletta has published twenty books and over one hundred articles on political, diplomatic, and military subjects.

CLASSICS OF NAVAL LITERATURE

JACK SWEETMAN, SERIES EDITOR

Harwar Parker. Introduction and notes by Craig L. Symonds

The Riddle of the Sands, by Erskine Childers. Introduction and notes by Eric J. Grove

The Rise of American Naval Power, 1775–1918, by Harold and Margaret Sprout. Introduction by Kenneth J. Hagan and Charles Conrad Campbell

Running the Blockade, by Thomas E. Taylor. Introduction and notes by Stephen R. Wise

Run Silent, Run Deep, by Edward L. Beach. Introduction by Edward P. Stafford

Sailing Alone Around the World, by Joshua Slocum. Introduction by Robert W. McNitt

A Sailor's Log, by Robley D. Evans. Introduction and notes by Benjamin Franklin Cooling

Samurai! by Saburo Sakai with Martin Caidin and Fred Saito. Introduction by Barrett Tillman.

The Sand Pebbles, by Richard McKenna. Introduction by Robert Shenk

The Sinking of the Merrimac, by Richmond Pearson Hobson. Introduction and notes by Richard W. Turk

Two Years on the Alabama, by Arthur W. Sinclair. Introduction and notes by William N. Still Jr.

The Victory at Sea, by Rear Adm. William S. Sims and Burton J. Hendrick. Introduction and notes by David F. Trask.

White-Jacket; or, The World in a Man-of-War, by Herman Melville. Introduction by Stanton B. Garner

With the Battle Cruisers, by Filson Young. Introduction and notes by James Goldrick